A Mental Health Treatment Program for Inmates in Restrictive Housing

This treatment program targets the criminal, behavioral, and mental health problems of inmates in segregated housing that prevents them from living prosocially and productively within the general prison population.

The program makes use of a bi-adaptive psychoeducational and cognitive-behavioral treatment model to increase inmates' understanding about the psychological and criminal antecedents that contributed to their current placement, and to teach them the skills necessary for managing these problem areas. This flexible intervention assists inmates with significant problem behaviors by reducing psychological impairment and improving their ability to cope with prison life. This book includes a program introduction and guide for clinicians, the inmate workbook, and accompanying eResources to assist clinicians in both successful program implementation and evaluation of treatment outcomes.

Designed to account for the safety and physical limitations that make the delivery of needed mental and behavioral health services difficult, this guide is essential reading for practitioners working with high-needs, high-risk inmate populations.

Ashley B. Batastini, Ph.D. is an assistant professor in the School of Psychology at the University of Southern Mississippi.

Robert D. Morgan, Ph.D. is the John G. Skelton Jr. Regents Endowed Professor in Psychology, chairperson for the Department of Psychological Sciences, and director of the Institute for Forensic Science at Texas Tech University.

Daryl G. Kroner, Ph.D. is a professor in the Department of Criminology and Criminal Justice at Southern Illinois University at Carbondale.

Jeremy F. Mills, Ph.D. is a regional manager for the Institutional Mental Health for the Ontario Region of the Correctional Service of Canada and an adjunct research professor at Carleton University.

A Mental Health Treatment Program for Inmates in Restrictive Housing

Stepping Up, Stepping Out

Ashley B. Batastini, Robert D. Morgan, Daryl G. Kroner, and Jeremy F. Mills

Routledge
Taylor & Francis Group
NEW YORK AND LONDON

First published 2020
by Routledge
52 Vanderbilt Avenue, New York, NY 10017

and by Routledge
2 Park Square, Milton Park, Abingdon, Oxon, OX14 4RN

Routledge is an imprint of the Taylor & Francis Group, an informa business

Library of Congress Cataloging-in-Publication Data
Names: Batastini, Ashley B., author. | Morgan, Robert D., author. | Kroner, Daryl G., author. | Mills, Jeremy F., author.
Title: A mental health treatment program for inmates in restrictive housing : stepping up, stepping out / Ashley B. Batastini, Robert D. Morgan, Daryl G. Kroner, and Jeremy F. Mills.
Description: New York, NY : Routledge, 2019. | Includes bibliographical references and index. rsion record and CIP data provided by publisher; resource not viewed.
Identifiers: LCCN 2019009031 (print) | LCCN 2019010720 (ebook) | ISBN 9781315180755 (E-book) | ISBN 9781138745100 (hardback) | ISBN 9781138745117 (pbk.) | ISBN 9781315180755 (ebk)
Subjects: | MESH: Mental Disorders—therapy | Prisoners—psychology | Criminal Behavior
Classification: LCC RC451.4.P68 (ebook) | LCC RC451.4.P68 (print) | NLM WM 400 | DDC 616.890086/927—dc23
LC record available at https://lccn.loc.gov/2019009031

ISBN: 978-1-138-74510-0 (hbk)
ISBN: 978-1-138-74511-7 (pbk)
ISBN: 978-1-315-18075-5 (ebk)

Typeset in ACaslon
by Apex CoVantage, LLC

Visit the eResources: www.routledge.com/9781138745117

Contents

About the Authors viii
Acknowledgments x

Part I An Introduction and Guide for Clinicians **1**

Layout of This Book 3
Introduction to *Stepping Up, Stepping Out* 3
Program Goals 4
Theoretical Rationale and Evidence Base for *Stepping Up, Stepping Out* 4
Provider Qualifications 7
Program Structure and Logistics 8
Taking Personal Responsibility for Mental Health Problems and Criminalness 9
The Role of Hope 10
Basics of Goal-Setting 11
Participant Rules 12
Completion and Graduation Policies 13
Adjunctive Services and Interventions 14
Assessment 14
Required and Recommended Pre-Post Measures 14
Module Content Quizzes 16
Assessment Schedule 17
Program Outline 18
Module 1: Understanding Change and Making It Happen: An Introduction 18
Module 2: Surviving Segregation: What to Expect and How to Cope 19
Module 3: Suicide and Self-Injurious Behavior: Protecting You From You 19
Module 4: Understanding My Emotions: Identifying and Dealing With Anger, Fear, and Other Frustrating Feelings 21
Module 5: Exploring My Mental Distress and Criminalness: Where It Comes From, What It Looks Like, and How to Recognize It 21
Module 6: Managing My Mental Distress and Criminalness: Improving Functioning and Preventing Relapse 22

Module 7: Seeking Supportive Allies: Finding Helpful Others Among the Crowd 23
Module 8: Integrating "Us" and "Them": Improving Inmate-Staff Relations 23
Module 9: Road Map to Recovery: Creating Your Relapse Prevention Plan 24
References 24

Part II Inmate Workbook 27

Program Introduction and Expectations 29
Program Outline 30
Module 1 Understanding Change and Making It Happen: An Introduction 33
Handout #1 The Basics of This Program 34
Handout #2 Setting Personal Goals 37
Module 2 Surviving Segregation: What to Expect and How to Cope 41
Handout #3 Understanding Restrictive Housing 42
Handout #4 Occupying the Mind and Body 45
Handout #5 Being in Good Favor 47
Handout #6 Accepting Your Anger 49
Handout #7 Catching Some ZZzz's 51
Handout #8 Reducing Sensory Deprivation 54
Module 3 Suicide and Self-Injurious Behavior: Protecting You From You 59
Handout #9 Knowing Your Suicide Risk 60
Handout #10 Suicide vs. Self-Injurious Behavior vs. Morbid Rumination 62
Handout #11 False Suicidal Intent and SIB as Manipulation 65
Module 4 Understanding My Emotions: Identifying and Dealing With Anger, Fear, and Other Frustrating Feelings 69
Handout #12 Roots of Aggression and Violence 70
Handout #13 Assessing Your Anger 72
Handout #14 Attacking Anger at the Source 76
Handout #15 Moving From Aggressive to Assertive 81
Handout #16 Aggression, Assertiveness, and Being Tough 83
Handout #17 Passing Up Passive-Aggression 85
Handout #18 Digging Deeper Into Anger 88
Handout #19 Fighting With Fear 90
Handout #20 Stopping Shame and Sadness 95
Module 5 Exploring My Mental Distress and Criminalness: Where It Comes From, What It Looks Like, and How to Recognize It 103
Handout #21 Defining "Mental Distress" 104
Handout #22 Common Diagnoses: Part I 107
Handout #23 Common Diagnoses: Part II 114
Handout #24 Stigma and Mental Illness 120
Handout #25 Defining "Criminalness" 123
Handout #26 Signs of Criminalness 127
Handout #27 The Road to Recovery 135
Handout #28 Watching for Warnings and Tackling the Triggers 138
Module 6 Managing My Mental Distress and Criminalness: Improving Functioning and Preventing Relapse 143
Handout #29 Awareness of Automatic Thoughts 144

Handout #30 Altering Automatic Thoughts 149
Handout #31 Signs of Stress 155
Handout #32 Stopping Stress the Green Light Way 158
Handout #33 Learning to Cope With Cognitive Problems 160
Handout #34 Learning to Cope With Negative Moods 163
Handout #35 Learning to Cope With Psychotic Symptoms 168
Handout #36 Learning to Cope With Interpersonal Problems 171
Handout #37 Learning to Cope With Criminalness 175
Handout #38 Sticking With Your Medications 179
Module 7 Seeking Supportive Allies: Finding Helpful Others Among the Crowd 187
Handout #39 Separating the Good From the Bad 188
Handout #40 Moving Away From Antisocial Associates 192
Handout #41 Making the First Move 196
Handout #42 Avoiding Prison Gangs as Social Supports 200
Handout #43 Don't Befriend the Bully 203
Module 8 Integrating "Us" and "Them": Improving Inmate-Staff Relations 211
Handout #44 Keeping Order Among Disorder 212
Handout #45 The Nature of Inmate-Staff Relations 216
Module 9 Road Map to Recovery: Creating Your Relapse Prevention Plan 223
1. Where I've Been 225
2. Going for the Goal 226
3. Always Alert 230
4. Playing Favorites 231
5. Quick Thinker 232
6. People Picking 233
7. Busy, Busy, Busy 234
8. Medication Management 235

Index 238

About the Authors

Ashley B. Batastini is an assistant professor in the School of Psychology at the University of Southern Mississippi. She earned her doctorate in counseling psychology at Texas Tech University after completing a predoctoral internship at Western State Hospital in Tacoma, Washington. She received her master of science degree in psychology with a focus in forensic psychology from Drexel University and her bachelor of science degree in psychology from the University of Pittsburgh. Dr. Batastini's research focuses on intervention strategies for criminal justice–involved populations with mental health issues, reentry and vocational barriers for returning citizens, violence risk assessment, and the use of telepsychology in the legal system. Dr. Batastini has authored or coauthored several peer-reviewed publications related to topics such as the psychological effects of administrative segregation, barriers to offender employment upon release, nature of antisocial thinking patterns, and violence risk assessment. She has also authored or coauthored three book chapters related to the correctional psychology and the treatment of offenders with mental illnesses. Dr. Batastini is a licensed psychologist in the State of Mississippi and currently serves on the Mental Health Task Force under the State Attorney General's Office.

Robert D. Morgan completed his Ph.D. in counseling psychology at Oklahoma State University and a postdoctoral fellowship in forensic psychology in the Department of Psychiatry at the University of Missouri-Kansas City and the Missouri Department of Mental Health. He is currently the John G. Skelton Jr. Regents Endowed Professor in psychology, chairperson for the Department of Psychological Sciences, and director of the Institute for Forensic Science at Texas Tech University. Dr. Morgan's research and scholarly activities include treatment and assessment of justice-involved persons with mental illness; effects of incarceration, including in restricted housing units; and forensic mental health assessment. His research has been funded by the National Institute of Mental Health, the National Institute of Justice, and the Center for Behavioral Health Services and Criminal Justice Research. He has authored or coauthored over 95 peer-reviewed articles and book chapters, and authored or edited 4 books, including *A Treatment Program for Justice Involved Persons with Mental Illness: Changing Lives and Changing Outcomes* and *A Clinician's Guide to Violence Risk Assessment*. He has over 20 years of experience in correctional and forensic psychology, and consults with state and private correctional agencies to inform practice.

Daryl G. Kroner completed his Ph.D. at Carleton University, Ottawa, Canada. He is a professor in the Department of Criminology and Criminal Justice at Southern Illinois University at Carbondale. He has published over 70 peer-reviewed papers and 3 books covering a variety of topics related to offender psychological and risk assessment. His primary areas of scientific inquiry include violence risk assessment, criminal attributions, and crime desistance. He has been centrally involved in the evaluation of a number of nationally based offender programs. In addition, he has co-developed psychometric instruments that have been employed in national evaluations and assessment protocols of the Correctional Service of Canada. Dr. Kroner has served on the Executive of the Criminal Justice Section of the Canadian Psychological Association both as the co-editor of their newsletter and as chair of the section. His accomplishments have been recognized in his appointment as fellow of the Canadian Psychological Association.

Jeremy F. Mills completed his Ph.D. at Carleton University, Ottawa, Canada. He is a regional manager for the Institutional Mental Health for the Ontario Region of the Correctional Service of Canada. Dr. Mills is also an adjunct research professor at Carleton University where he supervises both undergraduate and graduate students. He has served on the Executive of the Criminal Justice Section of the Canadian Psychological Association in the capacity of co-editor, editor, and chair of the section. Dr. Mills was also the chair of the first North American Correctional and Criminal Justice Psychology Conference held in Ottawa, Canada. He has published over 30 peer-reviewed papers and a book (*Clinician's Guide to Violence Risk Assessment*) covering a variety of topics related to offender assessment. His primary areas of scientific inquiry include offender suicide, violence risk assessment, antisocial attitudes, and the perception of violence risk. He has developed a depression-hopelessness-suicide screening instrument that has been incorporated into a nationally administered mental health screening for all offenders entering the Correctional Service of Canada.

Acknowledgments

We would like to acknowledge the following individuals for their contributions to this user's manual and inmate workbook. First, we thank Dr. Amanda Seirup (director of behavioral health at Maine State Prison) for her willingness to initiate *Stepping Up, Stepping Out* within her facility, as well as providing thorough feedback and recommendations to improve the inmate workbook. Her background in education was particularly beneficial to improving the readability of program content. The following graduate and undergraduate students also deserve recognition for their careful and detailed efforts in editing, proofreading, and formatting program materials: Kray Scully, Madison Pike, Alexandra Repke, and Ja'Nisha Robinson.

We are also grateful for the mental health staff and administrators at Corizon Health Inc. and the Missouri Department of Corrections for their willingness to partner with us on program implementation. In particular, we thank Dr. Mariann Atwell (formerly at Corizon) and Dr. Elizabeth Atterberry for opening the lines of communication and advocating for the use of our program in the state of Missouri and elsewhere. Thank you for giving us a chance to turn this idea into a reality. And we thank Michael Lester for his assistance in managing program evaluation efforts.

Lastly, we thank the inmates who volunteered to complete this program and opened themselves up to the process of change.

Part I

An Introduction and Guide for Clinicians

Layout of This Book

This book is laid out in two primary parts. Part I speaks directly to you—the clinician—in describing the goals and implementation of the *Stepping Up, Stepping Out* program. This part will also provide guidance on how to track client progress and assess overall program impact at the institutional level. The audience for Part II of the book is the inmate participants themselves. Part II includes a list of program expectations to set the stage for the level of work and commitment required, an outline of the upcoming modules, and all module handouts, which can be photocopied for distribution. Prior to distributing module handouts, it is recommended that clinicians first provide inmates with the list of program expectations and outline, and allow participants to ask any questions. At this pre-treatment stage, clinicians can challenge and foster inmates' motivation for treatment.

In addition to Parts I and II, the purchase of this book gives clinicians free access to a number of eResources. Among these resources are copyrighted but nonproprietary pre- and post-treatment assessment measures; a spreadsheet for clinicians to track treatment progress and engagement, pre- and post-module quizzes, modules; program completion certificates; a quick-reference glossary of key terms; and supplemental materials that accompany module content. Clinicians are encouraged to introduce these supplemental materials in conjunction with respective modules and to provide copies to inmates on a recurrent basis. When and how to use these supplemental materials is described in further detail in the following sections. In general, eResource materials are listed online in the order in which they will be used. Use of eResource material is referenced throughout the clinician's guide (Part I).

Introduction to *Stepping Up, Stepping Out*

Following a similar theoretical framework as the *Changing Lives and Changing Outcomes* program developed by Morgan, Kroner, and Mills (2018; also part of the International Perspectives on Forensic Mental Health book series), *Stepping Up, Stepping Out* uses a bi-adaptive intervention model to address both mental health issues and antisocial (or criminal) patterns with the goal of reducing behavioral problems of inmates detained in restrictive housing settings, such as disciplinary segregation (DS) and administrative segregation (AS), and other types of units that limit access to resources and/or programming. Specifically, *Stepping Up, Stepping Out* aims to prevent inmates from remaining in and returning to long-term isolation by reducing behavioral misconducts and psychological impairment, and improving their ability to cope with prison life. Like *Changing Lives and Changing Outcomes*, *Stepping Up, Stepping Out* also uses both a psychoeducation and psychotherapeutic approach to teach and train inmates in skill acquisition. Principles of various empirically supported treatments, including Linehan's Dialectical Behavior Therapy (1993), Hayes and colleagues' Acceptance and Commitment Therapy (Hayes, 2004), Mueser's Illness Management and Recovery (2002), and the Substance Abuse and Mental Health Services Administration's Anger Management and Assertiveness Training (Reilly & Shopshire, 2015), are emphasized throughout. Although the program is primarily geared toward inmates with a history of more serious mental health concerns, inmates with less severe psychiatric symptoms (e.g., heightened levels of general stress, externalizing behaviors commonly associated with antisocial personality disorder, adjustment issues, problematic coping) are also appropriate candidates for program participation, perhaps with some modification to program content as determined by pre-treatment assessment results and clinical judgment. Further, this program may be used with inmates who are prone to restricted housing placements or at-risk of such placement, but not currently housed there.

Stepping Up, Stepping Out includes nine treatment modules: (1) Understanding Change and Making It Happen: An Introduction; (2) Surviving Segregation: What to Expect and How to Cope; (3) Suicide and Self-Injurious Behavior: Protecting You From You; (4) Understanding My Emotions: Identifying and Dealing With Anger, Fear, and Other Frustrating Feelings; (5) Exploring My Mental Distress and Criminalness: Where It Comes From, What It Looks Like, and How to Recognize It; (6) Managing My Mental Distress and Criminalness: Improving Functioning and Preventing Relapse; (7) Seeking Supportive Allies: Finding Helpful Others Among the Crowd; (8) Integrating "Us" and "Them": Improving Inmate-Staff Relations; and (9) Road Map to Recovery: Creating Your Relapse Prevention Plan. Because *Stepping Up, Stepping Out* describes relatively complex psychological concepts throughout the program, a glossary of terms (eResource Appendix I) is also included to aid understanding.

The delivery of *Stepping Up, Stepping Out* is flexible and is intended to be implemented as a largely self-directed program, with inmates completing the handouts and exercises embedded in each module on their own with as little or as much staff contact as is available. At a minimum, it is recommended that clinicians provide written feedback following each handout to ensure completeness and understanding, and schedule in-person contact at least once per week to discuss progress or review stuck points. Although each module focuses on a specific problem area, modules are represented in a developmental progression—that is, basic treatment concepts and goals are discussed first, then immediate stressors related to segregation, then more global issues within the individual, and, finally, relapse prevention. None of the modules are designed as stand-alone modules; rather, broader concepts from all nine modules are integrated within each individual module to create a developmentally coherent and consistent program for inmates detained in segregated housing units.

Program Goals

The goal of *Stepping Up, Stepping Out* is not to cure mental illness, eliminate criminal risk, or even to negate the need for continued care. Instead, this intervention is designed to maximize compliance with institutional rules and foster adaptive behavioral change so inmates with mental health concerns (or those at risk of developing them) can successfully serve their time in segregation with fewer incidents of misconduct, return to the general prison population where more intensive services can be provided, and remain there. That is, *Stepping Up, Stepping Out* is conceptualized as a gateway intervention, meaning that inmates who complete the program are not expected to be "recovered" or "fixed." This program is intended to reduce an inmate's risk enough to allow for safe transition to the general population (GP). It is in GP where inmates must continue to build upon the skills learned while in segregation by engaging in treatment services that otherwise are unavailable to them in secure placement. The ultimate outcome for all inmates is to get out and stay out of segregation. Accomplishing this goal is not only dependent on the inmate's willingness and motivation to do the necessary work but also on the ability of correctional staff to see change as possible.

Theoretical Rationale and Evidence Base for *Stepping Up, Stepping Out*

Although solitary confinement was first implemented in the late 1700s as a measure of criminal justice reform, the contemporary use of restricted housing (to include disciplinary and AS) in North American prisons and jails is a growing and controversial correctional practice. A survey out of Yale University Law School estimated that nearly 80,000 to 100,000 inmates were held in restrictive housing across the country (Liman Program & Association of State Correctional Administrators, 2015). Yet this number is likely an underestimate, as it did not include local jails, juvenile facilities, or military and immigration detention centers. Although the range of activities to which inmates have access varies depending on the facility (Suedfeld, Ramirez, Deaton, & Baker-Brown, 1982), all restricted housing units closely monitor inmate movement and limit access to mental health programing, educational and library services, religious services, personal possessions, and physical exercise (O'Keefe, 2008; Pizarro & Stenius, 2004). It is not uncommon for inmates to spend years, even decades, in these restricted units (see, for example, Goode, 2015; Landau, 2015). Typically, long-term or indefinite stays are most associated with AS. DS, on the contrary, is usually reserved for shorter-term, determinate sanctions in response to disciplinary infractions.

Efforts to better understand the impact of segregation on the well-being of inmates have been occurring for decades. To help clarify the effects of restricted housing, a team of researchers (Morgan et al., 2016) undertook two independent meta-analytic reviews in which over 40,000 search results relating to solitary confinement, protective custody, DS, and AS were identified. These researchers reported small to moderate effects across most physical, behavioral, and mental health outcomes. The largest of these effects (compared to non-segregated inmates) were for increased hostility, anxiety, hypersensitivity, general mental health functioning, and post-release criminal recidivism. Although these researchers concluded that the adverse effects of restricted placements might be over-stated, they also acknowledged two of the major limitations in the literature: (a) the limited time that study participants spent in these units (i.e., one year or less; see Coid et al., 2003; Haney, 2003; O'Keefe, Klebe, Stucker, Sturm, & Leggett, 2010; Suedfeld et al., 1982) and (b) the lack of pre-post testing to determine baseline functioning of inmates and rule out the possibility that psychological impairment and/or behavioral problems existed prior to segregated placement.

A subsequent study (Chadick, Batastini, Levulis, & Morgan, 2018), which included assessments at initial booking and at least one-year post-booking, inmates detained in AS for up to four years, and a comparison group of GP inmates, similarly concluded that AS alone did not appear to cause debilitating psychological effects. While segregated inmates reported higher levels of distress (particularly on measures of anxiety, depressed mood, posttraumatic stress, and somatic complaints) compared to the GP at post-assessment, scores did not reach the clinical cutoff. Further, inmates did not deteriorate as time in restrictive housing increased. However, compared to those in GP who showed some improvement over time, AS inmates remained relatively stable from baseline to follow-up. The authors concluded that, rather than causing significant psychological damage, it is more likely that segregation is a barrier to opportunities for continued growth. Notably, this study was limited by its small sample size (AS = 24; GP = 24) and lack of severely mentally disordered offenders (e.g., 30% had no psychiatric diagnosis at booking, and none were diagnosed with a psychotic disorder). Another study published in 2018 by Walters revealed that prison inmates with a history of mental health need were more likely to experience severe psychological consequences from restricted housing than those without such a history. However, these differences in psychological reactions also held for GP placement, suggesting that aversive outcomes for those with mental health problems may have more to do with incarceration generally than restricted housing specifically.

Although the totality of consequences for inmates placed in segregation remains unclear and likely depends on other institutional factors (e.g., staff-inmate dynamics, emphasis on punishment, physical conditions; e.g., Gendreau & Labrecque, 2015), it appears that at least small to moderate adverse effects are associated with segregation (Morgan et al., 2016; Chadick et al., 2018). Thus, correctional systems must strive to minimize the risk of inmate decompensation that could result from segregated placement. Furthermore, prevention of harm is not just an aspirational goal—it is a legal obligation. That is, correctional departments are responsible for the well-being and care (including the provision of mental health services) of inmates (Ruiz v. Estelle, 1980). Perhaps even more concerning is that inmates with preexisting and serious mental health problems tend to be over-represented in restricted units, often to contain their odd or disruptive behaviors (Haney, 2003; O'Keefe, 2007, 2008; Metzner & Fellner, 2010). The fact that inmates with mental health concerns are at greater risk for restricted placements may be the product of misguided responses to behavioral issues by untrained correctional staff and/or insufficient treatment options. Little empirical data exists regarding the additive effects of segregated placement on this high-needs and unique group, especially for those with longer placement periods. Unfortunately, the availability of mental health services in general is limited in segregation due to higher safety and security restrictions (Beven, 2005; Metzner & Fellner, 2010), and interventions that uniquely target the needs of this population are lacking. Though there is a trend in the United States to remove inmates with serious mental illnesses from segregation units—following a number of law suits (*Madrid v. Gomez*, 1995; *Disability Law Center v. Massachusetts Department of Corrections*, 2007)—many correctional agencies struggle to implement specialized units (e.g., Secure Treatment Programs, Behavioral Management Units) that are not simply alternative forms of restricted housing. Further, combating behavioral problems that are rooted in the cross-section between antisocial patterns and poor psychological coping remains a goal even in more treatment-oriented environments.

The few programs currently available for inmates prone to longer-term restricted placements are limited in scope and seem to address only one side of a two-sided problem. First, many mental health programs for offenders are based on the false assumption that mental distress or illness is the underlying cause of violence and behavioral misconduct. Yet a significant body of research suggests that known risk factors for crime (e.g., criminal history, antisocial attitudes, negative peers) are more predictive of justice involvement for those with mental health problems than psychological risk factors (e.g., symptom severity, diagnosis; e.g., Andrews & Bonta, 2017; Skeem & Louden, 2006; Andrews, Bonta, & Wormith, 2006). Therefore, many traditional programs for inmates miss the mark. Second, the gold standard CBT programs aimed at reducing criminal risk (e.g., *Thinking for a Change*, Golden, Gatchel, & Cahill, 2006; *Reasoning and Rehabilitation*, Ross, Fabiano, & Ewles, 1988) fail to incorporate related but unique psychiatric factors that, while less predictive, are nonetheless imperative to address if the goal is to stop or slow the recurrence of segregated placements. The notion of a "bi-adaptive model" focusing on both criminogenic and psychiatric risk was supported by a meta-analysis on effective treatments for offenders with serious mental illness (Morgan et al., 2012). Having few treatment options for one of the highest-risk inmate populations makes little practical sense.

Stepping Up, Stepping Out was developed to better serve the needs of this inmate population, unit providers, and administrators, particularly institutions with more limited staff availability. The nine modules that comprise *Stepping Up, Stepping Out* (described in detail next) are based on empirically supported criminogenic and psychiatric risk factors, as well as risk factors that appear particularly relevant to segregated inmates, such as the prevalence of assaultive behaviors, increased self-harm, and more frequent contact with correctional staff (Dvoskin & Spiers, 2004; O'Keefe, 2008; Patterson & Hughes, 2008; Sánchez, 2013; Way, Sawyer, Barboza, & Nash, 2007). *Stepping Up, Stepping Out* is unique in that it *holistically integrates* the bi-adaptive model with other principles from the correctional best practice literature base, including the need to provide structured, intensive, and CBT-informed interventions that use easy-to-follow treatment concepts and heuristics (Andrews & Bonta, 2017; Andrews et al., 1990; Bourgon & Armstrong, 2005; Burdon, Messina, & Prendergast, 2004; Gendreau, 1996a, 1996b; Leak, 1980; Lipsey, 1989; Mills, Kroner, & Mongrain, 2005; Morgan & Flora, 2002; Morgan, Kroner, & Mills, 2006). The uniqueness of *Stepping Up, Stepping Out* is in the *integration* of best practices in mental health and correctional rehabilitation practices that is reinforced throughout the entire program. For example, refusing to take medication for psychiatric symptoms reflects the same lack of responsibility (i.e., prosocial decision-making) that often precedes criminal behavior and may in fact lead to disruptive behavior resulting from unmanaged mental illness.

Stepping Up, Stepping Out was also designed to give clinicians the ability to circumvent the safety and physical limitations that make the delivery of needed mental and behavioral health services difficult. The self-directed nature of this program reduces the need for confidential space that is often limited or not possible due to security concerns (e.g., transportation of an inmate; Chaiken & Shull, 2007), as verbal communication can be minimal. Again, *Stepping Up, Stepping Out* is intended to be a gateway program aimed at maximizing rule compliance and adaptive behaviors so that inmates, especially those with mental health concerns (or those at risk of developing such concerns), can begin working their way out of segregated placement and return to the general prison population better stabilized and with a broader skill set to reduce the likelihood of decompensation and rule noncompliance. Given the cost of housing an inmate in segregated placements compared to GP (approximately two to three times higher in many states; Mears, 2006; Rodriguez, 2011), reducing time in those units has financial benefits as well.

The theoretical model underlying *Stepping Up, Stepping Out* was born out of Morgan and colleagues' *A Treatment Manual for Justice Involved Persons with Mental Illness: Changing Lives and Changing Outcomes*, first edition (2018), which has shown to produce reliable reductions in psychiatric symptoms, criminal thinking, and relevant behavioral markers (e.g., see Morgan et al., 2014; Gaspar, Brown, Ramler, Scanlon, & Morgan, 2019). Importantly, participants were actively engaged in and satisfied with the treatment program (Morgan et al., 2014), and retained core treatment content (Van Horn et al., in press). It is anticipated that *Stepping Up, Stepping Out* will produce similar outcomes. Anecdotal reports from clinicians using the program in the Maine Department of Corrections (personal communication with staff) suggested good acceptability among providers and participants. At the time of this publication, *Stepping Up, Stepping Out* was also adopted by the Missouri Department of Corrections (whose mental health services are contracted with Corizon Health, Inc.) across multiple facilities. Clinical staff reported that the program has been generally well received within their institutions. Staff has further noted positive responses regarding both inmate engagement and behavioral functioning for program participants. In one case, for example, an inmate who had spent over four years in segregation was permitted to return to GP as a result of his progress in the program. Perhaps most importantly, initial analyses of 32 program completers revealed reductions in emotional distress and fewer endorsed criminal attitudes directly related to criminal activity from pre- to post-treatment. Effects were both statistically significant and in the medium range ($p = .002$, $d = .60$ and $p < .001$, $d = .65$, respectively). Given these initial outcomes and the matching of program content to the "what works" literature, *Stepping Up, Stepping Out* is a promising practice. Further, the integration of the best available research in correctional psychology with clinical expertise that takes client characteristics into account is in line with the definition of an evidence-based practice (APA Presidential Task Force on Evidence-Based Practice, 2006).

Provider Qualifications

Individuals who guide inmates through the *Stepping Up, Stepping Out* protocol should be mental health professionals with formal education and training in the provision of psychotherapy or counseling services. Although this program does not necessarily require significant in-person contact by mental health providers, the material it covers incorporates a variety of evidence-based interventions and skills that are best understood by those with a demonstrated competence in theories of psychotherapy (primarily cognitive-behavioral theories), mechanisms of client change (e.g., strong working alliance, instillation of hope and motivation), and assessment of treatment needs and progress. Providers' ability to effectively teach inmates about complex psychological concepts presented within *Stepping Up, Stepping Out*; provide accurate and comprehensive corrective feedback; determine inmate understanding and application of learned concepts; and continually monitor changes in symptomology is imperative to successful program implementation.

While non-mental health professionals (e.g., correctional officers, unit managers) may have a basic understanding about the psychological and behavioral problems that are often experienced by inmates in segregation, their understanding about the specific interventions used as part of *Stepping Up, Stepping Out*, including the aims and expected outcomes, is insufficient. Therefore, mental health training at the master's (e.g., M.A. in clinical or counseling psychology, master's in social work, M.A. in counseling or clinical mental health, licensed professional counselor program) or doctoral (e.g., Ph.D. or Psy.D. in clinical or counseling psychology) level is a prerequisite for facilitating *Stepping Up, Stepping Out*. In some cases, bachelor's level providers may assist with program implementation under the direct supervision of a more advanced, post-graduate-level practitioner.

Program Structure and Logistics

Program implementation is flexible and can be completed at a pace conducive to the needs of the inmate and/or to the availability of the provider; however, to encourage efficient completion and to maintain treatment progress, it is recommended that the inmate complete at least three handouts routinely each week with at least brief check-ins (preferably in-person) between each handout to provide feedback on completed tasks and assignments, and to discuss specific challenges or personal areas of growth. Because knowledge accumulation and skill development build from previous handouts, inmates must demonstrate sufficient understanding of the topics presented in each handout before moving on to the next handout. Inmates who begin *Stepping Up, Stepping Out* but return to GP prior to completing the program can (and should) continue working toward completion; however, additional interventions may be supplemented as needed and as available. Given the specific attention to issues associated with placement in segregation, exposure to the full program, even though the inmate has returned to GP, may prevent a more immediate return to restricted housing.

Figure 1.1 illustrates the basic layout of the modules. Modules typically begin with a pre-module content quiz (Appendix G in the eResource materials contains quizzes for distribution while Appendix H includes the quiz answer keys), followed by a series of interactive handouts related to the module's general topic. Handouts include brief explanations of concepts and skills, with exercises designed to help reinforce learned concepts and skills. Modules conclude with a recap worksheet in which learned concepts and skills are summarized. This recap worksheet is followed by the post-module content quiz. The exceptions to this progression are Modules 1 and 9. Module 1 is a relatively brief introduction to the program and, as such, does not include a content quiz or a recap worksheet. Module 9 focuses on developing a relapse prevention plan and no new material is presented. As part of Module 9, participants are also instructed to compose a letter to the review panel responsible for determining their release from restricted housing. This letter serves as an opportunity for inmates to highlight their progress toward goals and specify how they will continue to work on these goals if transferred to GP.

Ideally, inmates should be exposed to one handout at a time rather than the program or any one module in its entirety. However, if it is not logistically feasible to distribute and review one handout at a time, at a minimum, modules must be distributed individually. It is not advisable to provide access to the entire program. Working through the program handout by handout is ideal for several reasons. First, providing handouts in a singular fashion will help the inmate maintain focus on the task at hand and prevent the

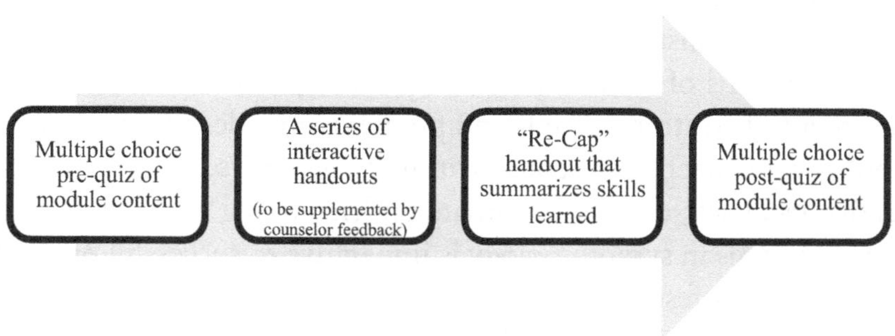

Figure 1.1 Sequence for Modules 1 through 8

urge to move ahead in the program prematurely. Second, having exposure to all materials would invalidate scores on the module content quizzes, as these quizzes are not meant to be open book. It is for this same reason that completed and corrected materials within a module should only be returned (assuming this is permitted by institutional policy) to the inmate indefinitely after he successfully passes the module. Therefore, it is recommended that, once feedback on a particular handout is returned, reviewed, or discussed with the inmate, the provider retake possession of the material and return all module handouts to the inmate for his own record keeping once he earns a passing score on the post-module quiz (scoring of module quizzes is discussed next). The Relapse Prevention Packet contained in Module 9 should be viewed as one large handout. Thus, all pages of the Relapse Prevention Packet are distributed to the inmate at the same time. Because the length of the Relapse Prevention Packet is significantly longer than any other handout, inmates may require a longer period of time to complete it thoroughly. Inmates should have access to all program materials up to this point to assist them in completing the Relapse Prevention Packet. The glossary of terms (see Appendix I in the eResource materials) can be provided at the beginning of program implementation for continued reference throughout.

Although *Stepping Up, Stepping Out* is designed to be implemented in its entirety to maximize treatment gains, the program can be dissected when time limitations and/or the need to address more imminent concerns requires a truncated or modified version of the treatment program. That is, providers can select and assign specific handouts on an as-needed basis under these special circumstances. However, regardless of any modifications to the program, all inmates must complete both handouts within Module 1, as this module presents the program's foundational therapeutic concepts and teaches effective goal-setting. Furthermore, handout selection decisions should be based on initial assessment results that highlight inmates' specific mental health and criminogenic needs, as well as sound clinical judgment. For example, if an inmate scores high on suicidal risk (using the Depression Hopelessness Suicide Screening [DHS]; see the following), Module 3 should be implemented.

Although designed as a self-guided program, *Stepping Up, Stepping Out* can be used in a group treatment format, if space and staff availability allow. Implemented in a group setting, the program will increase provider time and efficiency by enabling the treatment of multiple inmates simultaneously, while also encouraging positive social interactions among participants and offering real-time opportunities to practice learned skills. When delivered in a group setting, an interpersonal process-oriented approach is recommended. For guidance on integrating this approach within a CBT and psychoeducational framework, clinicians are referred to *A Treatment Manual for Justice Involved Persons with Mental Illness: Changing Lives and Changing Outcomes*, first edition (Morgan et al., 2018; see Chapter 9), in this book series.

Importantly, reading and writing abilities should be assessed prior to program participation. Because *Stepping Up, Stepping Out* will be self-directed under most circumstances, it requires sufficient ability to read, write, and understand English independently at about the fifth-grade reading level. At this time, the program is not yet available in any other languages or an audio version. Inmates who understand English but cannot read or write well enough to complete handouts on their own may still participate in the program so long as providers are able to offer more one-on-one assistance to ensure content understanding and assess skill acquisition. In these cases, inmate responses to handout exercises may be expressed orally to providers. If possible and available, inmates may also select a prosocial, literate peer to assist them with each handout.

Taking Personal Responsibility for Mental Health Problems and Criminalness

Like *Changing Lives and Changing Outcomes*, *Stepping Up, Stepping Out* was developed on the premise that inmates with mental problems are ultimately responsible for avoiding crime or behavioral misconducts and managing the symptoms of their illness or distress. While it is relevant to discuss antecedents to crime (e.g., growing up in a high-crime neighborhood) and mental impairment (e.g., biological predisposition), these are not excuses for continuing a life of crime. This is not to say that people are to "blame" or are "at fault" for developing mental health issues, or even going down the path of crime, but they are responsible for learning and using new prosocial coping skills to avoid negative consequences in the future. That is, inmates are responsible for whether or not they change. Accepting responsibility for their own thoughts and behaviors and managing their symptoms or maladaptive coping is imperative to treatment success. Inmates who continue to blame others or their circumstances will not progress. However, full acceptance of responsibility is not necessary at the outset of *Stepping Up, Stepping Out*; rather, this is a quality that can be taught and instilled throughout the program.

Failure to take responsibility for oneself—whether it relates to mental health management, criminal desistance, or something else entirely—is an example of "criminalness." Reducing inmates' instances of criminalness is a central focus of *Stepping Up, Stepping Out*, and the construct is defined in the same manner as in Morgan et al. (2018). That is, criminalness is

> behavior that breaks laws and social conventions and/or violates the rights and well-being of others. . . . Criminalness is not the same as criminogenic risk. . . . Criminalness is a trait that can vary in degree over time, can present in numerous ways and can be found in varying levels in all members of society. (p. 6)

In other words, criminalness may or may not lead to offenses that are against the law. Criminalness can range from cheating at a board game and abusing sick leave to drug possession, property crime, and/or violent crimes. Consider a time when you engaged in criminalness and how that decision may have impacted others (e.g., taking unnecessary time off from work leaves more work for others in your absence). Those who live a criminal lifestyle, however, engage in more *frequent* and more *severe* forms of criminalness. However, we argue that all instances of continued criminalness (whether lawlessness or not) increase the risk of continued criminal involvement.

As the authors of *Changing Lives and Changing Outcomes* warn: the term "criminalness" is likely to be viewed as pejorative and stigmatizing to participants, yet it provides a useful strategy for discussing all behaviors (even those that are not illegal or rule violating) that keep inmates in restricted placements. Furthermore, for therapeutic purposes, criminalness is a term that can be normalized (i.e., we all do it to some extent) and, based on field testing of *Changing Lives and Changing Outcomes*, participants appear to have little difficulty integrating it into their everyday vocabulary. The use of this term also serves as a device for segregated inmates to evaluate their behavior. Thus, when program participants show a lack of responsibility for change, their choice to forego responsibility should be promptly labeled as criminalness and appropriately processed within the therapeutic framework of *Stepping Up, Stepping Out*, with particular emphasis on its relation to participants' goals.

The Role of Hope

In the recovery literature, hope is an attitude of maintaining positive expectations about wellness that is considered critical for achieving optimal treatment outcomes (Weinberg, 2013). Importantly, hope is not only a useful attribute for those who participate in treatment programs but also for the providers who deliver it. While hope is necessary for treatment engagement and building a collaborative therapeutic relationship, "faith in a treatment mode can in itself be therapeutically effective" (Yalom, 1995, p. 4). Thus, having and instilling hope that *Stepping Up, Stepping Out* can be beneficial and lead to positive change may very well improve the likelihood that it does. Yet this should not be interpreted to mean that hope is sufficient for treatment success. Rather, hope keeps participants (and providers) invested in a program so they can gain full exposure to all mechanisms of change within an intervention model.

In correctional settings, having hope that inmates can get better by engaging with treatment—both in terms of mental distress and antisocial behavior—extends to a broader systems level. For segregated inmates specifically, when prison staff and administrators fail to see these individuals as capable of prosocial change, opportunities for upward mobility or progression are limited, if not completely obstructed. Therefore, inmates who participate in *Stepping Up, Stepping Out* must at least be presented with the possibility of release from these units following successful completion of the program, even if not released directly into GP (e.g., mental health ward, therapeutic community, or other least restrictive alternative). If release from segregation is highly unlikely, participating in the program is essentially setting up false hope, which could trigger frustration, lack of motivation, or, in the extreme, violent retaliation. In other words, for *Stepping Up, Stepping Out* to have initial buy-in from inmates and a lasting effect, they must be able to see a light at the end of the tunnel, no matter how distant it may be. To avoid false hope, and any negative consequences that may accompany it, providers should be honest and transparent about which outcomes are possible for a given inmate and what criteria must be satisfied for that possibility to become reality.

Basics of Goal-Setting

Goal-setting is a primary component of *Stepping Up, Stepping Out*. While the ultimate goal of release to a lesser restrictive setting (and no more returns to segregation) is the same for all program participants, each individual will have several unique sub-goals that they must work toward for release to become a possibility. Although goals are established in Module 1 (Understanding Change and Making It Happen: An Introduction), participants' goals should be continually emphasized throughout the program. Modifications to these goals may be made whenever appropriate; for example, inmates may reach a particular goal before treatment ends, determine that a new goal should be added, or may realize that an initial goal is not achievable as-is and needs to be redefined or broken down into smaller goals.

Goal attainment should not be viewed as a pass/fail outcome; rather, when goals are not achieved as originally defined, providers, and inmates are encouraged to view this as an opportunity for self-evaluation and reflection, not a failure. In other words, ask, "Why was this goal not obtained?" Perhaps the goal was not specific enough to evaluate whether it was achieved or not, or perhaps it would have been achieved if given more time. To better assist the goal-making and goal-achieving process, *Stepping Up, Stepping Out* (like its sister program, *Changing Lives and Changing Outcomes*) emphasizes the need for realistic, meaningful, and clearly defined goals. Goals that are unrealistic, overly ambitious, or too abstract or vague are not likely to be achieved and may create a sense of false hope. "False hope prevents people from objectively assessing their status and goals . . . and might suggest that people [can] pursue . . . goals that exceed true abilities" (Corrigan, 2014, p. 424). Conversely, simple, concrete, and measurable goals are likely to provide a source of motivation and a more accurate sense of hope, as inmates can clearly see and evaluate their progress.

The following are examples of "good" versus "bad" goals as reproduced (with some modifications to have relevance for segregated inmates) from Morgan et al. (2018):

Examples of "Good" (or More Productive) Goals

- I will remain free of rule violations for one year following my release from segregation (as an initial marker).
- I will have no crisis holdings in the month that I am back in the GP.

- I will obtain a job within 30 days of my release and maintain full-time employment at this job for one calendar year.
- I will miss no more than two required parole appointments in the first six months of release, and I will notify my parole officer in advance every time I am going to miss an appointment.

Examples of "Bad" (or Less Productive) Goals

- I will never go back to prison (or segregation).
- I will never go to the infirmary again.
- I am going to go to medical school and be a doctor to help people like me.
- I will be a great dad to my children.

Less productive goals are stated in absolutist terms (e.g., never, always), are not clearly defined (e.g., what does being a "great" dad entail?), may not be feasible for the inmate (e.g., would he or she really be able to earn a medical degree with a criminal record?), and lack a specified time frame. Time frames are, again, helpful for prompting evaluation of the goal—was it achieved, and if not, what got in the way? Providers will likely need to assist inmates in developing goals that are more productive in nature, which can require significant patience on the part of providers. Many inmates will not be accustomed to such a highly specific method of goal-setting and may even show frustration over the fact that their goals are composed of several smaller, short-term goals. However, instillation of hope and reinforcement of completed goals will likely help inmates understand why this type of goal-setting is more beneficial than setting lofty or abstract goals for themselves.

Participant Rules

If delivered in a group setting, the rules outlined by Morgan and colleagues in *A Treatment Manual for Justice Involved Persons with Mental Illness: Changing Lives and Changing Outcomes*, first edition, should be followed. These rules address confidentiality, attendance, and participation, promptness, respect, homework, and other rules to be determined by group participants (e.g., no cursing). However, many of these rules are applicable to a one-on-one delivery format, as well.

First, while a schedule for completing handouts will be determined on an individualized basis according to provider availability and inmate level of functioning, it is expected that *program participants will complete assigned handouts by the established deadlines.* Multiple failures to turn in completed handouts should prompt a discussion aimed at assessing the factors related to this behavior—including, but not limited to, lack of motivation, decompensation, language or reading difficulties, or an inability to understand concepts presented, completion expectations, or general handout instructions. When such a discussion takes place (e.g., after the first or third missed handout) is a matter of clinical judgment.

Related to handout completion is the quality of work and adherence to handout instructions. That is, not only are participants expected to complete each handout promptly but also they are *expected to complete them well—that is, thoroughly and completely to the fullest extent of their capability.* A high versus low quality handout is assessed by the provider and should generally consider whether the inmate (1) addressed all aspects of the handout (particularly the embedded exercises), (2) responded in a way that demonstrates understanding of the concepts or skills taught, and (3) provided thoughtful, relevant, and effortful answers overall. The second tab in eResource Appendix A (Assessment Schedule and Behavioral Log for Clinicians) will help you track each completed handout, level of engagement with feedback, and work quality. The third tab in this Excel spreadsheet provides a key for rating engagement levels and scoring inmates' work quality. Lower-quality work should again be discussed with inmates so that they have an opportunity to improve responses to that particular handout and are clear on the expectations for future handouts. In the event of continued poor work ethic, providers may discuss the need for special accommodations (e.g., extra time, more one-on-one instruction), program fit with inmate abilities, or termination from the program.

Third, inmate *participants are expected to treat providers with the utmost respect.* There will be times throughout program implementation when inmate behaviors and attitudes need to be challenged or corrected; this is no excuse for disrespect. All participants are expected to take all feedback (positive or otherwise) openly and nondefensively. Consequences for disrespectful behavior should, of course, be based on institutional policies and procedures. Similarly, inmates are *expected to stay free of all institutional rule violations (or disciplinary infractions) throughout their participation and beyond.* Rule violations are counter to program goals and indicate that inmates are not practicing the prosocial skills learned in the program. While behaviors that violate institutional policy are no doubt serious, inmates should not necessarily be dismissed from the program. Before considering program dismissal, it is recommended that providers first use rule violations as a teaching tool. Because rule violations represent criminalness, they can be addressed therapeutically in the context of treatment goals. For example, an inmate may have employed his go-to criminal thinking style to rationalize an undesirable behavior. Pointing this out and having the inmate work through a corrective thought process based on a salient personal example will likely reinforce the need to implement new skills the next time he is faced with a similar choice. Furthermore, research shows that justice-involved individuals benefit from being in treatment (Kroner & Takahashi, 2012), and it would be detrimental and therapeutically counterproductive to dismiss participants for rule violations. Inmates in segregation need to develop skills for following rules, and dismissing them without first attempting to improve the behaviors that led to rule violations is contrary to the bi-adaptive goals of *Stepping Up, Stepping Out.*

Completion and Graduation Policies

Completion is assessed at the module and program levels. To complete a module, inmate participants must (1) successfully turn in all handouts within the module (judged by the provider based on the suggested criteria; see Participant Rules and Guide in Appendix A) and (2) earn at least a 75% on the content quiz, when applicable (note, Modules 1 and 9 do not include quizzes). Completion of Module 1 is determined by the inmate's performance on Handouts 1–2 and if these handouts were completed according to the provider's expectations. When a module is failed, the work needed to pass should be repeated before proceeding to the next module. However, to prevent failure at the end of the module, and reduce inmate frustration, insufficient or poorly completed handouts should be addressed immediately. As noted elsewhere, it is important that handout content is mastered before proceeding to the next handout given the additive nature of the program. Appendix J in the eResource materials include module completion certificates than can be personalized and awarded as inmates progress through the modules. Per anecdotal field reports from Missouri Department of Corrections (MDOC) staff, these intermittent rewards have been very favorably received by inmate participants and appear to serve as significant motivators for continued engagement.

To successfully complete the program in its entirety, participants must (1) pass Modules 1 through 8, (2) complete the relapse prevention plan according to provider expectations, and (3) submit a letter to the review board responsible for the release from restricted housing. If an inmate is released from segregation prior to program completion, the third requirement to submit a letter can be modified. For example, clinicians may opt to have the inmate compose a letter to someone other than the review board who can hold him or her accountable for maintaining progress toward goals (e.g., the clinician, a significant other).

Upon successful completion of all program requirements, inmates receive a personalized completion certificate to reward and document their graduation status (see Appendix P in the eResources materials).

Adjunctive Services and Interventions

Stepping Up, Stepping Out addresses a number of mental health and criminal risk factors that are relevant to inmates in segregation, yet it is not sufficient by itself. In fact, there are a number of empirically supported factors predictive of continued crime and behavioral misconduct that are not directly included in *Stepping Up, Stepping Out*. This is because several such risk factors are more thoroughly addressed by others means. For example, there is no module dedicated to substance abuse—an obvious problem for many offenders. While *Stepping Up, Stepping Out* addresses problematic thinking that justifies antisocial behaviors, including substance misuse, it does not explicitly target drug and alcohol use because many institutions already have well-established addictions counseling services. Whenever possible and indicated, *Stepping Up, Stepping Out* should be supplemented with other services. For example, inmates with minor reading, writing, or language deficits may require additional tutoring or one-on-one assistance to progress successfully through the program. When needed services are available only in GP, enrollment in or initiation of these services should be planned ahead of the inmate's release from segregation, including meeting with new treatment providers and discussing the plan for continued care. Adjunctive services may include educational, recreational, religious/spiritual (e.g., chaplain) services, Alcoholics Anonymous (AA) or Narcotics Anonymous (NA) meetings, psychopharmacological regimens (e.g., antipsychotics or antidepressant medication), and other mental health–based services.

Because *Stepping Up, Stepping Out* encourages inmates in restricted housing to focus on what they have access to, rather than what they do not, it is also important that participants be given opportunities to engage in activities within the confounds of their restricted environment. Thus, it is suggested that inmate participants (barring any significant rule violations) have access to book carts, yard time, art or activities therapy, family visitations, or other activities that are typically afforded to segregated inmates. Increases in these privileges may also serve as a behavioral reward for working productively through the program. To maintain motivation, it is helpful for inmates to receive more immediate rewards following compliance with treatment, as opposed to waiting until the end of treatment. In fact, people in general show faster learning when rewards are given more proximally to the desired behavior. Any rewards outside module completion certificates should be monetarily small but satisfying enough to the inmate to encourage continued positive behavior. Behavioral rewards or incentives may also be used to encourage positive inmate behaviors that are not directly related to *Stepping Up, Stepping Out* participation, such as accepting opportunities to shower, eating all meals, compliance with staff directives, and maintaining a clean cell.

Assessment

Required and Recommended Pre-Post Measures

Assessment is critical when delivering any treatment, but perhaps especially so when a program is first adopted by an institution. Assessment has a number of benefits, including the ability to determine who is appropriate for a given intervention, whether the selected intervention is producing the intended effects on the intended population, knowing when to intervene in the process of someone's treatment (e.g., provide additional assistance, terminate involvement, or progress to the next stage of treatment), and ensuring that financial and staffing resources are not wasted on interventions that do not work. For assessment to be useful, measurement must be based on what is targeted within the intervention and the broader objective. Because the content of *Stepping Up, Stepping Out* addresses mental health and criminogenic needs, the selected assessment measures are those that have been shown to reliably and validly assess these domains. In addition, the assessment protocol described here includes a mechanism for evaluating knowledge acquisition via the module quizzes (that is, did inmates learn what they were supposed to learn from the program modules?), behavioral responses/reactions to the program and provider, and institutional markers (e.g., disciplinary infractions) that are relevant to consider when assessing whether change occurred as a result of program participation.

Several assessment measures are required, as they are part of the program itself. In other words, inmates' results from these assessment tools are used to illustrate their problem areas and point out individualized risk factors as they are related to the program material. The program can, of course, be run without these measures, but the personal applicability of the content will be greatly diminished. The ability to show and discuss assessment results can help with inmate buy-in, increase personal insight into functioning, and, ultimately, demonstrate tangible evidence of positive change. In addition to these required measures (noted in **bold**; see Appendix B in the eResources for copies), a number of optional, but recommended measures are listed next. All assessment inventories have adequate psychometric properties, have been used with offender populations, and are in the public domain (i.e., available free of charge for clinical use). For more information on how to score and interpret the Depression, Hopelessness, Suicide Screening (DHS), the Psychological Inventory of Criminal Thinking Style—Short Form (PICTS-SF), the Criminal Sentiments Scale—Modified (CSS-M), and the Working Alliance Inventory (WAI; a post-treatment-only measure), clinicians are referred to Appendices C, D, E, and Q, respectively, in the eResource materials. Information on how to access the Recovery Assessment Scale (RAS), Diagnostic and Statistical Manual Fifth Edition (DSM-5) Self-Rated Level 1 Cross-Cutting Symptom Measure, the Positive and Negative Affect Scale (PANAS), the Medication Adherence Rating Scale (MARS), the Measure of Criminal Attitudes and Associates (MCAA), and the Brief Situational Confidence Questionnaire (BSCQ) free of cost for clinical use is provided next. For further assistance, readers are encouraged to contact the first author (A. B.).

Measures of Mental Health Functioning

- ✓ **DHS**
- ✓ RAS (available at https://depts.washington.edu/ebpa/sites/default/files/RAS%20-%20double%20sided.pdf)
- ✓ DSM-5 Self-Rated Level 1 Cross-Cutting Symptom Measure (visit www.psychiatry.org/psychiatrists/practice/dsm/educational-resources/assessment-measures and select "DSM-5 Self-Rated Level 1 Cross-Cutting Symptom Measure, Adult")
- ✓ PANAS (available at www.toolshero.com/psychology/personal-happiness/panas-scale/)
- ✓ MARS (the MARS [see pg. 7 in the linked PDF] and other tools for assessing adherence to prescribed medications can be found at www.easacommunity.org/files/Medication%20Adherence%20Scale.pdf; note, if an inmate is not on any medications, this measure can be skipped)

Measures of Criminal Risk

- ✓ **PICTS-SF**
- ✓ **CSS-M**
- ✓ MCAA (contact first author A. B.)
- ✓ BSCQ (available at www.nova.edu/gsc/forms/appendix_d_brief_situational_confidence_questionnaire.pdf)

Measures of Program Satisfaction and Compliance

- ✓ **WAI**
- ✓ **Clinician-rated behavioral observations (to include handout completion, engagement, feedback time)**

Other Relevant Institutional Markers

- ✓ Status of mental health diagnoses
- ✓ Mental health sick-call requests
- ✓ Disciplinary infractions/rule violations, acquisition of new charges
- ✓ Crisis incidents (e.g., placement on suicide watch)
- ✓ Whether or not release from segregation was granted
- ✓ Time to release from segregation following program completion (if applicable)

Appendix F is an Inmate Score Report Template that can be completed and shown to program participants to enhance understanding of assessment results. This Score Report displays results of the DHS, PICTS, and CSS-M on separate tabs as a graphical presentation, along with basic interpretations for each scale. For the DHS, a number of critical items are also emphasized. Each tab can be printed for distribution to inmate participants. Once scale scores are entered into the "Score" column, they will auto-populate into the respective column in the bar chart. As outlined next, it is recommended that pre-treatment results be distributed to inmates within the designated modules. However, in the event that the DHS suggests a high and imminent risk for suicide, immediate clinical attention is warranted. For further assistance scoring these measures (see also Appendices C, D, and E) or using the Score Report Template, clinicians are welcome to contact the first author (A. B.).

Module Content Quizzes

Module content quizzes are intended to measure the extent to which inmates learned the material they were exposed to throughout the module. Quizzes are to be given at the beginning of each module (to assess baseline knowledge) and again after the module "recap" worksheet. In the top left-hand corner of each quiz, the clinician can check off the designated time point (i.e., pre- or post-module). Of note, Modules 1 and 9 do not include content quizzes—Module 1 is a brief overview of the program's theoretical model and focuses on individualized goal-setting; Module 9 focuses on a relapse prevention plan and does not introduce any new material. Quiz items are presented in a multiple-choice format and include 8–12 questions per module. Answer keys are provided for easy grading. When inmates pass the post-module quiz (75% or above), but do not answer all items correctly, correct responses should be further explained to ensure a full understanding of the concept(s) assessed by each test item, as it may be relevant to or be repeated in upcoming modules. To illustrate growth and encourage continued motivation, inmates who improve (even if below the 75% threshold) from the pre- to post-module quiz should be informed about their degree of improvement (if applicable).

However, inmates who fail post-module quizzes should not be provided with correct responses to specific question items, as they will need to retake the quiz after redoing designated handouts within a module, or if warranted, the entire module. Whether the inmate completes specific handouts or the module in its entirety is at the discretion of the counselor. As a general rule, more global failures would suggest a need to retake the module; failures centered on a specific concept may only warrant reassignment of select handouts. In the event of a failed post-module quiz, inmates may be told in a general sense whether they made some improvement (if in fact they did), but they may not see which questions were correct vs. incorrect until they pass the quiz. Likewise, inmates should not be given corrective feedback on the pre-module content quiz. To most accurately assess comprehension, quizzes are not open book. Thus, if institutional logistics allow, inmates should not have immediate access to any module materials while taking these quizzes. As noted earlier, it is recommended that module handouts be retained by the clinician following handout-specific feedback until the module is passed, at which time materials for a given module can be returned to the inmate's possession.

Module quizzes for inmate distribution can be found in Appendix G, and quiz answer keys for clinician use are provided in Appendix H of the eResource materials.

Assessment Schedule

To adequately track inmate improvement, it is strongly recommended that assessment take place at multiple time points and continue beyond program completion. To determine individualized treatment needs and gather baseline functioning, an assessment must take first place prior to the initiation of *Stepping Up, Stepping Out*. For a better understanding of the immediate effects of program participation, it is important to assess inmates again directly following treatment completion (i.e., once the letter to the review board is completed and approved by the treatment provider). Whenever feasible, longer-term treatment gains should then be evaluated 6- and 12-months after the inmate discontinues program involvement. The first tab in the Assessment Schedule and Behavioral Log (Appendix A) allows clinicians to track administration dates for each of the three required assessment measures at pre- and post-treatment, as well as at six-month follow-up. Additional follow-up time points are encouraged when feasible. Clinicians may also modify this log if additional outcome measures are added for program evaluation purposes.

For ease of administration, Table 1.1 also outlines which measures should be given at which time points. Module-level measurements are also shown here.

All self-report measures should be completed by inmates on their own in a quiet, distraction-free environment whenever possible. Clinicians are encouraged to skim all returned assessment measures for completeness and clarity. For the most accurate behavioral data, clinician-rated behavioral observations of feedback engagement and work quality should be recorded in the Assessment Schedule and Behavioral Log (Appendix A) immediately the after each worksheet is submitted and evaluated for completion.

Helpful Assessment Tip: Like most clinicians, you are probably overwhelmed with enough responsibilities and may be concerned about how you will manage to collect data on top of administering an intensive treatment program. One suggestion is to look for opportunities to collaborate with educators and researchers at local colleges and universities (see Batastini, Hill, Repke, Gulledge, & Livengood, 2018). Behavioral health researchers often have interests that align with treatment outcome research and program evaluation in correctional settings. A 2017 article in *Corrections Today* highlighted the mutual advantages of this type of collaboration for program development, implementation, and evaluation (Hallundbaek, 2017). In fact, the degree to which researchers are involved in treatment implementation can even impact the effectiveness of the intervention. That is, larger treatment effects are observed when programs are tied to a research initiative than when they are not (Landenberger & Lipsey, 2005). This is likely the product of better monitoring of inmate participation and treatment fidelity. Most researchers will be excited to share their expertise and resources in exchange for access to de-identified data that can be published and/or practical opportunities for their students. In return, correctional systems gain

Table 1.1 Schedule for Survey Administration

	Pre-treatment	*Module Start*	*Module Completion*	*Treatment Completion*	*6-Month Post-treatment (Optional)*	*12-Month Post-treatment (Optional)*
***Required* Program Measures**						
DHS	X			X	X	X
PICTS-SF	X			X	X	
CSS-M	X			X	X	X
Module Quizzes		X*	X			
Clinician Behavioral Observations		X	X			
WAI				X	X	X
Recommended Program Measures						
DSM-V Cross-Cutting	X			X	X	X
RAS	X			X	X	X
PANAS	X			X	X	X
MARS	X			X	X	X
MCAA	X			X	X	X
BSCQ	X			X	X	X
Institutional Markers	X			X	X	X

Note: If preferred, clinicians may administer all pre-module quizzes along with the other pre-treatment measures. However, the motivational and attentional capacity of the inmate should be taken into account, as longer assessments can cause fatigue, which can lead to less accurate responding. Post-module quizzes should always be given immediately after each module (not at program end), as the inmate's performance on each quiz determines whether or not he can advance to the next module.

valuable information (at little or no cost to them) about their current practices and where improvements are needed. While you will still need to track handout distribution and your personal interactions with each inmate participant, researchers may be able to help administer, score, manage, and interpret pre- and post-assessment measures, as well as maintain de-identified data and run relevant statistical analyses.

Program Outline

Module 1: Understanding Change and Making It Happen: An Introduction

(Handouts 1–2). This brief introduction is meant to provide inmates with an overview of the basic cognitive-behavioral concepts that will be emphasized throughout the program and to increase awareness of their immediate and long-term goals related to getting out and staying out of segregation. Two of the main concepts discussed in this module are THE Circle of Change and the Mental Traffic Light. THE Circle of Change illustrates the broad domains (thoughts, habits, and environment) that contributed to the inmate's current segregation placement. It is these domains that the inmate must work to change to get out and stay out of segregation. The Mental Traffic Light is an evaluative tool that helps inmates assess whether or not a thought, habit, or environment will help (green light) or hinder (yellow or red light) their efforts toward achieving personal goals. This module further assists inmates in developing effective goals that have a high likelihood of being accomplished.

Key Points

- As often as possible, integrate THE Circle of Change and the Mental Traffic Light into real-life examples of inmates' thinking and behavior as they arise. How was a particular behavior triggered by thoughts and/or the environment? Was it a red light or yellow light?
- In the exercise *Building Your Goals* (Handout 2), be sure to help inmates set "good goals" that follow all four steps. After you grade completion on this exercise, allow inmates to keep this page so that they can be reminded of these goals throughout the program.

Module 2: Surviving Segregation: What to Expect and How to Cope

(Handouts 3–8). This module is designed to prepare inmates for, and help them cope with, the mental and physical challenges they will experience in segregated housing. The module begins by discussing the functions and implications of segregation, as well as the inmate's personal concerns. The module then discusses ways in which the inmate can alleviate common difficulties, such as sleep, sensory deprivation, and negative affect by emphasizing what the inmate has rather than what he does not have. This module includes an activity log that should be used on a weekly basis (both during and after the completion of this module) to track inmates' use of available resources on the unit.

Key Points

- For inmates who have been in restricted housing before, they may initially feel like this module does not apply to them. Encourage an open mind. Challenge them to find and focus on what's new. There are sure to be things they have not heard about before.
- Handout 3 includes a section for you to address any lingering questions the inmates may have about their time in restricted housing. Be sure to return this handout with answers (even if the answer is "I'm not sure" or "I don't understand your question").
- Appendix K in the eResource materials is the *My Activities Log*. The log is best introduced after Handout 4. The log can be used on a weekly basis to track activities the inmates have participated in or refused. When inmates refuse to participate in activities, feel free to challenge them on why (and relate it back to their goals, THE Circle of Change, and the Mental Traffic Light). Please give the inmates multiple copies.

Module 3: Suicide and Self-Injurious Behavior: Protecting You From You

(Handouts 9–11). Given the high risk of suicide among segregated inmates with mental illness, and that suicide tends to occur within the first few weeks of segregated placement (Patterson & Hughes, 2008; Sánchez, 2013; Way et al., 2007), this module educates inmates about the risks and warning signs of suicide and self-harm using the Joiner model (Joiner, 2005). Inmates also assess their own level of risk using the Depression, Hopelessness, Suicide Screening Form (DHS; Mills & Kroner, 2004) and learn specific tools for preventing suicidal and self-harm behaviors. The DHS is currently used routinely on all offenders entering federal custody in Canada. The use and consequences of suicidal intent and self-injurious behavior (SIB) to manipulate others or their environment are also discussed.

Table 2.1 Suggested Rubric for Determining Overall Risk Level Using the DHS

Overall Risk Category	*Depression*		*Hopelessness*		*Critical Items*
Low Risk (no scale elevations and up to 1 critical item)	≤ 5 on depression	*AND*	≤ 1 on hopelessness	*AND*	≤ 1 endorsed
Moderate-Low Risk (no scale elevations but multiple critical items)	≤ 5 on depression	*AND*	≤ 1 on hopelessness	*AND*	≥ 2 endorsed critical item
Moderate-Low Risk (1 scale elevation but no critical items)	≥ 6 on depression	*OR*	≥ 2 on hopelessness	*AND*	0 endorsed
Moderate Risk (1 scale elevation and only 1 critical item)	≥ 6 on depression	*OR*	≥ 2 on hopelessness	*AND*	1 endorsed critical item
Moderate Risk (2 scale elevations but no critical items)	≥ 6 on depression	*AND*	≥ 2 on hopelessness	*AND*	0 endorsed critical item
Moderate-High Risk (1 scale elevation and multiple critical items)	≥ 6 on depression	*OR*	≥ 2 on hopelessness	*AND*	≥ 2 endorsed critical item
Moderate-High Risk (2 scale elevations and only 1 critical item)	≥ 6 on depression	*AND*	≥ 2 on hopelessness	*AND*	1 endorsed critical item
High Risk (2 scale elevations and multiple critical items)	≥ 6 on depression	*AND*	≥ 2 on hopelessness	*AND*	≥ 2 endorsed critical item

Key Points

- Some inmates may be annoyed about working through a module on suicide. They may fear what will happen to them if they endorse any level of suicidal ideation and respond defensively. Or they may not see this module as relevant to them if they've never considered suicide. For those at less risk, this module may be seen as more preventative in nature and increasing awareness of the signs of suicide and depression.
- If you (or the inmate) are concerned that talking about suicide will trigger suicidal thoughts, know that a large body of research has shown that being asked about suicidal thoughts actually decreases the intensity of negative emotions and suicidal thoughts, even for those who are experiencing thoughts of suicide or who have a prior history of suicide attempts (e.g., Dazzi, Gribble, Wessely, & Fear, 2014).
- Results of the inmate's pre-treatment DHS should be distributed along with Handout 9. The second page of Handout 9 allows the inmates to write down their scores, evaluate their overall risk level, and any thoughts, feelings, or behaviors that could explain their scores and may serve as warning signs in the future. The DHS User's Guide does not offer explicit cutoff scores for determining overall risk level; however, this can be determined based (1) on your own clinical judgment and knowledge of the inmate or (2) using the suggested rubric in Table 2.1.
- In the exercise *Creating Your Suicide Prevention Plan* (Handout 10), be sure to help inmates flesh out each section in as much detail as possible. After you grade completion on this exercise, allow inmates to keep this page so that they can have ready access to their plan.

Module 4: Understanding My Emotions: Identifying and Dealing With Anger, Fear, and Other Frustrating Feelings

(Handouts 12–20). Inmates in segregation often have assaultive or passive-aggressive tendencies that lead to disciplinary problems (O'Keefe, 2008). This module discusses the short-term functions and the long-term consequences of anger, as well as the secondary emotions (e.g., fear, sadness, shame, guilt) that lie under the surface of anger. Inmates learn how to recognize their own triggers for aggression and practice specific methods for coping with strong, negative feelings that lead to violence. Elements of emotion regulation, anger management, and assertiveness training also help inmates to control and communicate their frustrations in a prosocial manner. This module includes an aggression log that should be used on a weekly basis (both during and after the completion of this module) to increase awareness of anger-triggering events and personal reactions (cognitive, emotional, and behavioral).

Key Points

- Appendix L in the eResource materials is the *My Aggression Log*. The log is best introduced after Handout 13. Like the *My Activities Log*, this log can also be used on a weekly basis to track events that triggered an aggressive episode, including physical, behavioral, emotional, and cognitive clues that the inmate should have noticed and intervened. Relate these triggers or clues to THE Circle of Change and the Mental Traffic Light, and emphasize that the need to reduce these events (frequency and intensity) is important to their long-term goals. Inmates are also asked to rate and record the highest intensity of anger they reached for each day of the week using the Anger Meter. Reinforce inmates as this number decreases. Provide copies of the *My Aggression Log* as needed.
- In *Match the Story* in Handout 15, David is being aggressive, Mary is being assertive, and Robert is being passive.
- Because most inmates in segregated housing are men, Handout 16 focuses on the role of aggression in more traditionally masculine ways. This handout may have shortcomings for female inmates. However, like males, female inmates may view aggression as a sign of "toughness" or acting like one of the guys. As such, this handout could be presented to women as a way to show that their traditional views of being tough and masculine as a means to get ahead are faulty. Encourage women to think of how they have tried to assert power or dominance over others in ways that are more stereotypically masculine and what consequences (good or bad) this had for them.

Module 5: Exploring My Mental Distress and Criminalness: Where It Comes From, What It Looks Like, and How to Recognize It

(Handouts 21–28). This module is designed to increase inmates' understanding about how mental health problems develop, what specific symptoms they experience, and how these symptoms can contribute to the disruptive conduct that led to their segregation placement. Inmates discuss the stigma of mental illness by the general public, how behaviors related to mental distress and illness can often be misattributed as disciplinary problems by correctional staff, and the increased risk of being the victims of violence by other inmates due to their mental impairment. This module further educates inmates about the risk factors for criminal conduct and how it is maintained, particularly within the prison walls. Styles of thinking that have been shown to support an antisocial lifestyle are emphasized, and inmates are given feedback about the specific beliefs they hold that are most problematic for them using their results on the Psychological Inventory of Criminal Thinking Styles (PICTS; Walters, 2013). A supplemental description of the various criminal thinking styles is included to enhance understanding of this concept. Through this module, inmates learn the importance of playing a proactive role in their recovery process.

Key Points

- Some inmates may feel that most of this module does not apply to them. However, because this module is intended to be psychoeducational, point out that it's like a crash course on mental health (or abnormal psychology) and that it will be useful for them to understand other mental illnesses, so they can better understand the experiences of others.
- In helping inmates discuss their specific symptoms or diagnoses, you may need to provide them with information on what diagnoses they in fact have (including the presence of antisocial personality disorder).
- Results of the inmate's pre-treatment PICTS should be distributed along with Handout 26. Results should be accompanied by the *PICTS Supplemental Handout: Understanding Your Criminal Thinking Styles* that follows Handout 26 in the Inmate Workbook. This supplemental handout describes each thinking style scale in further detail and provides space at the end for inmates to write down their three most problematic styles and share personal examples of when they have used these styles. Now that inmates are aware of their own criminal thinking styles, you can directly challenge them when they are relying on these thinking styles going forward. Did the inmate get a rule violation? That's discontinuity! Is he doing the bare minimum on handouts? There's cognitive indolence! Blaming the system for current problems? Mollification! Thinking he doesn't need treatment? Superoptimism! And don't forget to connect criminal thinking to THE Circle of Change and the Mental Traffic Light when relevant.

Module 6: Managing My Mental Distress and Criminalness: Improving Functioning and Preventing Relapse

(Handouts 29–38). Once inmates learn about the risks associated with their mental health problems and criminalness, this module teaches them new skills for increasing their ability to function within GP. Emphasis is placed on cognitive-behavioral strategies for altering maladaptive thought processes that lead to disruptive behaviors, whether they are rooted in psychological impairment or criminalness. Given the prevalence of personality disorders (e.g., borderline, schizotypal, antisocial, and narcissistic; O'Keefe, 2008) among segregated inmates, Dialectical Behavior techniques, such as distress tolerance, are applied. The importance of following prescribed medication regimes to reduce the severity of symptoms is emphasized as well. Inmates also learn how to identify and use facility resources (e.g., book carts, recreational time) to get their needs met. This module includes a progress checkpoint to highlight accomplishments and strengths, supplemental relaxation exercises with instructions, and a medication monitoring card to track symptom relief and side effects for the purpose of facilitating effective doctor-patient communication.

Key Points

- Some inmates may need more time to understand the connection between thoughts, feelings, and actions. While this module includes a lot of practice exercises, be sure to work one-on-one with the inmate when needed.
- Appendix M in the eResource materials is the *My Automatic Log*. The log is best introduced after Handout 30. The log can be used on a weekly basis to track negative or maladaptive automatic thoughts and their consequences. The log also guides inmates through the process of challenging these thoughts to alter overall mood. Please give the inmate multiple copies of this log. It is also recommended that you periodically review their logs for accuracy and to provide feedback for improvement.
- Following Handout 30 is a *Progress Checkpoint* worksheet. This marks about the halfway point in the program and is a good place to reinforce the good things done up to this point. Once you grade

the completion of this worksheet and offer any positive affirmations, the *Progress Checkpoint* can be returned to inmates for reference and continued motivation.

- Appendix N in the eResource materials contains four *Extra Relaxation Techniques*. These additional exercises ("Using Your Breathing," "Progressive Muscle Relaxation," "Guided Imagery," and "Positive Self-Talk") are best introduced after Handout 32. Inmates can keep these exercises and should be encouraged to use them on a regular (e.g., daily) basis.
- Handouts 33–36 describe skills and techniques to address specific psychological problems. Most of these handouts will apply to everyone, but not in every case. For example, inmates may not have any history of or current problems with psychosis. Therefore, it is up to the discretion of the clinician whether handouts can and should be skipped.
- Appendix O in the eResource materials is the *Medication Monitoring Card*. A copy of this card should be given after Handout 38, and it is to be completed by the inmate prior to seeing the physician or health-care provider. Inmates should take this card with them to their appointments as a reminder of their concerns and to ensure that all questions are asked.
- Following this module, inmates will have a lot of new skills in their toolbox. Encourage continued use of these skills throughout the program and beyond.

Module 7: Seeking Supportive Allies: Finding Helpful Others Among the Crowd

(Handouts 39–43). This module highlights the role that other people play in the inmate's life. Other people can either help or hinder the inmate's goal of remaining within GP. Inmates learn to establish relationships with other inmates who are less criminal and who tend to follow institutional rules. The module also educates inmates about the warning signs (e.g., grooming) for becoming the targets of aggression and sexual assault, as well as the benefits and consequences of gang membership.

Key Points

- Handout 41 includes a specific mnemonic device (RITE or Ready, Introduce, Talk, Exit) for engaging in effective communication. If feasible, help the inmate role play the RITE technique or find a peer mentor to assist.
- In the exercise *The Gang Game* (Handout 42), inmates are asked to name common prison gangs to avoid. If there is fear of explicitly naming such gangs, this exercise can be modified. The inmate can be instructed to instead simply think about each gang, or they may come up with an unidentifiable nickname for the gang for purposes of completing the remaining columns.

Module 8: Integrating "Us" and "Them": Improving Inmate-Staff Relations

(Handouts 44–45). Given that correctional officers have the most contact with segregated inmates and are often the first to respond to mental health–related problems (Dvoskin & Spiers, 2004), this module is designed to help inmates understand the role of correctional staff in an effort to decrease an "us-vs-them" mentality. Inmates learn how correctional staff perceives the prison environment. The Criminal Sentiments Scale—Modified (CSS-M; Simourd, 1997) is used to demonstrate inmates' individual preexisting attitudes toward authority within the justice system. The primary objective of this module is to increase respect and empathy for authority figures, thereby increasing rule compliance. The importance of cooperating with staff, even when the inmate does not want to, is discussed. Inmates also learn to cope with dominant or power-seeking staff.

Key Points

- In the exercise *In Their Shoes* (Handout 44), inmates are asked to assume the role of a correctional officer and select the more appropriate response to each scenario while keeping security needs in mind. Because each institution has its own set of policies, you will need to decide which choice is most in line with your setting. Consult security staff if needed. You may find it helpful to maintain an answer key once you determine the best responses.
- Results of the inmate's pre-treatment CSS-M should be distributed along with Handout 45. The exercise *Attitude Check* within this handout requires inmates to copy their scores and identify which scales they were highest on, provide examples of how these attitudes showed up in their own lives, and consider more positive views toward authority and laws.

Module 9: Road Map to Recovery: Creating Your Relapse Prevention Plan

(Includes a Relapse Prevention Packet, template for a letter of progress to the segregation review board, and completion certificate). This module is designed to help inmates review and integrate what they have learned and accomplished throughout the program so that they can maintain treatment gains in the long term. Inmates must also prepare a written document highlighting their progress and will present that document to institutional staff responsible for determining the inmates' release from restricted housing. Upon successful completion of the program, inmates are awarded a personalized certificate.

Key Points

- First, consider congratulating the inmate for making it this far in the program and getting to the finish line!
- All materials from previous modules can be returned when the Relapse Prevention Packet is distributed. The entire packet should be distributed together.
- Remind inmates that no new information is presented here; rather, it is a place for them to summarize what they learned and make a promise to themselves that they will maintain progress. Be mindful that inmates may need more time to complete the packet than the typical handout.
- The final component of the program is the *My Letter of Progress*. To the extent possible, assist inmates in composing this letter. It may require a few rounds of edits. And you may need to help point out some aspects that are missing or that the inmate may not be aware of. For example, you may have noticed that he caught fewer infractions since starting this program or that medication dosage was reduced.

Now, celebrate and distribute the program completion certificate (see Appendix P)!

References

Andrews, D. A., & Bonta, J. (2017). *The psychology of criminal conduct* (6th ed.). New York, NY: Routledge Taylor & Francis Group.

Andrews, D. A., Bonta, J., & Wormith, J. S. (2006). The recent past and near future of risk and/or need assessment. *Crime & Delinquency*, *52*, 7–27.

Andrews, D. A., Zinger, I., Hoge, R. D., Bonta, J., Gendreau, P., & Cullen, F. T. (1990). Does correctional treatment work? A clinically relevant and psychologically informed meta-analysis. *Criminology*, *28*, 369–404.

APA Presidential Task Force on Evidence-Based Practice (2006). Evidence-based practice in psychology. *American Psychologist*, *61*, 271–285. doi:10.1037/0003-066X.61.4.271

Batastini, A. B., Hill, J. B., Repke, A., Gulledge, L. M., & Livengood, Z. (2018). Approaching correctional treatment from a programmatic standpoint: Risk-needs-responsivity and beyond. In M. Ternes, P. Magaletta, & M. Patry (Eds.), *The practice of correctional psychology*. New York, NY: Springer Publishing Co.

Beven, G. (2005). Offenders with mental illnesses in maximum and supermaximum security settings. In S. L. Charles & J. B. Gerbasi (Eds.), *Handbook of correctional mental health* (pp. 209–228). Arlington, VA: American Psychiatric Publishing, Inc.

Bourgon, G., & Armstrong, B. (2005). Transferring the principles of effective treatment into a "real world" prison setting. *Criminal Justice and Behavior, 32*, 3–25.

Burdon, W. M., Messina, N. P., & Prendergast, M. L. (2004). The California treatment expansion initiative: Aftercare participation, recidivism, and predictors of outcomes. *The Prison Journal, 84*, 61–80.

Chadick, C. D., Batastini, A. B., Levulis, S. J., & Morgan, R. D. (2018). The psychological impact of solitary: A longitudinal comparison of general population and long-term administratively segregated inmates. *Legal and Criminological Psychology, 23*, 101–116. doi:10.1111/lcrp.12125

Chaiken, S., & Shull, J. (2007). Mental health treatment of inmates in segregated housing. In O. J. Thienhaus & M. Piasecki (Eds.), *Correctional psychiatry: Practice guidelines and strategies* (pp. 7.2–7.21). Kingston, NJ: Civic Research Institute, Inc.

Coid, J., Petruckevitch, A., Begginton, P., Jenkins, R., Brugha, T., Lewis, G., . . . Singleton, N. (2003). Psychiatric morbidity in prisoners and solitary cellular confinement, I: Disciplinary segregation. *The Journal of Forensic Psychiatry & Psychology, 14*(2), 298–319.

Corrigan, P. W. (2014). Can there be false hope in recovery? *The British Journal of Psychiatry, 205*(6), 423–424. doi:10.1192/bjp.bp.114.151704

Dazzi, T., Gribble, R., Wessely, S., & Fear, N. T. (2014). Does asking about suicide and related behaviours induce suicidal ideation? What is the evidence? *Psychological Medicine, 44*(16), 3361–3363. https://doi.org/10.1017/S0033291714001299

Dvoskin, J. A., & Spiers, E. M. (2004). On the role of correctional officers in prison mental health. *The Psychiatric Quarterly, 75*(1), 41–59.

Gaspar, M., Brown, L. Ramler, T., Scanlon F., Gigax, G., Ridley, K., Morgan, R. D. (2019). Therapeutic outcomes of Changing Live, Changing Outcomes for male and female justice involved persons with mental illness. Manuscript submitted for publication.

Gendreau, P. (1996a). The principles of effective intervention with offenders. In A. T. Harland (Ed.), *Choosing correctional options that work: Defining the demand and evaluation the supply*. Thousand Oaks, CA: Sage.

Gendreau, P. (1996b). Offender rehabilitation: What we know and what needs to be done. *Criminal Justice and Behavior, 23*, 144–161.

Gendreau, P., & Labrecque, R. M. (2015). The effects of administrative segregation: A lesson in knowledge cumulation. In J. Wooldredge & P. Smith (Eds.), *Oxford handbook on prisons and imprisonment*. Oxford, UK: Oxford University Press.

Golden, L. S., Gatchel, R. J., & Cahill, M. A. (2006). Evaluating the effectiveness of the National Institute of corrections' "Thinking for a Change" program among probationers. *Journal of Offender Rehabilitation, 43*, 55–73.

Goode, E. (2015). *Solitary confinement: Punished for life*. Retrieved from www.nytimes.com/2015/08/04/health/solitary-confinement-mental-illness.html? r=29.

Hallundbaek, H. (2017). Art for a change: Innovative reentry program shows off practical implications. *Corrections Today, 79*(1), 56–61.

Haney, C. (2003). Mental health issue in long-term solitary and "supermax" confinement. *Crime & Delinquency, 49*(1), 124.

Hayes, S. C. (2004). Acceptance and commitment therapy, relational frame theory, and the third wave of behavioral and cognitive therapies. *Behavior Therapy, 35*(4), 639–665.

Joiner, T. E. (2005). *Why people die by suicide*. Cambridge, MA: Harvard University Press.

Kroner, D. G., & Takahashi, M. (2012). Every session counts: The differential impact of previous programmes and current programme dosage on offender recidivism. *Legal and Criminological Psychology, 17*(1), 136–150. https://doi.org/10.1111/j.2044-8333.2010.02001.x

Landau, E. (2015). *Solitary confinement: 29 years in a box*. Retrieved from www.cnn.com/2014/02/23/health/solitary-confinement-psychology/

Landenberger, N. A., & Lipsey, M. W. (2005). The positive effects of cognitive-behavioral programs for offenders: A meta-analysis of factors associated with effective treatment. *Journal of Experimental Criminology, 1*, 451–476.

Leak, G. K. (1980). Effects of highly structured versus nondirective group counseling approaches on personality and behavioral measures of adjustment in incarcerated felons. *Journal of Counseling Psychology, 27*, 520–523.

Liman Program & Association of State Correctional Administrators. (2015). *Time-in-cell: ASCA-Liman 2014 national survey of administrative segregation in prison*. New Haven, CT: Yale Law School.

Linehan, M. M. (1993). *Cognitive behavioral therapy of borderline personality disorder* (Vol. 51). New York: Guilford Press.

Lipsey, M. W. (1989, November). *The effectiveness of interventions for juvenile delinquency: Results from 400 studies*. Paper presented at the 41st annual meeting of the American Society of Criminology, Reno, NV.

Mears, M. P. (2006). *Evaluating the effectiveness of supermax prisons*. Washington, DC: The Urban Institute. Retrieved from www.urban.org/sites/default/files/publication/50846/411326-Evaluating-theEffectiveness-of-Supermax-Prisons.PDF

Metzner, J. L., & Fellner, J. (2010). Solitary confinement and mental illness in U.S. prisons: A challenge for medical ethics. *The Journal of the American Academy of Psychiatry and the Law, 38*, 104–108.

Mills, J., & Kroner, D. (2004). A new instrument to screen for depression, hopelessness, and suicide in incarcerated offenders. *Psychological Services, 1,* 83–91. doi: 10.1037/1541-1559.1.1.83

Mills, J. F., Kroner, D. G., & Mongrain, S. J. (2005). Deconstructing criminal networks: Intervening to break-down patterns of criminal associations. *Corrections Today, 67*, 46–49.

Morgan, R. D., & Flora, D. B. (2002). Group psychotherapy with incarcerated offenders: A research synthesis. *Group Dynamics: Theory, Research, and Practice, 6*, 203–218. doi:10.1037//1089-2699.6.3.203

Morgan, R. D., Flora, D. B., Kroner, D. G., Mills, J. F., Varghese, F., & Steffan, J. S. (2012). Treating offenders with mental illness: A research synthesis. *Law and Human Behavior, 36*, 37–50.

Morgan, R. D., Gendreau, P., Smith, P., Gray, A., Labrecque, R. M., MacLean, N., . . . Mills, J. F. (2016). Quantitative syntheses on the effects of administrative segregation on prisoners' well-being. *Psychology, Public Policy, and the Law, 22*(4), 439–461. doi:10.1037/law0000089

Morgan, R. D., Kroner, D. G., & Mills, J. F. (2006). Group psychotherapy in prison: Facilitating change inside the walls. *Journal of Contemporary Psychotherapy, 36*, 137–144. doi:10.1007/BF02729057

Morgan, R. D., Kroner, D. G., & Mills, J. F. (2018). *Changing lives and changing outcomes: A treatment program for justice involved persons with mental illness.* New York: Routledge.

Morgan, R. D., Kroner, D. G., Mills, J. F., Bauer, R., & Serna, C. (2014). Treating justice-involved persons with mental illness: Preliminary evaluation of a comprehensive treatment program. *Criminal Justice and Behavior, 41*(7), 902–916. doi.org/10.1177/0093854813508553

Mueser, K. T., Corrigan, P. W., Hilton, D. W., Tanzman, B., Schaub, A., Gingerich, S., . . . Herz, M. I. (2002). Illness management and recovery: A review of the research. *Psychiatric Services, 53*(10), 1272–1284. doi:10.1176/appi.ps.53.10.1272

O'Keefe, M. (2007). Administrative segregation for mentally ill inmates. *Mental Health Issues in the Criminal Justice System, 45*(1), 149–165.

O'Keefe, M. (2008). Administrative segregation from within: A corrections perspective. *The Prison Journal, 88*(1), 123–143.

O'Keefe, M. L., Klebe, K. J., Stucker, A., Sturm, K., & Leggett, W. (2010). *One year longitudinal study of the psychological effects of administrative segregation.* Report submitted to the National Institute of Justice, Washington DC.

Patterson, R. F., & Hughes, K. (2008). Review of completed suicides in the California department of corrections and rehabilitation, 1999 to 2004. *Psychiatric Services, 59*, 676–682.

Pizarro, J., & Stenius, V. (2004). Supermax prisons: Their rise, current practice, and effect on inmates. *The Prison Journal, 84*(2), 248–264.

Reilly, P. M., & Shopshire, M. S. (2015). *Anger management for substance abuse and mental health clients: A cognitive behavioral therapy manual.* Rockville, MD: U.S. Department of Health and Human Services Substance Abuse and Mental Health Services Administration Center for Substance Abuse Treatment.

Rodriguez, S. (2011). *Historic California assembly hearing on solitary confinement.* Retrieved from http://solitarywatch.com/2011/08/24/historic-california-assembly-hearingon-solitaryconfinement/

Ross, R. R., Fabiano, E. A., & Ewles, C. D. (1988). Reasoning and rehabilitation. *International Journal of Offender Therapy and Comparative Criminology, 32*, 29–35.

Ruiz v. Estelle, 503 F. Supp. 1265 (S.D. Tex. 1980).

Sánchez, H. G. (2013). Suicide prevention in administrative segregation units: What is missing? *Journal of Correctional Health Care, 19*, 93–100.

Simourd, D. J. (1997). The Criminal Sentiments Scale-Modified and Pride in Delinquency Scale: Psychometric properties and construct validity of the two measures of criminal attitudes. *Criminal Justice and Behavior, 24*, 52–70. doi: 10.1177/0093854897024001004

Skeem, J. L., & Louden, J. E. (2006). Toward evidence-based practice for probationers and parolees mandated to mental health treatment. *Psychiatric Services, 57*, 333–342.

Suedfeld, P., Ramirez, C., Deaton, J., & Baker-Brown, G. (1982). Reactions and attributes of prisoners in solitary confinement. *Criminal Justice and Behavior, 9*(3), 303–340.

Van Horn, S. A., Morgan, R. D., Brusman-Lovins, L., Littlefield, A., Hunter, J. T., & Gigax, G. (in press). Changing lives, changing outcomes: "What works" in an intervention for justice-involved persons with mental illness. *Psychological Services.*

Walters, G. D. (2013). *The Psychological Inventory of Criminal Thinking Styles (PICTS) professional manual.* Allentown, PA: Center for Lifestyle Studies.

Walters, G. D. (2018). Checking the math: Do restrictive housing and mental health need add up to psychological deterioration? *Criminal Justice and Behavior, 45*(9), 1347–1362. https://doi.org/10.1177/0093854818780177

Way, B. B., Sawyer, D. A., Barboza, S., & Nash, R. (2007). Inmate suicide and time spent in special disciplinary housing in New York State prison. *Psychiatric Services, 58*(4), 558–560.

Weinberg, C. M. (2013). Hope, meaning, and purpose: Making recovery possible. *Psychiatric Rehabilitation Journal, 36*(2), 124–125.

Yalom, I. D. (1995). *Theory and practice of group psychotherapy* (4th ed). New York, NY: Basic Books.

Part II
Inmate Workbook

Program Introduction and Expectations

Welcome to *Stepping Up, Stepping Out*! The goal of *Stepping Up, Stepping Out* is not to cure you of experiencing mental health problems or stop all bad behavior from happening; rather, this program will help you better deal with the thoughts and behaviors that brought you to this unit, so you can successfully serve you time here, return safely to GP or a less restrictive unit, and stay there. You will start with an assessment of your treatment needs—that is, what are some of your personal areas for growth? These assessments will also help track your progress throughout the program. Because your treatment and progress are determined by these assessments, it is important that you answer each question honestly.

After these assessments, you will complete a series of modules that will help you follow the rules and change your typical pattern of thinking and acting so that you have the best shot of being infraction-free. Your success matters. The way this program works is that you will do a lot of the work on your own with the help of a counselor. You will be asked to read information and then complete activities based on that information. To really learn it, you should practice the skills you read about in your everyday life on the unit. You will also take quizzes before and after each module to make sure you learned key information. Passing these quizzes means you will be able to move on to the next module. If you do not pass, it simply means you need to review some material before moving on.

As you work through the program, you will earn completion certificates that will go in your file. If you do well, you may even be able to get some of your privileges back or be eligible for early release from seg. Ask your counselor about the options that are available to you if you finish this program. If you need help reading, ask your counselor if a peer mentor can work with you.

Before You Get Started, Here Are Some Important Expectations to Keep in Mind

1. This program is LONG. Why? Because you've been thinking and doing things the same way for a long time. So, to make a new way of thinking and behaving become natural, it's going to take a long time and a lot of practice. Persistence is key. Push through it. Think about change as climbing a mountain. It's steep, but you can go at your own pace.
2. Information is repetitive, meaning you will read about and be asked to do the same things more than one time. Why? Because doing things over and over again will help you learn it better. How did you learn to memorize your phone number as a kid? You had to say it many, many, many times. New habits stick when you practice them.
3. Some new skills will be challenging and test your abilities. Try it anyway. You won't be punished for giving it your best effort. Or ask for help if you don't understand what you're being asked to do.
4. You may read something that you don't agree with or that challenges the way you think about yourself. For example, many people struggle with the term "criminal," but that's what you are as a person in the system, and you must learn to rise above this label. Some people also have a difficult time hearing that they must now take responsibility and look inward at themselves. This is a normal feeling. Accept the challenge anyway.
5. Some material may be less true of you than other material. Why? Because *Stepping Up, Stepping Out* was made for lots of people in your situation. So while some things you read about or are asked to do may not apply as directly to you, they do to other people. If you find yourself saying, "This isn't me," first consider whether you are being too quick to dismiss or ignore the information. Maybe it is true, but you're having a hard time hearing it (see expectation #4). If it truly isn't about you, do your best to get through it with an open mind. Who knows—maybe you'll end up learning something you didn't expect!

6. If you start to feel discouraged or annoyed, think about why you need to do this program. Do you want to have better control over your mood, feel less stressed, make a better life for yourself, or not repeat the same mistakes again? Keep climbing the mountain.

Program Outline

Module 1 Understanding Change and Making It Happen: An Introduction

This brief introduction is meant to provide you with an overview of the basic cognitive-behavioral concepts that will be emphasized throughout the program and to increase awareness of your immediate and long-term goals related to getting out and staying out of segregation.

Module 2 Surviving Segregation: What to Expect and How to Cope

This module is designed to prepare you for, and help you cope with, the mental and physical challenges you will experience in segregated housing. The module begins by discussing the functions and implications of segregation, as well as your personal concerns. The module then discusses ways in which you can alleviate common difficulties, such as sleep, sensory deprivation, and negative affect by emphasizing what you have rather than what you do not have.

Module 3 Suicide and Self-Injurious Behavior: Protecting You From You

Given the high risk of suicide for people in segregation, and that suicide tends to occur within the first few weeks of segregated placement, this module will educate you about the risks and warning signs of suicide and self-harm. You will also be assessed on your own level of risk and will learn specific tools for preventing suicidal and self-harm behaviors. The use of suicidal intent and self-injurious behavior (SIB) to manipulate others or your environment will also be discussed.

Module 4 Understanding My Emotions: Identifying and Dealing With Anger, Fear, and Other Frustrating Feelings

Inmates in segregation often have assaultive or passive-aggressive tendencies that lead to disciplinary problems. This module will discuss the short-term functions and the long-term consequences of anger. You will learn how to recognize your own triggers for aggression and will practice specific methods for coping with strong, negative feelings that lead to violence. Elements of emotion regulation, anger management, and assertiveness training will also help you control and communicate your frustrations in a prosocial manner.

Module 5 Exploring My Mental Distress and Criminalness: Where It Comes From, What It Looks Like, and How to Recognize It

This module is designed to increase your understanding about how mental health issues and mental illness develops, what specific symptoms you experience, and how these symptoms can contribute to the disruptive conduct that led to your segregation placement. You will also discuss the stigma of mental illness in the general public, how behaviors related to mental symptoms and illness can often be misattributed as disciplinary problems by correctional staff, and the increased risk of being the victim of violence by other inmates. This module will further educate you about the risk factors for criminal conduct and how it is maintained, particularly within the prison walls. Styles of thinking that have been shown to support an antisocial lifestyle are emphasized, and you will be given feedback about the specific beliefs you hold that are most problematic for you. You will learn the importance of playing a proactive role in your own recovery process.

Module 6 Managing My Mental Distress and Criminalness: Improving Functioning and Preventing Relapse

Once you learn about the risks associated with your mental health problems or illness and criminalness, this module will teach new skills for increasing your ability to function in the GP. Emphasis will be placed on cognitive-behavioral strategies for altering maladaptive thought processes that lead to disruptive behaviors, whether they are rooted in mental illness or criminalness. Given the prevalence of personality disorders (e.g., borderline, schizotypal, antisocial, and narcissistic) among segregated inmates, Dialectical Behavior techniques, such as distress tolerance, will be applied. The importance of following prescribed medication regimes to reduce the severity of symptoms is emphasized as well. You will also learn how to identify and use facility resources (e.g., book carts, recreational time) to get your needs met.

Module 7 Seeking Supportive Allies: Finding Helpful Others Among the Crowd

This module highlights the role that other people play in your life. Other people can either help or hinder your goal of remaining within the GP. You will learn to establish relationships with other inmates who are less criminal and who tend to follow institutional rules. The module also educates you about the warning signs (e.g., grooming) for becoming the targets of aggression and sexual assault, as well as the benefits and consequences of gang membership.

Module 8 Integrating "Us" and "Them": Improving Inmate-Staff Relations

This module is designed to help you understand the role of correctional staff in an effort to decrease an "us-vs-them" mentality. You will learn how correctional staff perceives the prison environment. The primary objective of this module is to increase respect and empathy for authority figures, thereby increasing rule compliance. The importance of cooperating with staff, even when you don't want to, will be discussed. You will also learn to cope with dominant or power-seeking staff.

Module 9 Road Map to Recovery: Creating Your Relapse Prevention Plan

This module is designed to help you review and integrate what you have learned and accomplished throughout the program so you can maintain treatment gains in the long term. You will also prepare a written document highlighting your progress and present that document to institutional staff responsible for determining your release from restricted housing.

Ready to begin?

Module 1

Understanding Change and Making It Happen: An Introduction

Handout #1
The Basics of This Program

There are a number of reasons why inmates find themselves in restrictive housing units, but the main problem is poor thinking skills that lead to rule breaking or destructive behavior. Inmates who are in these special housing units often have trouble handling stress in the first place and having to live in such a restrictive environment can add to that stress.

THE Circle of Change

The picture in the box that follows shows how different things in your life can lead to where you are at a given moment—right now you are in restrictive housing. **But how did you get here?** The way you think about your world led you to act in ways that are consistent with those thoughts, and those actions landed you in segregated placement. It's important to remember that this is a *cycle*. So being in restrictive housing (your environment) may, in turn, increase the kinds of thoughts that lead to your rule-breaking behaviors. This cycle makes it hard for you to get out of solitary and, more importantly, stay out.

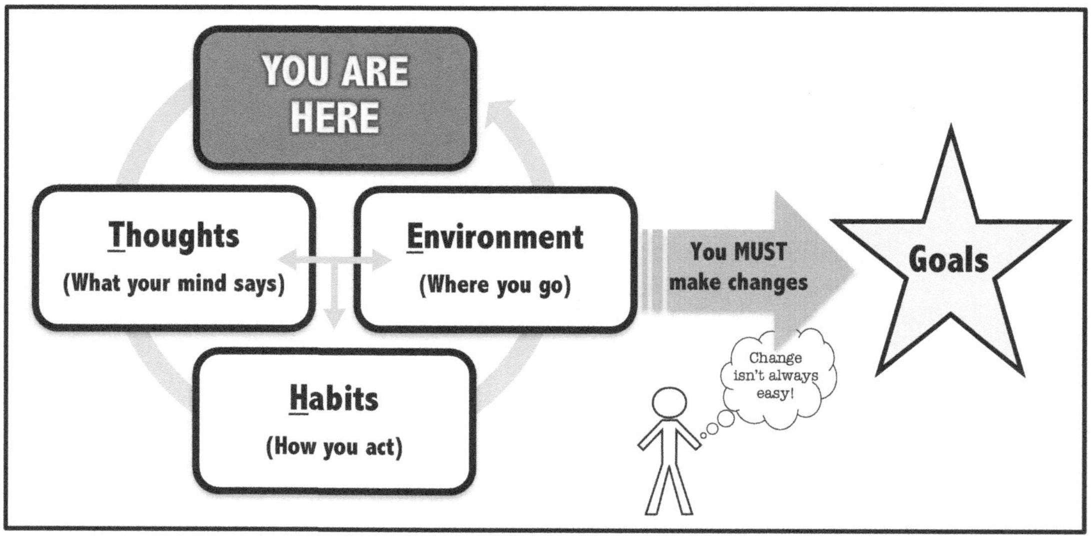

How do you get out of the cycle? *You must make changes*! To reach your goals, you must change how you think, how you act, and the places you go. You can apply this idea to any part of your life that you are not happy with and set positive goals for improving your situation. In this program, your main focus is to do the following:

> Successfully serve your time in restrictive housing and learn new skills to manage the problems that led you here, so you **do not come back**.

Mini Exercise 1

To get the hang of THE Circle of Change, try an example. Read the story that follows about Marcus and complete the pieces of the circle in the diagram that comes after it.

> *Marcus is a 35-year-old man. He grew up in a poor neighborhood where many of his friends did illegal things to make money and survive. Marcus often robbed people whom he thought were wealthy and could afford to lose their personal belongings. He figured if he could get access to their items, then those people didn't deserve to have them anyway. One night, he broke into a family's home believing that the house was empty. He was wrong! The police were called, and Marcus was placed under arrest. He already has a criminal record, and there was evidence of his break-in, so there is a good chance he will serve jail or prison time for his crime.*

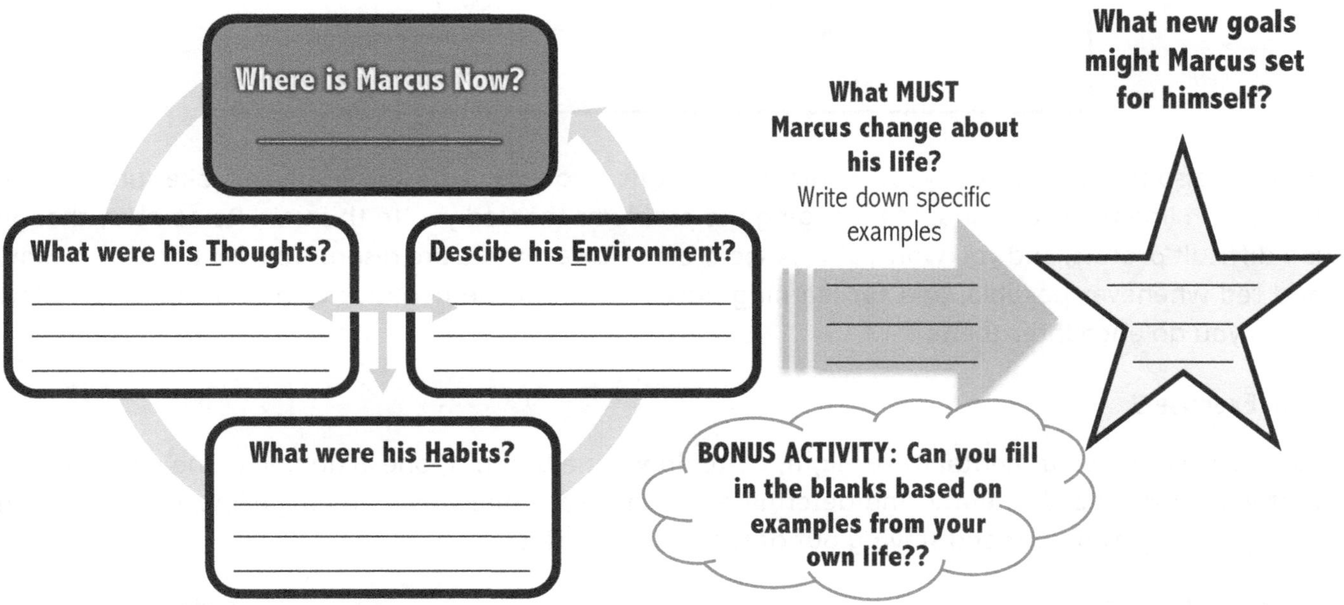

Throughout the program, you will be applying **THE Circle of Change** to your personal situation—that is, where you are now. You will be introduced to new skills that will help you identify and change the thoughts, actions, and environments that lead you to your rule-breaking behaviors. The different parts of **THE Circle of Change** for you may be related to the way you are as a person with criminal tendencies and/or as a person with a mental health problem. We will explore both.

The Green Light to Goals

So how do you know which thoughts, habits, and environments (remember, this can also include the people you hang around) are not helpful for achieving your goal of staying out of restrictive housing once you leave here? One way to start doing this is to use a mental traffic light. Just as traffic lights in the real world help keep people safe by enforcing the rules of the road, your mental traffic light can help you stay safe in your recovery from criminal conduct and mental illness (two problems that have brought you to where you are right now). The mental traffic light gives you awareness of your thoughts, habits, and environments, as well as a method to evaluate how helpful or not helpful they are in reaching your goals. Again, this model can be applied to other aspects of your life to help you stay on track with all of your goals. But for now, your focus is to get out and stay out of restrictive housing.

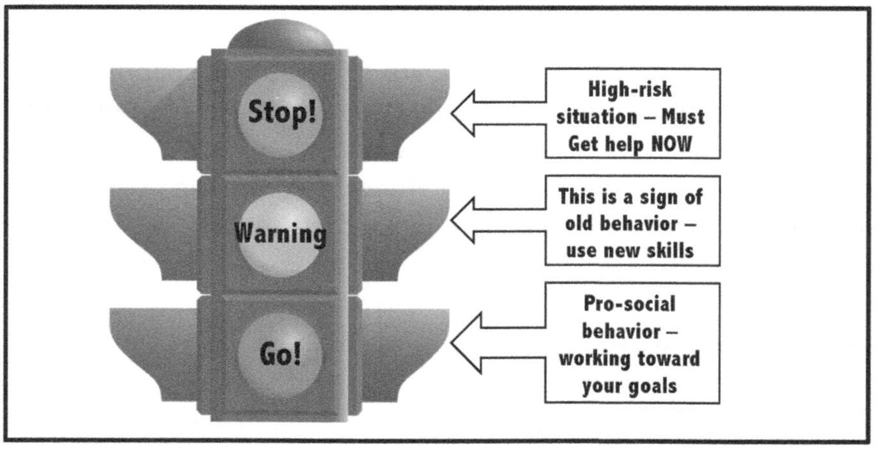

You will also be asked to use your mental traffic light throughout this program to make sure you are keeping in line with your goal of managing the problems that led you to this unit. Remember, change is a difficult process, and you won't always see green. However, you are responsible for avoiding yellow and red whenever possible, and for learning how to prevent the negative effects of red and yellow when you do encounter them.

Mini Exercise 2

To practice using your mental traffic light, write down one thought, one action, and one environment that you experienced recently, and determine whether each one was a green, yellow, or red light in your goal of getting out and staying out of restrictive housing.

I recently thought this: **Color:** ____________

____

____

I recently did this: **Color:** ____________

____

____

I was recently in this place and/or with these people: **Color:** ____________

____

____

Handout #2
Setting Personal Goals

Problems That Led You Here

Sometimes it's helpful to come up with goals when you first stop to think about the problems that led you to where you are now. Knowing *how* you got here can help you understand what goals are necessary to move you in a more positive direction—away from your old problems.

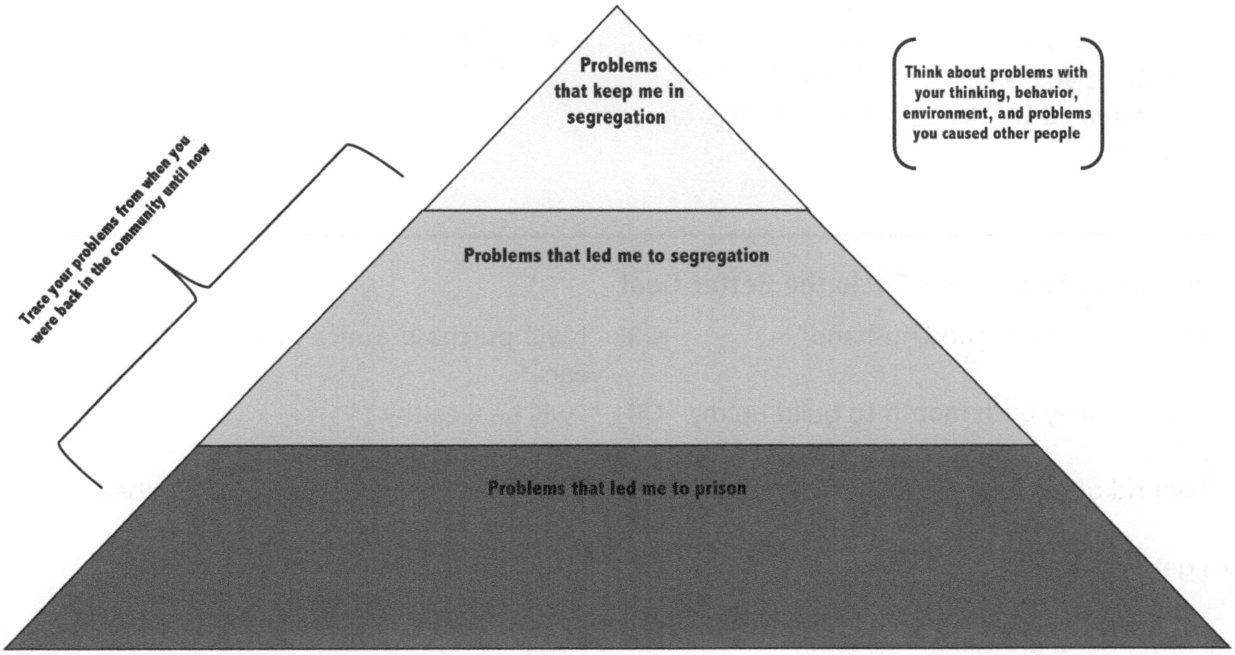

Do you notice any themes or common problems in each place?

____

____

____

____

Guidelines for Developing Good Goals

Good goals are ones that you are likely to stick with and achieve some day. Good goals give you something specific to work toward. What's *NOT* helpful about setting a goal of "staying out of trouble"? This is a perfectly fine place to start, but the way this goal is stated gives no information about **how** to achieve it, **how long** it will take to achieve it, or **when** it is achieved. Good goals are also something that you really want and are willing to work for. Have you ever set a goal because someone else wanted you to? How did that turn out for you? It's not surprising if things didn't go well. You will succeed at changing only if you want to change. This is not to say that others cannot help or support you with your goals, but they should not determine them for you.

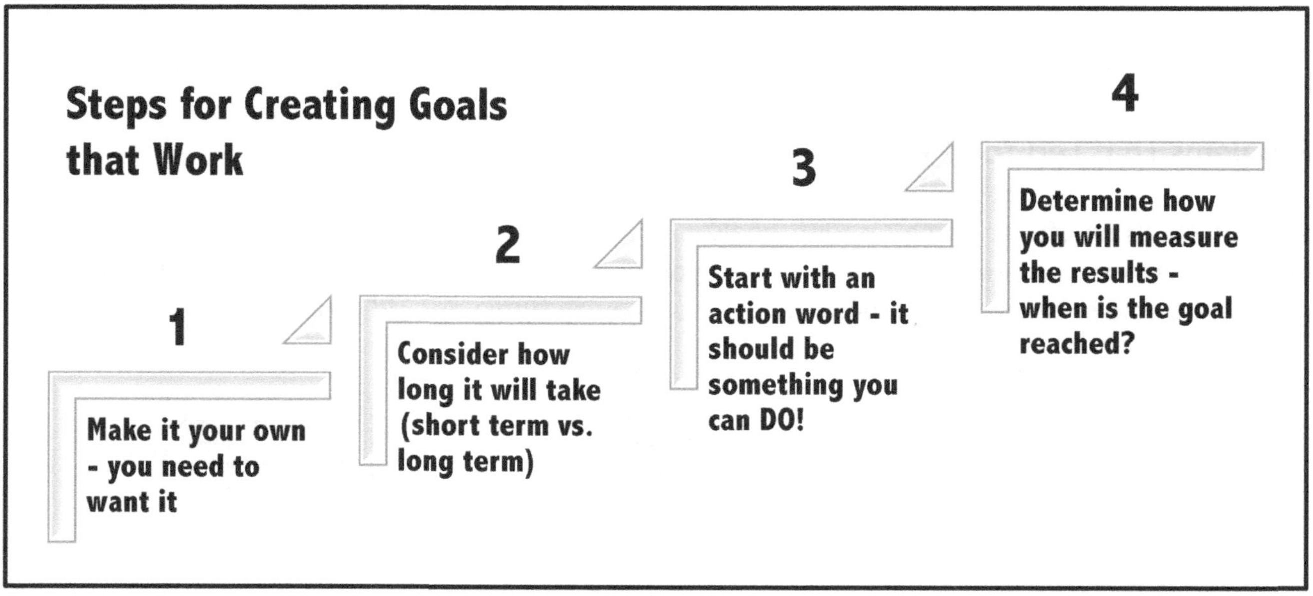

Here Are Some Examples—Circle the Better Goal

"I will be a great father and husband"	**OR**	"I will purchase a nice home for my family in two years."
"I will save money each month to build up my savings"	**OR**	"I will be wealthy."
"I will get rid of my mental health symptoms"	**OR**	"I will take my medication as prescribed."
"I will get in shape"	**OR**	"I will lose 20 pounds within 6 months."
"I will never get a disciplinary sanction"	**OR**	"I will spend one hour each day reviewing my relapse prevention plan."

For the goals you circled, think about **HOW** they fit the four steps described earlier.

Helpful Tip #1

Do not have goals that include the words "never" or "always." These are dead man's goals—only a dead guy could accomplish them! You're human; don't set impossible expectations. Cut yourself some slack.

Helpful Tip #2

If you set a time frame (two weeks, six months, five years) for achieving your goal, check to see if the goal is met when you get to that time frame. If it is—great! If it isn't—don't worry. You are not a failure. All you have to do is evaluate why you didn't reach the goal. Maybe the time frame was too short. Or maybe you needed to work harder or do something differently.

Knowing What You Need to Reach Those Goals

Writing down your goals is just the start. Now you have to begin planning for the goal. This may even require making smaller goals to achieve a larger goal. You also have to figure out what you need and who can help you. Let's look at a quick example:

> *Blake just got out of jail a few weeks ago, and he doesn't have a lot of money. He was sentenced to jail for gambling illegally and selling dope. This was how he earned a living. But these habits were also part of Blake's problems that landed him in jail. Blake wants to stay out of trouble, so his goal is to* ***find a full-time job within the next three months****. He can't just walk in anywhere and get hired. He needs help and resources. He takes the bus to the public library and looks through the local newspaper for job ads, uses the computer to make a résumé, and searches the Internet for job openings in his town. Blake also joins a support group for other job seekers and signs up at the employment agency. He asks his brother to help him practice interviewing for jobs—making eye contact, shaking hands, and answering questions. Blake uses money from his savings to buy some nice clothes so he can make a good impression at his interviews. He soon gets an interview for a job as a maintenance worker at an apartment complex. Blake's friend, Jake, lives in the same complex. So, he asks Jake to tell him more about the complex—what the residents like and dislike about living there. This information helps Blake play up his strengths (what he can add to the job). Before his interview, he also writes down questions he wants to ask so he will be better prepared. Blake doesn't have a car yet, so he again rides the bus.*

What steps did Blake take to find a job?

What resources or things did he need to help him?

Who did he need to help him?

Exercise: Building Your Goals

Using the information in this handout, come up with you own goals. Write them AS BIG AS YOU CAN. You will hang this on your wall as a reminder to keep you focused and on track. Under each goal, write down the steps you will take (which may include smaller goals) and what/who you will need to help you. Remember that you are working toward *getting out and staying out of restricted housing*.

Goal #1

- Steps:
- What/Who:

Goal #2

- Steps:
- What/Who:

Goal #3

- Steps:
- What/Who:

Goal #4

- Steps:
- What/Who:

Module 2

Surviving Segregation: What to Expect and How to Cope

Handout #3
Understanding Restrictive Housing

Why Am I Here?

Because of your negative actions, you are being housed in a restrictive unit of the prison. This unit is often called *administrative segregation, special management, disciplinary housing, solitary confinement*, or *"the hole."* Regardless of its name, the unit you are on now is separate from the majority of inmates. You may also be participating in this program if you are more frequently sent to live on these units than other inmates. In almost all cases, your placement on this unit is meant to be a punishment or consequence for how you chose to behave in the regular part of the prison, which is known as the GP. Many of your privileges and activities have been taken away, and you will spend nearly all day every day in your cell.

What Is the Purpose of Restrictive Housing?

Restrictive housing serves several functions. First, it is a way to increase the safety of the facility, including the safety of staff and other inmates, by removing certain inmates who are physically threatening to themselves or other people around them. Second, it is a way to encourage good behavior and hold inmates accountable for their disruptive behaviors. Without consequences for breaking the rules, the prison would be a more chaotic and dangerous place to live.

What Are the Implications of Restrictive Housing for My Sentence?

There are many possible implications of being in restrictive housing. Depending on what behaviors led you here, you could get more time added to your original sentence, you could get another criminal charge (for which you may go to trial), or you could be transferred to another facility or more intensive unit. You should be aware of the reasons why you were placed here and what legal consequences disciplinary housing could have for you and your time served in prison. *It is your right to know*. If you do not know, you must ask your counselor, your lawyer, or a knowledgeable staff person.

What disciplinary sanctions did you receive, or what rules did you break, that caused you to be placed in this housing unit?

____

____

What types of consequences (legal or otherwise) could you be facing because of the behaviors that led to your placement in this housing unit?

What Effects Will Restrictive Housing Have on Me?

There is mixed information about how this restrictive environment may affect you. Some people experience serious emotional problems, such as stress, suicidal thoughts, anxiety, depression, fear, and anger. Other people may react differently. But no matter what type of person you are, it will be mentally and physically difficult to live on this unit. ***It is important that you expect and prepare yourself for challenges*** .

Take a moment to write down how you expect your time on the unit will affect you mentally and physically, and/or how it has affected you in the past, if you've been placed here before:

Other Questions, Comments, or Concerns?

Use the space that follows to list any other questions that you have about spending time in restricted housing. Your counselor will be able to help you find the answers to your questions.

"**Q**" is for you to write down your question now. "**A**" is for you to write down the answer later.

Q_1: ____________________

A_1: ____________________

Q_2: ____________________

A_2: ____________________

Q_3: ____________________

A_3: ____________________

Q_4: ____________________

A_4: ____________________

Handout #4
Occupying the Mind and Body

When people don't know what to do with their time or when they use their time poorly, they can often find themselves in trouble. What happens when you have too much time on your hands? Chances are you get bored. And how do you solve the problem of being bored? You stir up some excitement! Sometimes this excitement leads to behaviors that break the rules of society and/or the prison facility.

Briefly describe a time when you felt bored or didn't know what to do, and you ended up doing something that you should *not* have done:

____

____

____

____

____

Researchers have shown that unplanned leisure time (leisure time is your free time to do things of your choosing; it does not include work or other required tasks, such as school or household chores) is a *risk factor for returning to criminal behavior*. In other words, people who are in the criminal justice system and do not learn to plan out or schedule leisure activities are likely to occupy their time with activities that could get them in trouble with the law again. Doing activities that you enjoy is important for your health, but you must use that time wisely!

Being in prison is no different. Prosocial activities are helpful for keeping inmates occupied and out of trouble. If you are already engaged in a positive activity, it is much easier to say "no" when an opportunity to violate the rules comes along. In addition, your mind and body will grow stronger if you use them regularly and in ways that are consistent with your goals. Let's look at an example:

Billy used to sit in his cell most of the day, only coming out for shower time and some meals. Over time, he started to feel tired. His muscles felt weak, he began to forget things easily, and he even thought about suicide. His counselor recommended that he take advantage of the book cart on the unit. Billy selected a book about meditation that helped him to relax. At first, it was difficult for him to read again; he had to sound the words out loud to himself, and it took him a while to finish the book. But soon, his reading and comprehension skills increased, and Billy was completing most books in no time. He liked how some of the books taught him new things, while other books

allowed him to escape his world for a little while and dive into the world of the characters in the story. Billy was also careful in his book choices—he did not read books about violence or aggression because he knew they might trigger something bad within him. He read books that were interesting but carried a positive message.

There isn't a lot to do in restricted housing; this is because it is meant to be a punishment for your actions. But there are some prosocial things you can do to exercise your mind and your body during your time here. Do you know what these things are?

Exercise: Activities Inventory

Complete the following table. Don't be afraid to ask for help; there may be more options and resources than you think. List all available possibilities, even if they don't interest you right away. Use this opportunity to explore your own imagination and creativity. *Focus on what you have, not on what you don't have.*

Activities that are available to me NOW	*How* do I get access this activity?	*Where* do I access this activity?	*When* am I allowed to access this activity?

Handout #5

Being in Good Favor

Part of surviving restrictive housing is not just about keeping your mind and body as busy as you can, but it is also about being on your best behavior. Sometimes, it may seem that staff pay the most attention to inmates who are acting out, causing problems, and being disruptive. But what happens to these inmates? *They stay in restrictive housing longer and have a greater chance of returning after release*. Believe it or not, staff will also notice inmates who are following the rules, being polite, working toward goals, and trying their hardest to make positive changes. In fact, staff members like these inmates better because they make their jobs easier, and they can focus on more important things like safety. Imagine how staff members must feel dealing with hundreds of inmates each day. Because poorly behaved inmates are so frustrating to the staff, well-behaved inmates are a welcome relief.

Think about this: Would you rather share a cell with someone who enjoys threatening and teasing you or someone who respects you and leaves you alone? You will actually ***stand out*** of the crowd if you don't act up or misbehave!

You may not realize it, but staff members at the prison—including correctional officers, unit managers, caseworkers, your counselor, nurses, and doctors—can influence your time in restrictive housing. When other people are able to give examples of your good and compliant behavior, you are more likely to get out faster and earn your privileges back sooner. You want staff members to be on your side, but you have to give them clear reasons to help and support you. Just like a jury looks at the evidence in a case, so do staff members when making decisions about where you need to be and what you can do.

What behaviors ARE NOT helpful for your goal of getting out and staying out of this unit?

Using your mental traffic light, what color are these actions?

____

____

____

What behaviors ARE helpful for your goal of getting out and staying out of this unit?

____

____

____

And, what color are these actions?

Avoiding Pressure From Others

In restrictive housing, you are living with many other inmates who have behavior problems. These behaviors keep them stuck where they are—in solitary. They are stuck and want you to be stuck with them. They can be aggressive, pushy, manipulative, scary, rude, and disrespectful. You may feel pressure to act out so you can fit in. It is common for these inmates to talk you into behaving badly or against the rules by calling you hurtful names (a "bitch") or threatening to cause you harm. Remember that they are only thinking about the short-term benefits (such as putting you down to make themselves feel better or looking important or powerful in front of others); they are NOT thinking about the long-term consequences (such as more time in restrictive housing, additional criminal charges, loss of commissary, social isolation, becoming the target of violence by rival inmates or gangs). If another inmate tries to pressure you into misbehaving, remember why he or she is here and what you need to do to get out. Behaving badly to quiet or calm other inmates will not make the problem stop; instead, it will encourage continued harassment. They will know that their behaviors worked to control you! Staff members are also aware of these troublesome inmates and do their best to make sure you, and everyone else on the unit, are safe.

Exercise: Segregation Scramble

Match up the actions in the box that follows with the appropriate circles. Good (ok) behaviors go in the circle with a ✓ mark and bad (not ok) behaviors go in the circle with an ✗ mark.

Throwing urine at staff **Sleeping through rec time** **Participating in other services/treatment**
Cutting your wrist **Spitting on an officer** **Making shanks or weapons**
Attending segregation or progress reviews with staff **Going on a hunger strike** **Complying with restraint procedures**
Cheeking medications **Gambling** **Not resisting cell searches**
Threatening other inmates **Being polite to staff** **Waking up for roll call** **Passing notes**

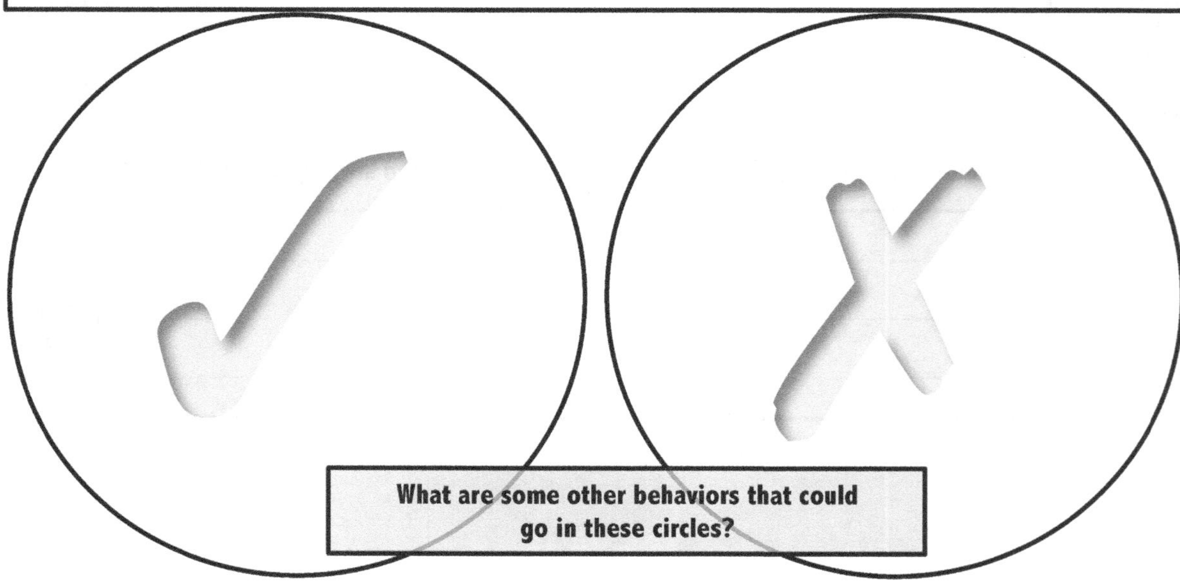

Handout #6

Accepting Your Anger

It's understandable that you may feel angry about being placed in restrictive housing. Your anger may be because you feel scared or nervous about spending time here, because you feel your placement here is unjust or unfair, or because you are frustrated with your own behaviors.

Briefly talk about your own feelings of anger or frustration about being on this unit. Where do you think these feelings come from?

____

____

Anger Meter, Part I: Circle Your Level of Anger Right Now

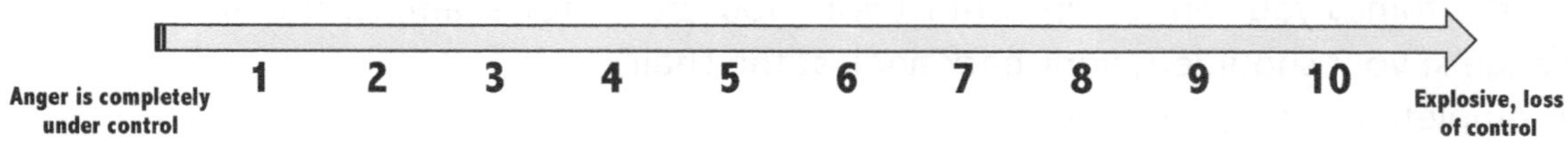

Anger is useful sometimes. It can help release tension, be used to control other people, and help you get what you want or trigger positive actions (consider people who protest in Washington, D.C., to make changes to our laws or economy). But many of these apparent payoffs can have serious long-term consequences.

> *Now, imagine that you are in a tug of war with a huge, ugly anger monster. You have one end of the rope and the monster has the other end. In between the two of you is a dark, bottomless pit. If you fall in, you will die. You're pulling and fighting as hard as you can, but the monster keeps pulling you closer and closer to certain doom. What's the best thing you can do in this situation? Your first guess might be to pull even harder. That's the natural choice. But the monster will also pull harder. What's another option?* ***Drop the rope****. When you drop the rope, the monster is still there, but you're no longer mixed up in a struggle with him. Your body and mind are free to do something more helpful for solving your problems.*

Just like in this story, if you keep fighting with your feelings of anger, you are not only going to become physically tired but also you're putting yourself at risk of getting into trouble. For example, uncontrolled anger could lead you to break other rules of the facility or avoid activities and in turn add to your time in disciplinary housing. ***Acceptance***, on the other hand, means opening up and acknowledging your feelings. This is what happens when you give up the fight. By doing this, you can make room for anger-related emotions, urges, and sensations while also having the energy to focus on what you need to do to get out and stay out of this unit. In other words, you can realize that anger is a normal response to a frustrating situation without letting your anger take over and stop you from accomplishing your goals. DON'T LET THAT ANGER MONSTER PULL YOU DOWN. We will revisit anger again in more detail later in the program.

Exercise: Dropping the Anchor

One strategy for reducing your anger is to make an active decision to focus on something else, like doing things that are in line with your goals. Try this exercise to release tension and begin refocusing yourself away from anger. Stick with it!

1. First, get ready by taking two slow, deep breaths. Focus on breathing all the way in through your nose and breathing out of your mouth as slowly as possible until your lungs are completely empty—then let them refill by themselves.
2. Next, take a seat and plant your feet firmly onto the floor.
3. Push your feet down—notice the feeling of the floor beneath you, supporting you.
4. Notice the muscle tension in your legs as you push your feet down.
5. Notice your entire body—and the feeling of gravity flowing down through your head, back, and legs into your feet.
6. Now look around you and notice the things you see—look at their texture and shape.
7. Notice the things you can feel in contact with your body (for example, the air on your face, your shirt against your shoulders, your back against the chair).
8. Now complete the Anger Meter.

Anger Meter, Part II: Circle Your Level of Anger Right Now

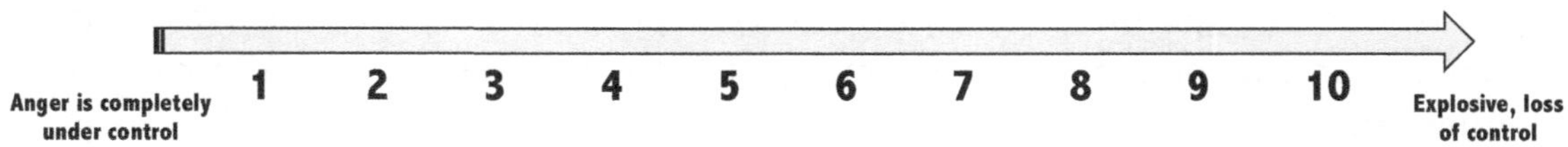

9. Compare your ratings at the beginning of the handout and now. Did your level of anger go up, go down, or stay the same after this exercise?

Old Rating: ________ **New Rating:** ________

Handout #7

Catching Some ZZzz's

Sleep can be a difficult task in disciplinary housing. The amount of sleep you get and how well you sleep each night can be complicated by your mood/emotions, the noise and chaos of other inmates, or prison safety procedures, such as nightly cell checks and the feeling that someone is always watching you. Over time, your mind and body will start to get used to all this stuff. It's also important to know that some types of medication cause poor sleep as a side effect; you may want to ask if this is true for any of the medications you are taking. Sleep disturbances can lead to emotional and physical problems, such as anxiety, depression, irritability, fatigue, and poor memory and concentration. Your brain and body need good, quality sleep to be healthy and to function properly. In fact, if you go too long without sleep, your mind can start to play tricks on you—you may even see or hear things that aren't really there.

If you're having serious difficulty with sleep, you may want to talk to a doctor in the prison. But there are some techniques that you can do on your own to help you sleep better.

Here Are a Few Tips to Start With

☑ **Don't nap during the day**—it's tempting to sleep all day because there isn't a lot to do in disciplinary housing, but don't forgot about your activity log! Sleeping during the day makes your brain feel like it doesn't need to rest at night.

☑ **Take advantage of exercise or rec time**—physical activity gives your body a reason to energize, which is what sleep does. But do not exercise too close to bedtime, or you will feel hyperactive.

☑ **Manage stress**—stress causes worry and racing thoughts, which can keep you up at night. Before you go to bed, write down what's on your mind to get it out of your head. Even thinking of a funny joke can relax you.

☑ **Stick to a sleep schedule**—try to go to bed and get up at the same time every day. So listen to staff when they tell you to wake up and when it's lights out; they're keeping you on a schedule. Being consistent helps your mind and body learn when to shut off each night.

☑ **Create a bedtime ritual or routine**—again, doing the same things at night lets your mind and body know when it's time to wind down. This could include reading a book, doodling a picture, writing down what's on your mind, quietly humming a song, stretching your muscles, or doing deep breathing exercises.

☑ **Use imagery**—when you close your eyes, think of something comforting, like a pleasant memory. Imagine that you are somewhere else and that the noises you hear belong to something else. Immersing yourself in a relaxing mental story is like starting your own dream.

Progressive Muscle Relaxation (PMR)

PMR has been around since the 1930s. Researchers have shown that PMR can be more effective than medication in reducing a number of problems, including anxiety, headaches, chronic pain, arthritis, and . . . poor sleep. It is even used to help patients who are diagnosed with cancer. PMR is a method of stress management that helps you to relax and quiet your mind. It requires you to alternate between tensing and relaxing groups of muscles. You have already practiced some aspects of PMR in Handout #6.

Exercise: Being Buddha

This is a series of self-guided PMR exercises. The first time you try it, it may seem strange or silly. With practice, you will likely find this exercise enjoyable. Allow yourself about 20–30 minutes before going to bed to complete the exercise. And make sure it is the LAST thing you do before going to sleep. Read ALL the instructions first so you have an idea how to do it and can focus more of your attention on relaxing. When you read the steps to yourself, talk in a slow, soothing voice.

Sit upright on your bed or in a chair with your legs hanging over the edge.

1. **Arms**
   - Clasp both hands into fists and roll your wrist with your knuckles pointing upward. Hold the tightness for ten seconds and notice the tension in your muscles. Now let go of the tightness and let your arms relax onto the bed/chair. Notice the change in how your muscles feel. Repeat by making fists again for 10 seconds and then relaxing for 20 seconds (be sure to count quietly to yourself).
   - Next, bend both your elbows and flex your biceps like a bodybuilder. Hold this pose for 10 seconds then let go of the tension for 20 seconds. Repeat.
   - Now, lock your elbows straight and stretch your arms toward the floor. Feel the tension up and down your arms. Release after 10 seconds and relax for 20 seconds. Repeat.
2. **Legs**
   - Flex your toes by bringing them toward your head while you tighten your shin and calf muscles. Hold for 10 seconds then release for 20 seconds by letting your feet hang loosely. Repeat.
   - Tighten your lower legs while pointing your toes outward. Hold the position for 10 seconds then return your toes to their natural place for 20 seconds. Repeat.
   - Tense your inner thigh muscles by pressing your knees together as hard as you can without causing pain for ten seconds. Release and feel the sense of ease spread throughout your legs. Repeat.
   - Tighten your buttocks and thighs. Increase the tension by straightening your legs and pushing down hard through your heels. Hold this position for ten seconds then let go. Repeat.
3. **Midsection**
   - Gently arch your back. Hold the tension for ten seconds and then relax by letting your back go flat against the wall or chair. Repeat.
   - Take a deep breath and fill your lungs with air. Tighten all the muscles in your chest and abs. Hold your breath and then breathe out and release the air. Repeat.
   - Stretch your shoulders backward as though you were trying to touch your ears. Hold for ten seconds and then let your shoulders droop toward the floor. Repeat.

4. Head
- Tilt your head backward and stretch your chin toward the ceiling. Hold for ten seconds and then release and bring your chin to rest on your chest. Repeat.
- Clench your jaw and push your tongue up to the roof of your mouth. Hold and then release. Notice the relaxation of your lips. Repeat.
- Close your eyes tightly and smile, stretching your mouth as wide as you can. Hold it for ten seconds and then relax. Repeat.
- Raise your eyebrows as high as you can and feel the tension across the top of your head. Hold and then relax. Repeat.

Repeat these steps as many times as you want and then slowly lower your body down into your bed and place your head gently on the pillow. Close your eyes.

The Morning After

Rate your quality of sleep the next morning after you've tried the PMR exercises and the other tips listed earlier.

Sleep Meter

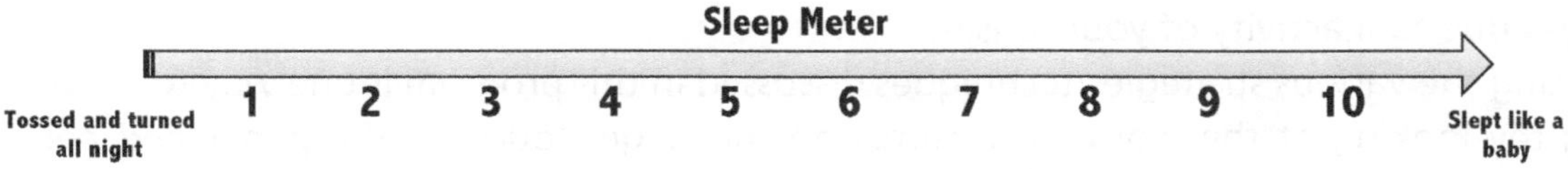

As you continue to practice new strategies, continue to rate how well you slept each night.

Handout #8
Reducing Sensory Deprivation

What Is Sensory Deprivation?

There are five different senses we use to help us understand our world: **(1) taste, (2) touch, (3) smell, (4) hearing, and (5) sight**. Sensory deprivation means that you are in an environment that gives you little opportunity to use these different senses. Short-term sensory deprivation can be relaxing, but long-term sensory deprivation can cause problems. For example, when your mind and body are deprived of information that activates the senses (such as a pretty picture to attract the attention of your eyes) for too long, they can begin to make up sensations without your permission. This is called hallucinating. Sensory deprivation can also lead to anxiety, problems controlling behavior, bizarre beliefs, paranoia, depression, and suicidal thoughts.

Disciplinary housing units are not meant to be pleasant or exciting; they are dull, dark, colorless, and closed off. Prolonged periods of time in this type of environment may present mental and physical challenges due to inactivity of your senses.

Practicing the various strategies/techniques discussed in this program is one way to keep your senses working (by looking at the words or pictures on this page, touching the paper and pencil, talking out your responses, participating in activities available on the unit, attending to muscles movements in your body, etc.). You must also take advantage of every opportunity to interact prosocially with other people, such as caseworkers, correctional officers, your counselor, lawyer, visitors, and other rule-abiding inmates. Do not skip meals, shower time, or time in the rec yard. These are all opportunities to exercise your five senses. But *do not try to eliminate sensory deprivation by touching, tasting, or smelling anything that is unhealthy, dangerous, or against the rules*. This might include coming in contact with your excrement (waste that comes out of your body), putting your hands on someone, or hurting yourself.

When you don't have access to real sensations, ask your mind to help you remember different sensations. This is called ***guided imagery***. You saw earlier how imagery can help you fall asleep, but you can practice this technique at other times as well. Try to imagine yourself in this story:

It is a bright summer day. It is late in the day. You decide to go for a walk along the beach. The sun is beaming warmth and comfort as it shines brightly. The sky is crystal clear without a cloud in sight. The grains of sand beneath your feet shine from the sunlight and warm the bottom of your feet. The sound of the waves crashing against the shore echoes in the air. You feel the warm, light breeze brush against your face as you walk through the sand. Far off in the distance, you can hear the cries of sea gulls. . . . You watch them glide through the sky, swoop down into the sea, and then fly off once again.

As you walk further along the shore, you decide to rest. You sit down on a mound of pure white sand and look out at the sea, staring intently at the rhythmic, soothing motion of the waves rolling into shore.

Each wave breaks against the coast, rising slowly upward along the beach, leaving an area of white foam. Slowly, the wave retreats back out to sea, only to be replaced by another wave that crashes against the shore . . . working its way up the beach . . . then slowly retreating back out to sea.

With each motion of the wave as it glides in and then out, you find yourself feeling more and more relaxed. The tranquility creates a sense of calmness, peace.

As you stare off into the distance, you see that the sun is beginning to sink into the horizon. The sky is turning brilliant colors of red . . . orange . . . yellow . . . while the sunsets, sinking down . . . down into the horizon.

You feel very relaxed and soothed. You continue to watch the sun as it descends.

The beating of the waves, the smell and taste of the sea, the salt, the cries of the gulls, the warmth against your body—all of these sights, sounds, and smells leave you feeling very calm, refreshed, and relaxed.

Describe some of the senses you experienced from the story:

See?

____

____

Hear?

____

____

Touch?

____

____

Taste?

____

____

Smell?

____

____

You can do other types of guided imagery with any place you want to go. Just close your eyes and use your brain to remember the sensations—where are you, what do you see, what do you hear, what do you smell, what do you touch? Explore those senses in detail. This is also a good way to relax and reduce stress.

Exercise: Finding the Big Five

In addition to guided imagery, you can also be more attentive to your use of senses throughout the day. For each of the five senses, an example of how to do this is provided to you. In the blank space, provide a second example and then place a ✓ mark in the box next to both strategies once you have tried them.

Sight:

☐ Get a nature book or magazine from the book cart or facility library that has bright and colorful pictures, and look closely at the beauty of the animals, trees, sky, etc.

☐ ______________________________

Hearing:

☐ Listen carefully to any sounds that come your way, letting the noise travel in one ear and out the other.

☐ ______________________________

Smell:

☐ During shower time, lather soap on your hands and breathe in the fresh scent.

☐ ______________________________

Taste:

☐ Find the part of your meal that you enjoy the taste of. Let the food/drink sit on your tongue a few seconds longer before you begin chewing or swallowing it.

☐ ______________________________

Touch:

☐ In the rec yard, take notice of the beads of sweat on your body and feel how they roll down your face, neck, and arms.

☐ ______________________________

Module 2
Recap

In This Module You Learned About

- ☑ **Restrictive housing—its purpose, implications, and effects**
- ☑ **Keeping your mind and body active in helpful ways**
- ☑ **Managing feelings of anger related to your placement on this unit**
- ☑ **Overcoming sleep problems**
- ☑ **Reducing sensory deprivation**

Now, place an ✗ mark next to the techniques that you will continue to practice, and write down WHEN you will practice them, WHAT you will do, and HOW they will help you. Give your counselor permission to hold you accountable for following through with your plan.

Technique	I WILL do this (place ✗ here)	Whenever I . . .	This is how I will do it . . .	This is how it will help me . . .
Talk about my concerns with my counselor				
Ask questions when I don't understand my situation				
Keep track of my daily activities				
Accept my anger and save my energy for accomplishing my goals				
Use PMR				
Stick with a schedule for falling asleep and waking up				
Create a bedtime ritual				

Technique	I WILL do this (place ✗ here)	Whenever I . . .	This is how I will do it . . .	This is how it will help me . . .
Reduce stress before bedtime				
Use guided imagery				
Pay more attention to the five senses I experience				
Take advantage of exercise time				
Seek prosocial interactions with others when possible				
Participate in meal and shower times				
Avoid naps during the daytime				

Module 3

Suicide and Self-Injurious Behavior: Protecting You From You

Handout #9
Knowing Your Suicide Risk

The Basics of Suicide Risk

People think about suicide (the purposeful act of killing oneself) when they feel unbearable emotional pain in their minds or conscience. This feeling is called **Psychache**. Like a headache or heartache causes pain to your head or heart, Psychache causes pain to your minds and emotions. There are things about your history (even your family history), your mood, and your ways of handling stress that put you at greater risk for suicide. There are also things about your environment—such as social isolation in restrictive housing—that can add to your risk. In fact, inmates who live in disciplinary housing units have suicidal thoughts and behaviors more often than inmates who live in the GP. People who have a strong intent to commit suicide and who have easy access to materials that can be lethal (guns, sharp objects, rope, drugs) are likely to succeed at dying.

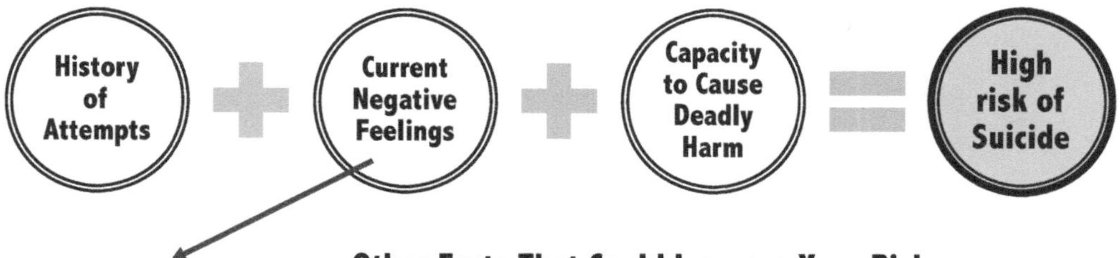

Hopelessness	Anger
Shame	Dread
Guilt	Wishes of death
Humiliation	Pain
Fear	Loneliness
Helplessness	Emptiness

Other Facts That Could Increase Your Risk:

- Why does the past matter? Because it shows that you have the capacity to tolerate pain and a lower fear of death. It also means that you've had practice, and practice makes people better at doing things.
- Men are more likely to succeed at killing themselves with fewer attempts, but women will try more often.
- Suicides in restrictive housing are highest within the first 3 weeks of placement.

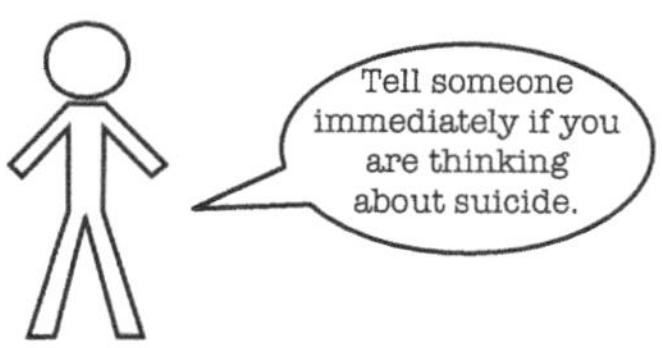

Name some of <u>your</u> specific risk factors
(These could be thoughts/feelings, behaviors, things in your environment, or traits)

____

____

____

____

Assessing Your Own Risk

Prior to taking this program, you completed a measure called the DHS or Depression-Hopelessness-Suicide scale. This is a screening tool used to look at people's risk for suicidal thinking. Your clinician will share your scores with you. Complete the black spaces that follow based on your scores. Even if you are not currently thinking about hurting yourself, what are some thoughts, feelings, and behaviors that could be a warning sign for you?

Depression: __________

Your Overall Risk Level Is:

Hopelessness: __________

Cognitive suicide indicator: __________

Current suicidal ideation indicator: __________

Historical suicidal indicator: __________

Previous diagnosis of depression (Y/N)? __________

Known others who have committed suicide (Y/N)? __________

Thoughts, feelings, or behaviors to look out for:

____

____

____

Handout #10

Suicide vs. Self-Injurious Behavior vs. Morbid Rumination

Suicide

Suicide is serious. People who attempt suicide want to end their lives and have a clear plan to do so. You read a little bit about suicide in Handout #9. Your level of suicide risk depends not only on the number of risk factors—such as having a suicide history, negative emotions, environmental stress, or access to sharp objects—but also on the severity of these factors (how bad are they?). There are two specific categories of feelings that, along with some of the risk factors mentioned earlier, are believed to increase the likelihood of suicidal behavior. Researchers have fancy names for these feelings: (1) **Thwarted Belongingness** and (2) **Perceived Burdensomeness**. See the figures in the following box.

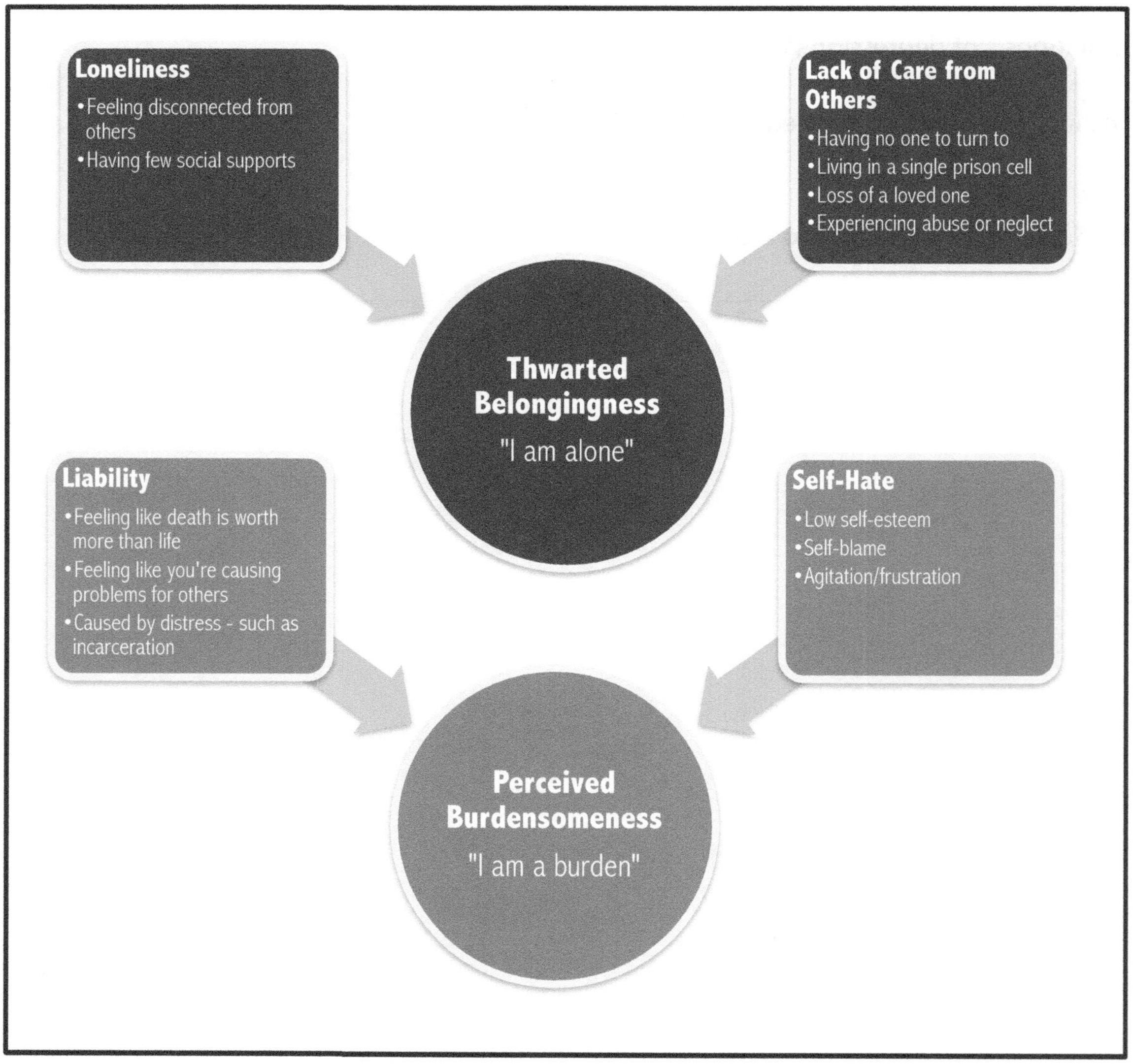

Remember: There is hope. You can take charge of your life and make positive changes, even if you are incarcerated.

Self-Injurious Behavior (SIB)

SIB is a broad definition that may or may not include the desire to die. Self-harm is anything a person does to intentionally cause injury to him or herself, such as cutting or burning the skin (arms, wrists, legs), choking the neck area, pulling out hair, or head banging. There are many different reasons why people engage in SIB. For example, someone who causes self-injury, but does not want to die, may be trying to seek help for his problems, punish or get back at others, fit in/belong to a group, or gain attention. This is called non-suicidal self-injury. In disciplinary housing, some inmates may even turn to self-injury to reduce sensory deprivation because it gives them a new sensation to feel. But you have other skills you can use.

Self-injury can be dangerous whether you intend to kill yourself or not—it can result in physical disability, disfigurement, scars, brain damage, or accidental death.

Morbid Rumination

The word **morbid** means gloomy, unhealthy, or gruesome and **rumination** means to think about something. Morbid rumination includes thoughts about death or dying that do not convey a true desire to end one's life. Examples of morbid rumination are as follows: "I should have never been born," "I wish my parents never met," "Things would be easier if I were dead," and "No one would care if I died." These thoughts may eventually lead to suicidal thinking, but not always. People may have these thoughts because they feel depressed, anxious, afraid, hopeless, lonely, or frustrated. But doctors and staff in the prison will take these words seriously, so do not use them freely or as a joke.

Practicing Positive Self-Talk

You have the power to reverse the type of thinking that supports suicidal or SIB.

Example: "I have the strength to cope with the challenges of segregation."

Now, think of a few more statements on your own:

1. ______________________________
2. ______________________________
3. ______________________________
4. ______________________________
5. ______________________________

Exercise: Creating Your Suicide Prevention Plan

Having a plan in place for when you experience suicidal thoughts allows you to take immediate action to prevent deadly future behaviors—you don't have to feel stuck when those feelings happen or take the time to think of a plan because you will already have one.

This Prevention Plan Belongs to: ______________

Know how to recognize your warning signs: List your warning signs for suicidal thinking/behavior (for example, thinking negatively about yourself or the future, being awake in the middle of the night, asking for potentially lethal objects, like pencils). Be specific!

Communicate your warning signs to others: List people you will tell when you notice your warning signs.

Find out what resources are available to you: List the sources of help (could be people or things) that are available to you when you feel suicidal and write down the procedures for getting these resources. Take advantage of these resources.

Handout #11

False Suicidal Intent and SIB as Manipulation

SIBs are typically considered serious problems and should be treated as such. But sometimes people use these behaviors to manipulate other people or their situation. For example, talking about dying by suicide could get you special attention, sympathy, or other rewards, such as the opportunity to leave your cell and get a change of scenery. These benefits may seem nice but using suicide to get what you want will get you into trouble. In fact, inmates act out using suicidal intent and SIB so often (up to 50% of inmates say that manipulation is a goal of their SIB) that some prison staff see these behaviors as a disciplinary problem that requires punishment. This is particularly true if you have a number of rule violations already. Even one incident of self-injury can increase your chances of getting a disciplinary sanction.

Spot the Snake

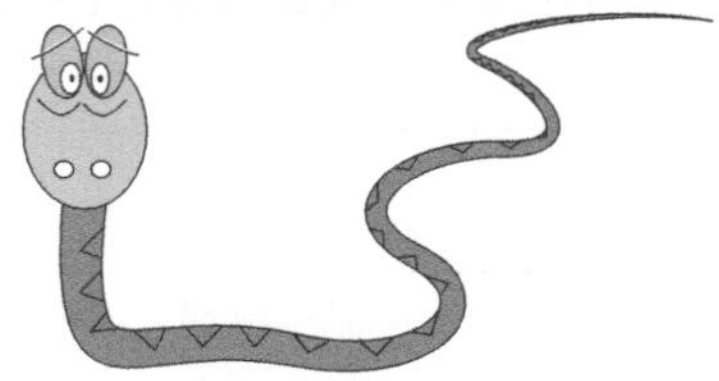

Can you tell which inmate is experiencing serious suicidal intent/SIB and which one is using it for personal gain?

Janet is 35 years old. She is currently incarcerated for selling heroin on the streets—this is her third offense. She not only sold drugs, but she also used them frequently. She often robbed people to support her habit, including her mother and brother. When she needed money for drugs, she often told her family that she needed to pay her bills or school-related expenses. Once, Janet even convinced her mother to drive her to buy a new supply of heroin. She said she needed a ride to a job interview—that was a lie. Janet was arrested when she sold $500 worth of heroin to an undercover cop. She was booked into the prison and began experiencing withdrawal symptoms from her heroin use. Janet felt frustrated by her situation and decided to smuggle in a pencil from the intake process. She dug the pencil point deep into her arms, causing bleeding. She made sure the nursing staff saw her wounds, and they did. She was soon transferred to a psychiatric hospital to get help. Janet escaped from the hospital. The police put a warrant out for her arrest, and she is now being prosecuted to the fullest extent of the law for her behaviors . . . in addition to her original sentence.

Real or fake? ______________________________

What is Janet's motive for her SIB?

____

____

What did Janet get as a result of her SIB?

____

____

Peter is a 42-year-old man. He has been incarcerated for three years now for attempted murder. He tried to rob a grocery store clerk at gunpoint and ended up shooting the clerk in the neck, causing paralysis. Peter has bipolar disorder, which sometimes makes him feel sad and sometimes makes him feel hyper and on top of the world. One time when he was feeling hopeless and alone, Peter tried to hurt himself by stabbing his chest with a letter opener. He survived and was hospitalized; he now has difficulty breathing. Peter also had an uncle who shot himself to death when Peter was ten years old. Sometimes, Peter stays up most of the night thinking of ways to kill himself. He also knows that if he commits suicide at night, there will be fewer staff or other inmates to notice him and stop him. He has been known to say things like, "There is nothing left for me in this world." Peter recently stole a razor blade during shower time when a correctional officer was not looking. A fellow inmate noticed Peter's sneaky behavior and told a staff person. Peter's counselor was called. Peter and his counselor had a long conversation about his suicidal feelings. Being able to talk and come up with a prevention plan reduced Peter's depression.

Real or fake? ______________________________

What is Peter's motive for his suicidal intent?

____

____

What did Peter get as a result of his suicidal intent?

____

____

Exercise: Pros vs. Cons

List the pros and cons of using suicidal intent/SIB as a manipulation tool. Then think of better, less criminal ways to achieve a similar "pro" **without** using suicidal/SIB intent.

Pro (Benefits)	Con (Consequences)	Better Method
1.		
2.		
3.		
4.		

Module 3
Recap

In This Module You Learned About

- ☑ **Common factors that increase suicide risk**
- ☑ **Your personal risk for suicide**
- ☑ **The differences between suicidal intent, self-injurious behavior, and morbid ruminations**
- ☑ **The effects of faking suicidal intent and self-injurious behavior**

Now, place an ✗ mark next to the techniques that you will continue to practice, and write down WHEN you will practice them, WHAT you will do, and HOW they will help you. Give your counselor permission to hold you accountable for following through with your plan.

Technique	I WILL do this (place ✗ here)	Whenever I . . .	This is how I will do it . . .	To help me cope with . . .
Talk to my counselor or staff about my suicidal thoughts				
Continue to assess my personal risk for suicide				
Practice positive self-talk				
Follow my suicide prevention plan				
Figure out prosocial ways to get what I need so I don't misuse suicidal intent/ self-injury				

Module 4

Understanding My Emotions: Identifying and Dealing With Anger, Fear, and Other Frustrating Feelings

Handout #12

Roots of Aggression and Violence

Aggressive behaviors are a lot more common in restrictive housing units than in the general prison population. Inmates act out for a number of reasons, such as expressing an emotion (anger, fear, anxiety), seeking revenge, getting something they want, or feeling powerful. Acting aggressively can have immediate benefits, but those benefits are ***never*** worth the serious consequences.

Violence is a poor way to handle problems, but if inmates do not learn better ways, they will resort to what they know. Violent behavior can be influenced by the environment—your family, friends, neighborhood, or prison. Many people learn how to think, act, and feel from their parents or caregivers during childhood. For example, children whose parents hugged them and expressed their feelings are likely to be warm and affectionate adults. Other types of family experiences encourage aggression and violence that can carry over into adulthood.

Take a moment to write down how different emotions (happy, angry, sad, afraid) were expressed in your family.

How were you disciplined as a child? What was that like for you?

How do these experiences in childhood help explain how you interact with other people today?

Although experiencing violence and aggression at a young age can affect how you respond to problems as an adult, your life history is only one explanation for your current behaviors. Aggression can also be a symptom or side effect of brain damage, medications you may be taking, or mental illness. *But this is not an excuse*. In other words, these factors do not give you the right to abuse, violate, harm, or offend another person. You are now responsible for learning more productive ways of expressing your anger, frustration, and other upsetting emotions without being physically, verbally, or sexually violent. Just like you learned to use violence, you can learn to use other methods.

Myths About Aggression and Violence

#1. **Aggression and Violence Are Inherited**—While you can learn to act violently from the people you grow up with or hang around, including your parents, you do not inherit this behavior like you inherit eye color, skin color, or height. Things that are inherited cannot be changed; you either have it or you don't. You CAN change your actions.

#2. **Anger Always Leads to Aggression**—You may think this is true if the only way you know how to express anger is through aggression. But there are better and healthier ways of dealing with anger. For example, you can learn to control the escalation of anger by using relaxation techniques (like PMR), changing negative and hostile thoughts, and practicing assertiveness skills (coming up in a later handout).

#3. **The Only Way to Get What You Want Is to Be Aggressive**—Wrong again. A better way to get what you want is to be assertive, not aggressive. The goal of aggression is to intimidate, dominate, show power, injure, or harm another person. But the goal of assertiveness is to express anger while also being respectful of others. Being assertive does not mean blaming or bullying other people; you can get what you want without causing physical or emotional harm. This IS possible. You will learn how to be assertive in another handout.

#4. **Venting Anger Is Always Helpful**—Many people used to believe that screaming into or beating on pillows, smashing objects, or pounding a punching bag were healthy ways of blowing off steam. Now researchers know that people who vent their anger aggressively, even if they are not harming another person, just get better at being angry. That is, when you vent your anger in this way, all you're doing is encouraging more aggression. It feels good to vent, so you come to learn that it feels good to be aggressive.

Which myths did you believe before reading this?

Handout #13
Assessing Your Anger

Anger vs. Aggression

Anger is a feeling or emotion that can be experienced as mild irritation to intense fury and rage. You completed the Anger Meter in Handout #6; this was a check for your level of anger. Many people confuse anger and aggression (see Myth #2 in the previous handout). **Aggression** is meant to cause harm or injury to a person or their belongings. Anger can be handled in ways that do not get you into trouble and are not dangerous to others. The diagram that follows shows how anger can turn into aggression.

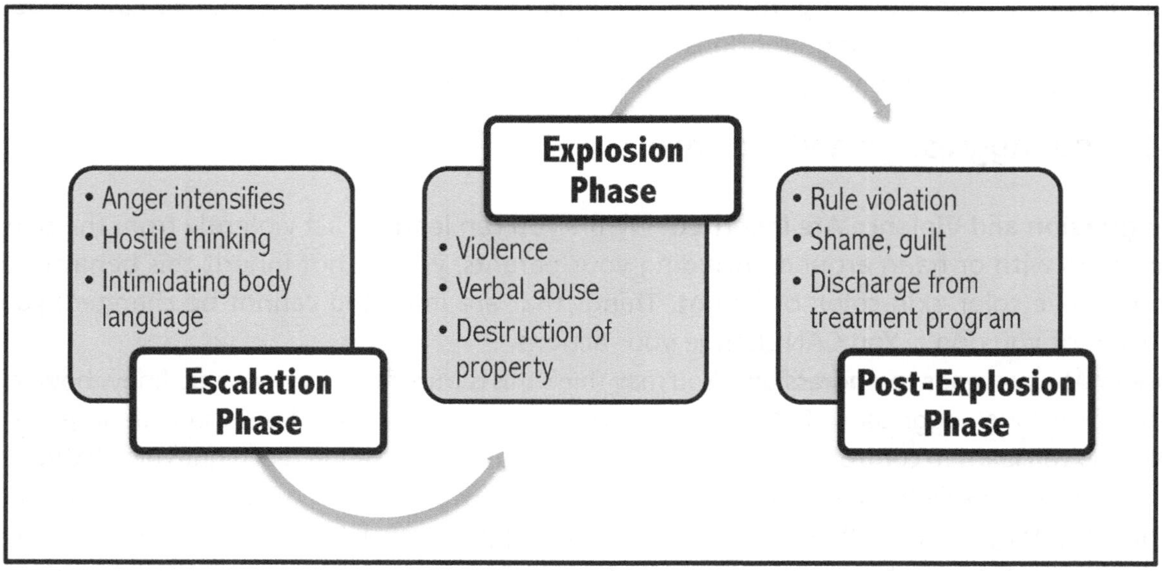

The escalation phase is the beginning of the cycle—this is where you see the first signs of anger. If the escalation phase is allowed to continue, you will soon lose control. Uncontrollable anger leads to verbal and physical aggression—this is the explosion phase. The anger episode eventually ends, and there are negative consequences—this is the post-explosion phase.

When Anger Is a Problem

Anger is a problem when it is felt too intensely, too often, or is expressed poorly (such as through violence). As discussed earlier, intense anger has some payoffs, like releasing tension or controlling others. But as you know by now, these payoffs are far outweighed by the negative consequences. Intense or inappropriate anger can cause problems for you or for other people. List some payoffs and consequences in the table that follows. Think about ways in which intense anger can affect your beliefs, actions, environment, relationships, and body.

Payoffs of Anger for YOU	Payoffs of Anger for OTHERS	Negative Consequences for YOU	Negative Consequences for OTHERS

Anger as a Habit

Think back to THE Circle of Change. "H" stands for habit. If anger is a habit of yours, it probably played a role in where you are right now—restricted housing. Your thoughts can lead to anger. Very hostile and negative thoughts can then turn anger into aggression. By definition, habits are behaviors that we perform so often that they become natural to us; we do them without thinking. Habits become routine and familiar. Some people have a habit of going to the gym. Others have a habit of brushing their teeth before bedtime. Still others have a habit of smoking cigarettes, drinking alcohol, or using drugs. Anger that is expressed often and aggressively can become a habit too. You can break this habit by making changes to how you think or interpret situations, how you act, where you go, and who you hang around. But remember, change is hard. Think about how difficult it is for people to quit smoking or to stay sober. Be prepared to work for it. The payoffs for learning to control your anger will be worth it.

Is anger a habit for you? How do you know?

____

____

____

____

First Steps

You may be asking yourself how you will break the cycle of anger and aggression. The first step is uncovering the clues to your anger. What triggers your anger? What warning signs should you pay attention to? Anger is often provoked by an event in your life. Your mind then tells you negative or hostile things about that event. Your habit is to respond in an aggressive way. Now picture yourself standing in the ocean. You have your feet planted in the sand where the water just hits your ankles. You see a shark in the waters ahead. All you have to do is take a few steps back, and you are on shore. Now imagine being further out and spotting the shark. Instead of just a few steps, you have to move your arms and legs harder, battling the waves and currents to get out. The deeper you are, the harder it is to get back to shore safety. Similarly, the longer you let your anger go on, the more difficult it will be to calm yourself down. So focus on preventing the escalation of anger from becoming an explosion of anger. Stopping it early requires you to be aware of the early clues.

Exercise: Detecting the Clues

There can be many events that trigger anger and aggression. Next are some common examples. Circle the ones that are true for you and then think of at least five more personal examples. This is a chance for you to use your mental traffic light.

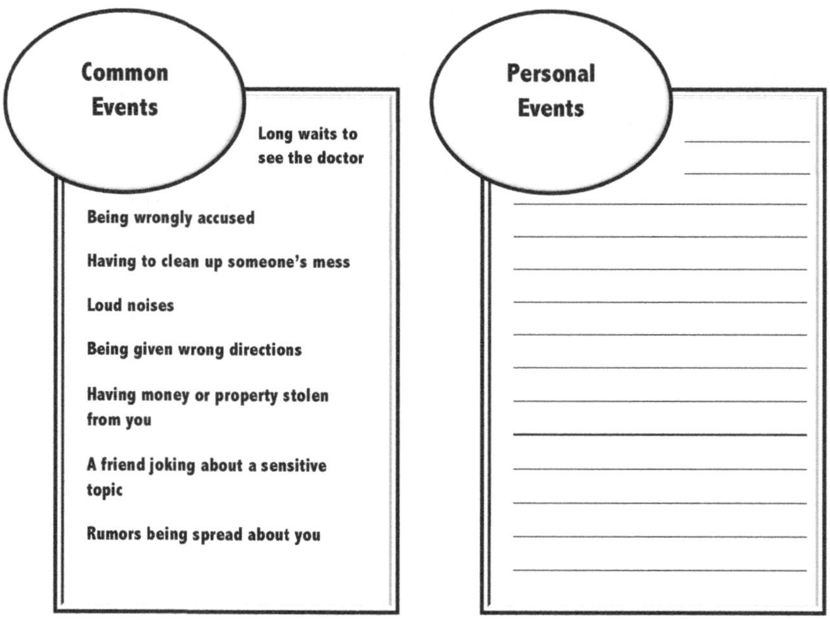

You can also learn clues from your body's reaction to anger before you become aggressive. There are four categories of clues: **(1) physical** (how your body reacts), **(2) behavioral** (what you do), **(3) emotional** (other emotions that go along with anger), and **(4) cognitive** (what you think). Just like you did earlier, circle common clues in each category that fit you and then come up with at least five other personal examples.

Common Physical Clues

- Tightness in chest
- Increased heart rate
- Feeling hot or flushed
- Shaky hands

Personal Physical Clues

____
____
____
____
____
____

Common Behavior Clues

- Clenching your fists
- Raising your voice
- Staring at others
- Pacing back and forth in your cell

Personal Behaviors Clues

____
____
____
____
____
____

Common Emotional Clues

- Disrespect
- Hurt
- Jealousy
- Depression
- Fear
- Frustration
- Anxiety

Personal Emotional Clues

____
____
____
____
____
____

Common Cognitive Clues

- "I want revenge"
- Hurt
- "He meant to hurt me"
- "I see red"
- "I look weak"
- "I want to beat her"
- "My manhood is threatened"

Personal Cognitive Clues

____
____
____
____
____
____

Quick Tips for Controlling Anger

1. **Take a time out or walk away from the situation—come back to it once you've calmed down.**
2. **Take deep breaths or use progressive muscle relaxation (PMR)** (see Handouts #6 and #7).
3. **Talk to someone you trust—your counselor, doctor, case manager.**
4. **Exercise—go to the rec yard if you can or do pushups in your cell.**
5. **Focus on your treatment plan—practice new strategies that you've learned and *remember your goals.***
6. **Explore what's hiding under the anger—are you actually feeling sad, afraid, hurt, annoyed, bored . . .?**

Handout #14
Attacking Anger at the Source

Cognitive Restructuring

As you read in Handout #13, anger can be triggered by certain events in your life, but it's really about how your mind understands or explains these events to you that takes you to the explosion phase—the point where you experience aggression or an outburst of anger. In other words, how you think about an event may cause you to behave in ways that are against your goals. One method for stopping anger before it gets the best of you is to challenge or dispute the thoughts your mind comes up with. This method is called **cognitive restructuring**. "Cognitive" is another word to explain the things that go on in your mind. "Restructuring" is a word that means you are going to change something about what goes on in your mind. So cognitive restructuring is one way you could change your thoughts about an anger-triggering event. The idea is to replace your negative thoughts with thoughts that are more helpful and tell a better story of the situation. Here's an example:

> *Tony has been working in the mess hall as a cook for about six months now. Another inmate, Jeff, is new to the kitchen and doesn't know his way around just yet. The guys are preparing sloppy joe sandwiches for lunch that day. Tony asks Jeff to make the sauce. Jeff doesn't know what he's doing, so he asks Tony where the bowls are . . . then he asks for the ingredients . . . then he needs to know how much salt to use. Tony is frustrated that Jeff is being such a pain in the ass and thinks that he might as well make everything himself! Then, just as Tony begins to walk away to prepare another food dish, Jeff splashes Tony with the sauce while mixing everything together. That's it! Tony turns around, shoves Jeff, and yells "What the fuck, man?! Can't you do* ***ANYTHING*** *right?" Jeff pushes back at Tony, and before you know it, the two of them are in a physical fight. The guard on duty shows up, and both men get suspended from their jobs and a disciplinary write-up.*

What were some of Tony's thoughts that led to his anger and aggression?

____

____

What was the consequence of Tony's thoughts?

____

____

Do you think Tony's thoughts were helpful/justified in this situation? Why or why not?

____

____

What are some other ways Tony could have thought about the situation to prevent anger?

____

____

How do you think these other thoughts would have helped Tony in this situation?

____

____

Thought Stopping

Another way to prevent anger from escalating is to just stop the thought. Here, rather than changing the thoughts that make you angry, what you are doing is talking yourself out of having the thoughts that make you angry. You don't dispute the thoughts; you simply command yourself to stop thinking those thoughts. Here are some examples of things you can tell yourself:

"Don't go there."

"I need to stop thinking these thoughts, or I will get in trouble."

"Don't buy into this situation."

"These thoughts aren't worth it."

What other self-commands can you think of to stop anger?

____

____

____

____

____

Acting Opposite

Yet another way to change difficult emotions, like anger, is to act the opposite of what you are feeling. But you should ONLY do this if the emotion is not helpful. To know when it's ok to act opposite, you first need to remind yourself of your goals. Got 'em? Good. Here's what you do:

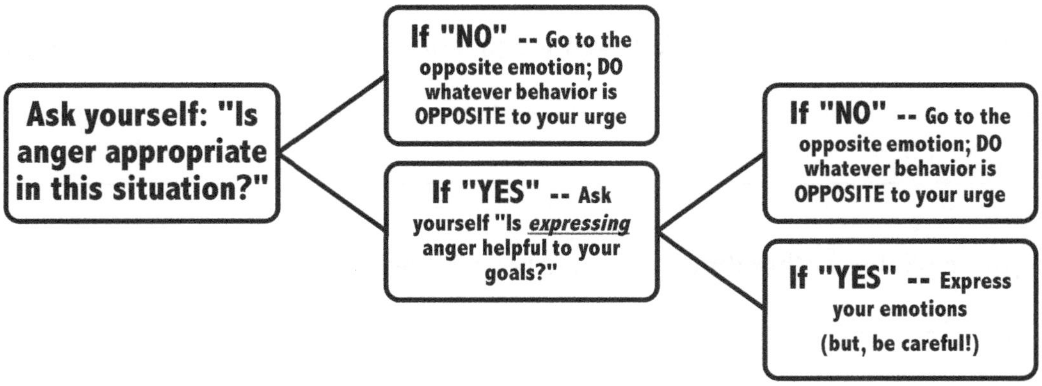

What emotions or behaviors are OPPOSITE of being angry?

____

____

This may seem like a strange thing to do, but acting opposite of how you are feeling, even if you don't start out feeling that way, can change your attitude. Don't believe it? Smile right now J. Did you do it? Even if you weren't happy before you smiled, you probably feel at least a little bit happier after you smiled. That's the idea here.

Write down how controlling anger with cognitive restructuring, thought stopping, and acting opposite will help you reach your goals.

Goal #1 ____

Goal #2 ____

Goal #3 ____

Goal #4 ____

Exercise: Highlighting Helpful Thoughts

To get more practice changing your thoughts, come up with *two* NEW and more helpful ways of thinking for each statement that follows.

"I am always right."

New thought #1: ______________________________

New thought #2: ______________________________

"That guy meant to disrespect me."

New thought #1: ______________________________

New thought #2: ______________________________

"That's unfair—I have been wronged."

New thought #1: ______________________________

New thought #2: ______________________________

"This situation has ruined my day."

New thought #1: ______________________________

New thought #2: ______________________________

"It's all his fault!"

New thought #1: ______________________________

New thought #2: ______________________________

"I should have gotten what I wanted."

New thought #1: ______________________________

New thought #2: ______________________________

"It's not my responsibility to fix other people's mistakes."

New thought #1: ______________________________

New thought #2: ______________________________

"That idiot knows better than that!"

New thought #1: ______________________________

New thought #2: ______________________________

"He needs to be set straight."

New thought #1: ______________________________

New thought #2: ______________________________

"That officer knows that shit pisses me off."

New thought #1: ______________________________

New thought #2: ______________________________

Think of a common thought you have that leads to anger (see Detecting the Clues exercise from Handout #13) **and write it here:** ______________________________

New thought #1: ______________________________

New thought #2: ______________________________

Handout #15
Moving From Aggressive to Assertive

As you know, one apparent benefit of aggression and violence is getting control over others or getting what you want from others. Aggression can also be used to solve problems or deal with conflicts between people. When you feel that someone has violated your rights or well-being, your first reaction might be to fight back or retaliate. You want revenge. Aggression sends the message that "***my*** feelings, thoughts, and opinions are very important, but ***your*** feelings, thoughts, and opinions are **not** important." People don't like to feel less than or worthless. So a few consequences of aggression may include losing close relationships or putting yourself at risk for a physical altercation. But there is a better way to express your feelings and still get what you want without hurting others or getting yourself in trouble.

The opposite of acting aggressively is to act passively. Being passive isn't helpful either. By acting in a passive way, you allow others to violate your rights and take advantage of you. You're a doormat for people to walk on. You may come to despise the person who is violating your rights or be upset with yourself for not standing up for your rights. Passivity sends the message that "***your*** feelings, thoughts, and opinions are very important, but ***my*** feelings, thoughts, and opinions are **not** important." People who are passive generally do not feel good about themselves. They may have low self-esteem and feel inferior to other people. They are also likely to be disrespected and treated unfairly by others.

The BEST way to resolve conflicts with other people or to express your negative feelings (like anger, frustration, sadness, pain) is by acting assertively. Assertiveness involves standing up for your rights while also showing respect for other people. Assertive behavior sends the message that "***my*** feelings, thoughts, and opinions are **just as** important as ***your*** feelings, thoughts, and opinions." It's ok—and even normal—for people to disagree with you. That doesn't mean their beliefs are any more or less important. You can still be respectful. Assertiveness allows you to share your feelings and reactions to the person who offended or hurt you without suffering the negative consequence of aggression or passivity.

Match the Story (Left) to the Behavior Used (Right)

Passive	*"Another inmate called David a 'bitch' for not participating in a gambling ring on the unit. David made a shank out of a pen that he stole and stabbed the inmate in the mess hall as payback."*
Aggressive	*"Mary is a young, attractive woman. As she's walking down the street, she hears a man yell something sexual about her body. Mary tells the man in a calm voice that she is offended by his words and would have appreciated it more if he started a nice conversation with her instead."*
Assertive	*"Robert is spending his first time in segregation. He's scared and refuses to cuff-up for shower time. The officer on duty sees this behavior as defiant and threatens to write up a disciplinary report. Robert takes the write-up and lays back down on his bed."*

The Conflict Resolution Model

The conflict resolution model is a method for acting more assertively. There are **five steps**.

Identify the Problem
What issue is causing the conflict?

Identify Your Feelings
How is the conlifct making you feel?

Identify the Impact
What's going to happen if the problem continues?

Decide Whether to Resolve the Conflict
Is the conflict important enough to bring up or should you let it go?

Address and Resolve the Conflict
Talk about your view of the problem, your feelings about it, and possible solutions.

What are the advantages of this model? What do you get by doing this?

How will other people react or respond to you if you follow this model?

Exercise: Calm the Conflict

Think of a conflict you had with someone in the past that didn't turn out well—either because you were too aggressive or too passive. Use the conflict resolution model to rethink how you would handle the situation assertively.

Describe what happened (who was involved, where were you, what were you doing?)	What was the big problem or disagreement that led to the conflict?	How did the original problem and the resulting conflict make you feel?	What consequence or overall impact did the problem have on your life at the time?	Was the conflict worth resolving or letting go (the intensity of your feelings and the consequences of the problem are clues)?	What could you have said or done differently and what solutions could have solved the conflict more peacefully?
	1	2	3	4	5

Handout #16

Aggression, Assertiveness, and Being Tough

Tough Guys Do It

So far, you have been reading a lot about feelings and how you should openly talk about them—either with yourself or with someone you trust. You may be thinking that tough people don't share their feelings or that feelings are for weak people. This is a common belief. You may have gotten this message from your family, friends, neighborhood, or the prison environment. Especially in restrictive housing units, you may be teased or called hurtful names for trying to express feelings. Anger, aggression, violence, and bad behavior in general are so common here that other inmates may try to put you down for not behaving like they are. Remember, they are stuck in a negative cycle that keeps them in trouble, and they want you to be stuck with them.

Aggressive anger may seem like the badass or tough thing to do because it shows power and control. But the truth is, anger is the easy way out. It's easier to let anger escalate and to bully people into getting what you want than it is to manage your anger and solve your problems prosocially. You may scare and intimidate other people, but they don't see you as superior like you would want them to. Even though your victims may step aside when you walk in the room, they do not see you as the better person. Instead, they see you as an "asshole" or "bitch" who is out of control, crazy, and irresponsible. You do not gain respect this way—at least not from the people who matter. You may be respected by other violent inmates or gang members but remember where they are and where you don't want to be. Aggression is cowardly and lazy—it doesn't require any real work to get things, and the things you do get are shallow and not meaningful. Real tough people (those who are successful) aren't lazy. They work hard for what's important, even if it means they have to think and act in ways that are challenging or uncomfortable. People who are strong will push through and make it happen.

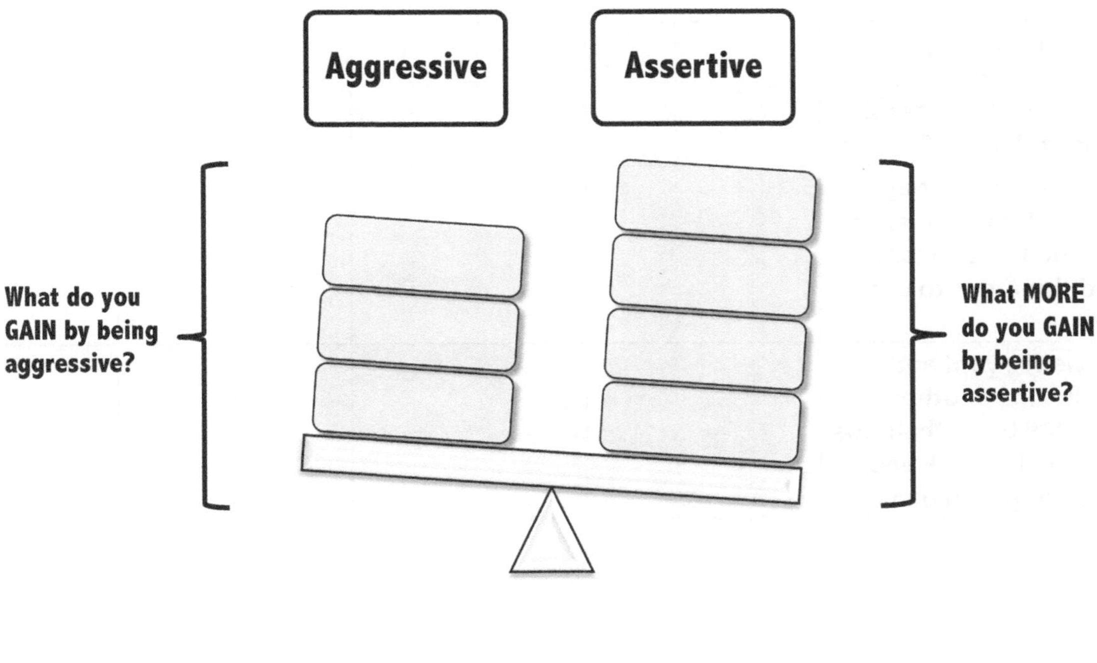

Rolling With Resistance

In Handout #15, you learned how to resolve conflicts more peacefully by being assertive (not aggressive or passive). But the reality is that you are living in a restricted housing unit where many inmates do not know or do not practice this skill. So when you try to be assertive, they may not respond well. They may yell at you, call you names, tell you to "fuck off," or threaten to harm you. Understand that this is THEIR problem. They are being lazy and feel more comfortable handling problems the only way they know how—through aggression. They wrongly believe that being tough and strong means bullying others. Don't get upset by these inmates; it will only make you lose sight of your goals. You are stronger and capable of controlling your anger. You have the ability to get out and stay out of segregation. When other people resist your attempts to be assertive and to solve the problem peacefully, you may just need to walk away. It's not worth the fight. Tell yourself it is their loss. Don't let them keep you stuck.

Exercise: Who's Tougher Than Nails?

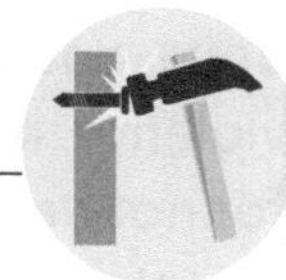

Read the short stories that follow and determine who is acting more like a badass. Discuss how you see each person and how other people, like staff at the prison, would see them. Then guess the likely result of their behavior (what did they get, or what did they lose?).

Story	What do you think about him?	What might others think about him?	What might happen because of his actions?	How much of a badass is he/she? (not at all, a little bit, or very much)
Troy is cooking out on the grill. He has a beer or two and plays catch with his son in the yard.				
Wayne throws urine at a correctional officer because he's angry about being in prison.				
Monica is threatening another inmate in segregation, yelling that she should just kill herself.				
Larry's coworker is always late getting things done, so Larry tells him he's "a lazy slob" and threatens to get him fired.				
Joe is in the rec yard and accidentally hits another inmate with a basketball. Joe asks the guy if he's ok and invites him to play a game.				

Handout #17
Passing Up Passive-Aggression

What Is Passive-Aggression?

You learned about being aggressive, being passive, and being assertive in Handout#15. But, what about passive-aggression? Inmates who are passive-aggressive are more likely to find themselves in restricted housing units. So it's another important behavior to learn about and get control over. People who are uncomfortable being openly aggressive will often use passive-aggression to get what they want by indirectly saying or doing something that makes others feel bad, guilty, embarrassed, or ashamed. It allows people to have things their way and still be liked. Passive-aggression is sneaky; instead of being verbally abusive or physically assaultive, you are hiding your aggression under a sly comment or behavior. Passive-aggression doesn't always appear as angry or resentful. Actually, it can sometimes sound polite, friendly, or well-meaning. Sometimes people don't realize that they've been victims of passive-aggression until later on. But the more you behave this way, the more people will see the truth—that you are using this strategy to manipulate them or your situation. Correctional staff knows this behavior well and see it as a reason for disciplinary action. To them, you are showing noncompliance and an overall bad attitude. Just because you are not verbally threatening or physically hurting someone doesn't mean you aren't causing harm.

Here's an example:

> *Harry and his coworker, Greg, went out for a beer at the corner bar after work. It was a Tuesday night, and both men had to get up early for a job the next morning. Greg asked Harry to drive that night because he "had a rough day" and needed to distract himself. Harry agreed, but on the condition that they leave around 10:00 pm. Harry wanted to be rested for work in the morning. It was 9:45 pm and Harry warned Greg that it was almost time to go. At 9:55 pm, Harry asked Greg to grab his coat and pay his tab. By 10:00 pm, Harry announced, "All right, Greg, it's time to go. I need to get home." Greg had just purchased another beer and said "Oh . . . ok . . . well . . . um . . . I guess we can leave." Harry responded, "Did you want to stay? Is that what you're getting at?" Greg replied, "Huh? Oh, no. We can leave if you want to. It's just that I have all this beer left," Greg said. Harry agreed to stay for one more round, which turned into three. He was tired the next day and showed up late for work.*

Who was being passive-aggressive in this story? ____________________

Who was the victim in this story? ____________________

What did Harry get? ____________________

What did Greg get? ____________________

How do you think their relationship will be affected?

____

____

Is It *That* Bad? What Are the Consequences?

Yes, passive-aggression can hurt your reputation and relationships over the long term. Here are some things that could happen:

Cover up real issues	Create poor self-image	Create tension between people
Create resentment	Create confusion or frustration	Problems build up

What Can I Do Instead?

Use assertiveness! Be clear about what you want and understand that other people may want something different. Here are some other tips:

- ☑ **Explore the feelings that are causing your behavior (are you pissed off, hurt, jealous?).**
- ☑ **Remember how your behaviors affect other people—trying to defeat someone else, get back at them, or annoy them creates even more discomfort in the relationship.**
- ☑ **Take responsibility! Show others that you are the bigger person by acknowledging your role in the situation. It will only make people like you more if you are honest and can admit your mistakes.**
- ☑ **Don't feel attacked when a problem comes up—problems happen in life, and you just have to deal with it.**

When other people are being passive-aggressive, use your assertiveness skills to talk about how their behaviors are making you feel. If they don't want to hear it, ask to talk when the person has calmed down, or you may have to let it go and know that their behaviors are not really about you.

Exercise: Pinpointing Passive-Aggression

The following are some other examples of passive-aggression. Write about a time when you did this to someone and a time when you were the victim of this by someone else.

Example	I have done this to someone	I have been a victim of this
Not communicating something when there really is a problem		
Avoiding or ignoring when you feel angry, putting up a wall to your feelings		

Example	I have done this to someone	I have been a victim of this
Intentionally putting off important tasks		
Avoiding situations where someone else will be seen as better at something		
Always being late and making others wait on you		
Always coming up with reasons for not doing something		
Sulking to get attention		
Not getting too attached to other people		
Self-pity, feeling "poor me"		
Blaming other people for things you are responsible for		
Withholding things like sex, money, or love from other people		
Acting like you can't help yourself and need others to do a task for you		
Rolling your eyes or giving angry looks at someone		

Handout #18
Digging Deeper Into Anger

Anger can mean that someone is simply frustrated or pissed off (like someone cutting you in line for the commissary). But most of the time, anger is covering up something more serious. As noted earlier, anger can be a sign that someone is really feeling emotional pain—such as sadness, shame, guilt, or fear. Just like an iceberg, anger is on the surface. It's what other people can see, and it only shows a small part of the problem. All those other emotions are hiding beneath the surface. That's where the danger lies—***IF*** you don't watch out for them. But knowing that there is more to anger than meets the eye, you can begin to focus on these other emotions. Understanding what your anger is covering up will help you get to the real root of the problem so you can start to come up with solutions that work. By doing this, you will feel less angry and act less aggressively.

So, Why Is Anger the Go-to Emotion When It's Not the Emotion You Are *Really* Feeling?

As you read earlier, anger is a lazy way to express yourself. It can be challenging and uneasy to think about all those other emotions—you may have to bring back old memories and go outside of your comfort zone. But you can handle it. Anger is also more accepted, especially among men. It sends a message of power and superiority. As you now know, this is just a front. Anger actually makes people look out of control.

If These Other Emotions Are So Uncomfortable, Why Should I Put Myself Through That?

Because the payoff will be worth it. At first, it will feel strange to talk about shame, sadness, hurt, fear, guilt, humiliation, or any other negative emotion. This may be because you've never talked about it before, because you are worried about trusting other people, because you're afraid your manhood will be questioned, because you have to think about something bad that happened to you in the past, or because you have to admit that you sometimes need help. But being able to overcome difficult challenges makes you stronger and smarter in the end. Eventually, you will be able to recognize these other emotions and work through them rather than relying on anger to solve your problems (which it hardly ever does). In the process, you will learn more about who you are. Knowing yourself can help you develop better goals—you will know what you want and what you need to do to get it. In addition, when people finally let down their guard and talk about these deeper emotions, they say things like "a weight has been lifted." It feels good to be able to see what is really going on.

Exercise: Emotional Fact or Fiction

Having a misunderstanding about the emotions hiding underneath your anger can stop you from exploring any further. The following are some myths about emotions. In the blank spaces, write counter-statements—more accurate beliefs.

1. **There is a right way to feel in every situation.**

   ____

2. **Letting others know that I'm feeling bad is a weakness.**

   ____

3. **All negative feelings are bad and destructive.**

   ____

4. **Being emotional means being out of control.**

   ____

5. **Emotions can happen for no reason.**

   ____

6. **Talking or thinking about emotions doesn't help anything.**

   ____

7. **All painful emotions are the result of a bad attitude or mood.**

   ____

8. **If others don't like my feelings, then I shouldn't feel the way I do.**

   ____

9. **Other people are the best judges of how I am feeling.**

   ____

10. **Painful emotions are not really important and should be ignored.**

    ____

What's another misunderstanding you had about emotions?

____

Challenge that here:

____

Handout #19
Fighting With Fear

Fear is common in the restrictive housing unit. It's not a pleasant or happy place to be. Remember that this unit is a disciplinary placement for inmates who have violated the rules of the facility. Many are violent, aggressive, threatening, and intimidating. Fear may have also been a reason why you decided to violate the rules—so you could live in protective custody. But you didn't escape to paradise here. Fear is often expressed as anger because, in prison, inmates who look scared become victims of bullying and violence. However, you need to face your fears so you can reduce your risk for mental health problems and disciplinary sanctions.

What fears do you have about being on this unit?

What threats have you gotten from other inmates while living on this unit?
How did this make you feel?

What threats have you made to other inmates while living on this unit?
How do you think this made them feel?

There are many ways to describe fear. The bubble that follows lists other fear-related words. Circle the words that could have described how you felt at one time or another:

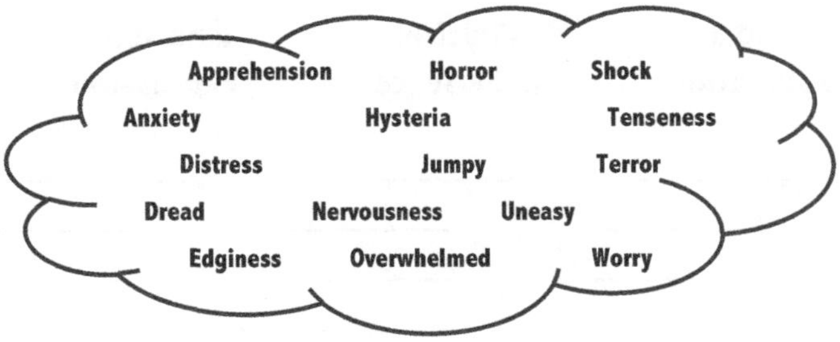

Just like anger, fear is caused by an event in your life. Your mind then tries to explain or understand the event. Depending on what explanation your mind comes to, your body reacts to it. You will then experience some kind of aftermath or consequence of your reaction. Here are some examples of what this process might look like:

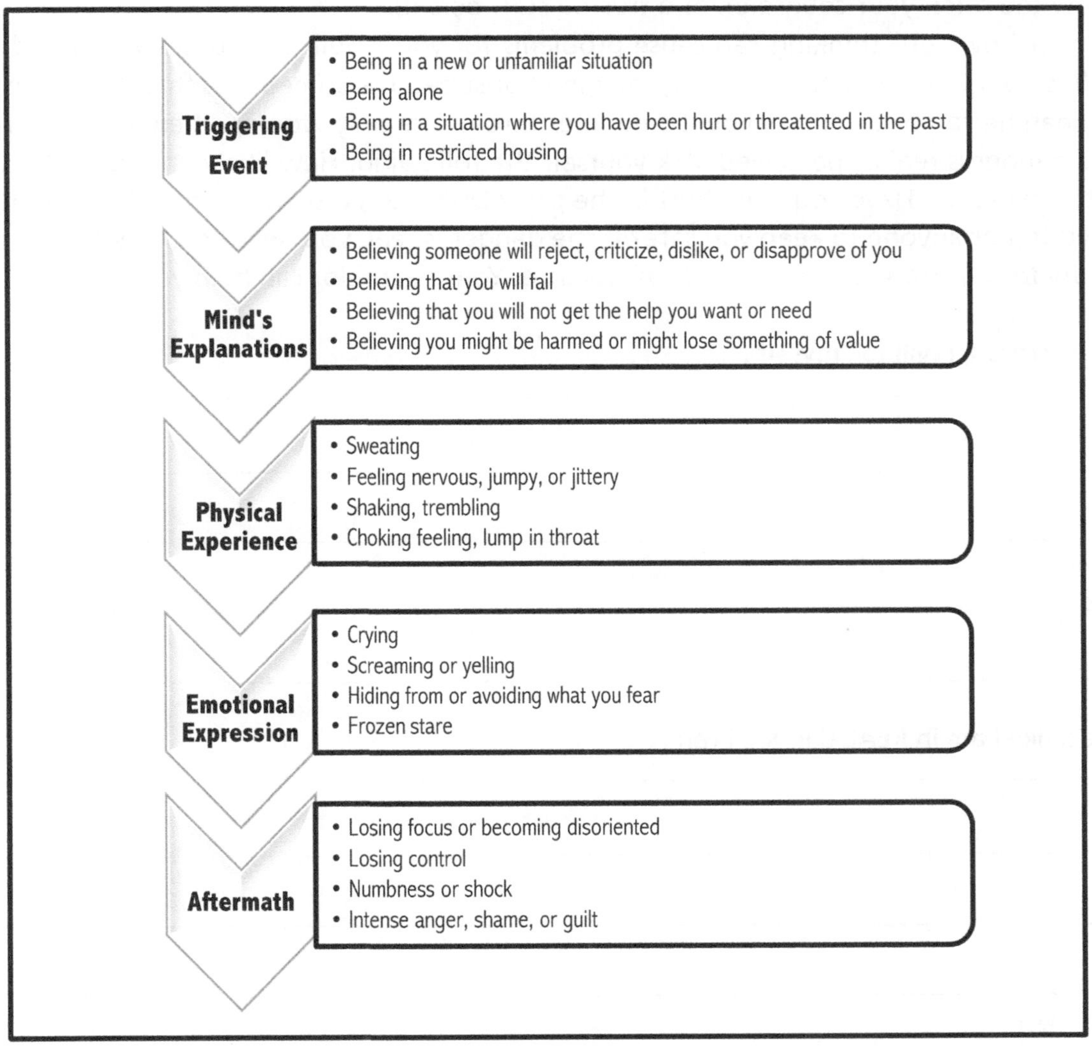

Now assess where your feelings of fear come from and how you experience it. Pick a triggering event you've experienced before and talk about how your mind tried to explain it, how you reacted physically and emotionally, and what consequences (or aftermath) you experienced because of your reaction.

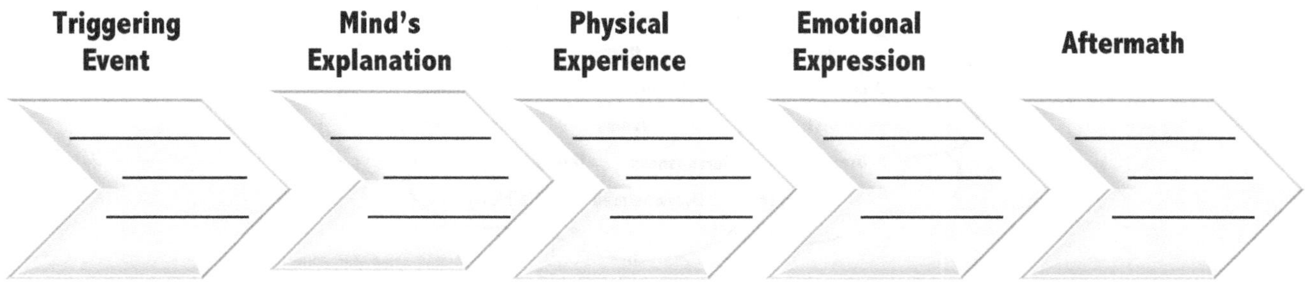

When you're scared, some inmates may try to be your friend—but be careful. These inmates may have a hidden motive. If they have a bad reputation, are getting into trouble a lot, or are in a gang, do not associate with them, even if they offer you protection or safety. These guys want something in return and will take you away from your goals! Instead, try to find people who are prosocial, such as inmates who follow the rules, your counselor, or a trusted staff person.

Remember how your thinking can cause problems for you? Well, sometimes your mind can make you feel like danger is real when it's really imagined. Just because someone is threatening to harm you doesn't mean he can or will harm you. Sometimes threats are only words. When you're scared, figure out if the danger is real or perceived. Ask yourself the following: How likely am I to REALLY be hurt? Look at the evidence. Have you been hurt in the past? Does the person have the ability to hurt you? Is there anything or anyone to keep you safe? If the danger is real, you need to *know the procedures at your facility for reporting serious threats of violence*. Your counselor can help you.

When I feel scared, I will tell myself . . .

When I feel like I am in REAL danger, I can . . .

Exercise: Lemons, Lemons, Lemons . . .

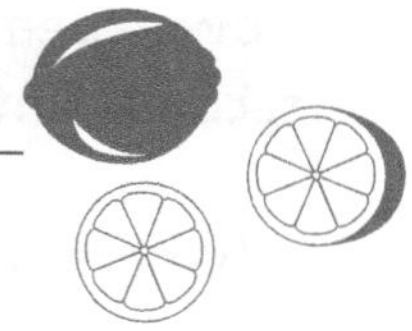

Sometimes, fear is caused when other inmates call you nasty names to try to provoke you and make you feel bad. But these are just words. Here is a strategy you can use to reduce the meaning of these words and how much of an impact they have on you. You can even use this strategy with the negative words you use to put yourself down (such as "bad" or "loser"). This may seem silly but stick with it!

1. **Say the word "lemon" out loud one or two times.**

   What are your ***thoughts*** about the word?

   What ***images*** come to mind?

   What ***smells*** come to mind?

   What ***tastes*** come to mind?

2. **Now, repeat the word "lemon" over and over out loud as fast as you can for 30 seconds until it's just a meaningless sound. You must do it out loud for it to be effective.**

3. **Next, think of a word that causes you to feel afraid, scared, or fearful. It could also be a two-word phrase.**
   Write the word(s) here: ____________

4. **Say the word(s) you wrote down earlier out loud one or two times.**

   What are your ***thoughts*** about the word(s)?

   What ***feelings*** are you experiencing?

   What ***images*** come to mind?

   What ***urges*** do you have after saying the word?

5. **Now, repeat the word(s) you wrote down earlier over and over out loud as fast as you can for 30 seconds until it's just a meaningless sound. You must do it out loud for it to be effective.**

   What are your ***thoughts*** about the word right now?

   ____

   What ***feelings*** are you experiencing right now?

   ____

   What ***images*** come to mind now?

   ____

   What ***urges*** do you have now?

   ____

6. **Have your reactions to the word changed the more you said it? Check the box that best fits you.**

   ☐ **More fearful?**
   ☐ **Less fearful?**
   ☐ **My level of fear stayed the same**

After this exercise, most people find that the word or phrase becomes meaningless within 30 seconds. Then you can see the word for what it really is: a strange sound, a vibration, a movement of your mouth and tongue. But when you hear that very same word from someone else or it pops into your head, you connect with it, and it can be very hurtful. Remember, it's just a sound.

Other Ways to Let Go of Negative Words That Are Hurtful or Scary

Close your eyes and . . .

- **Imagine the word on a cloud in the sky . . . watch it drift away**
- **Imagine the word in a bubble rising to the surface of a pond**
- **Imagine the word in the mouth of a bird flying across the sky**
- **Imagine the word on a leaf blowing lightly in the wind**
- **Imagine the word in a car driving away**

Handout #20
Stopping Shame and Sadness

Shame and sadness are two other common emotions that are often felt in restricted housing. You may feel ashamed or sad because of the behaviors that put you in this unit, because other inmates won't leave you alone, or because of many other reasons. They are difficult emotions to deal with, but if you ignore them, they can lead to anger, aggression, or mental health problems.

Do you have any feelings of shame and sadness about being on this unit?
Why or why not?

____

____

____

There are many ways to describe shame. The bubble that follows lists other shame-related words. Circle the words that could have described how you felt at one time or another:

Culpability Guilt Regret
Insult Embarrassment Remorse
Invalidation Disgraced Self-disgust
Mortified Humiliation Dejected
Demeaned Blameworthy Stigmatized

And here are some other sadness-related words. Circle the words that could have described how you felt at one time or another:

Grief Misery Despair
Hurt Woe Sorrow Unhappy
Rejection Gloomy Suffering
Melancholy Lonely Depression
Neglected Defeated Agony

Just like anger and fear, shame and sadness are caused by an event in your life. Your mind then tries to explain or understand the event. Depending on what explanation your mind comes up with, your body reacts to it. You will then experience some kind of aftermath or consequence of your reaction. Here are some examples of what this process might look like:

Shame

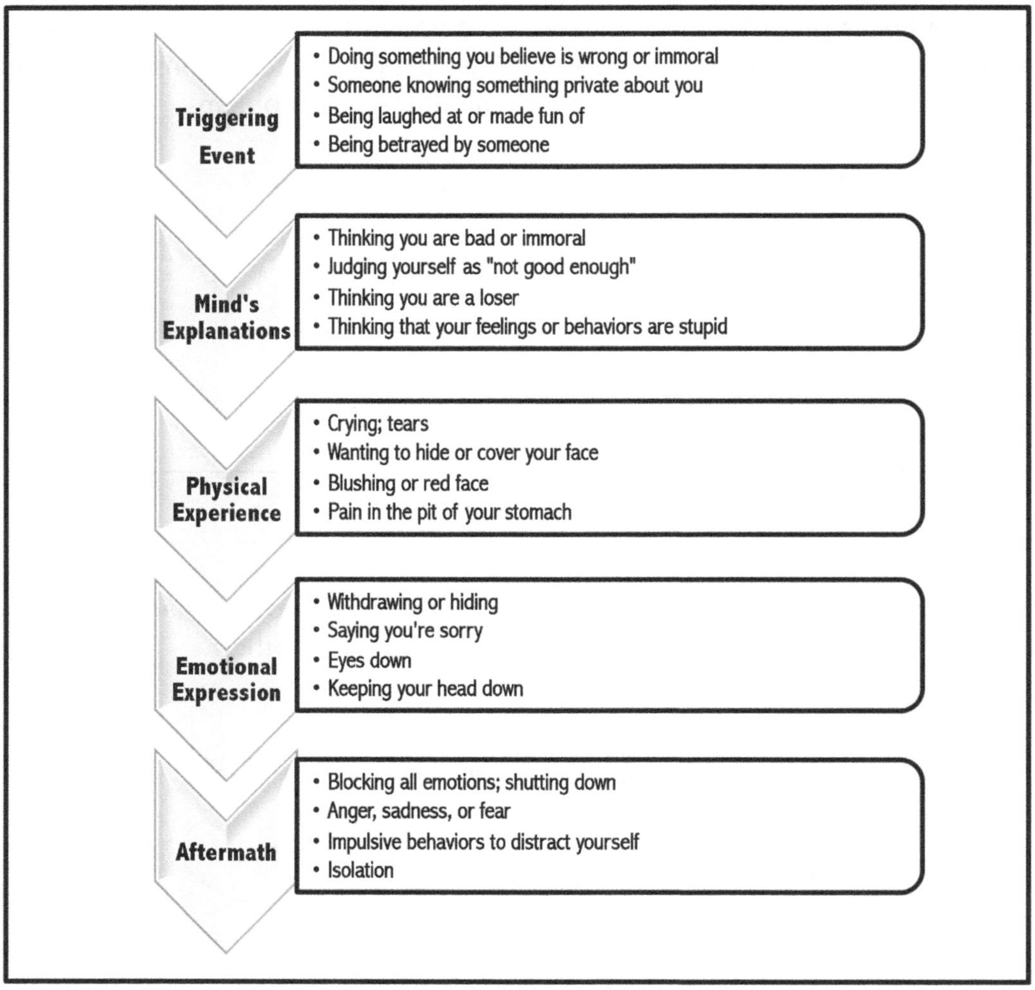

Now assess where your feelings of shame come from and how you experience them.

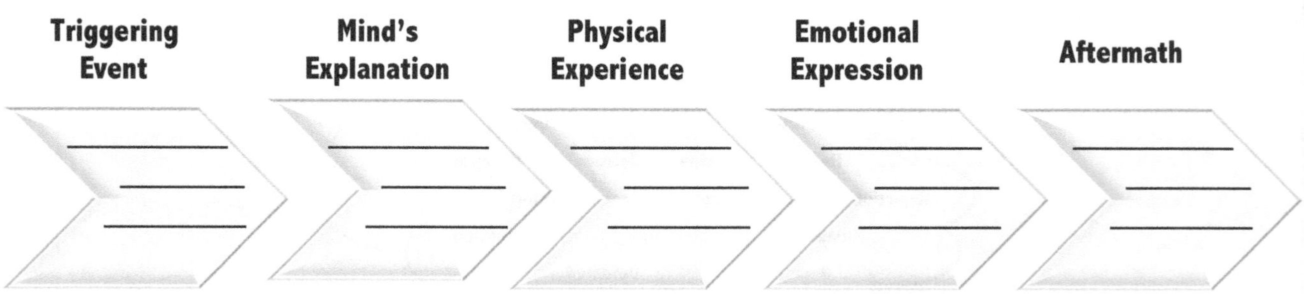

Sadness

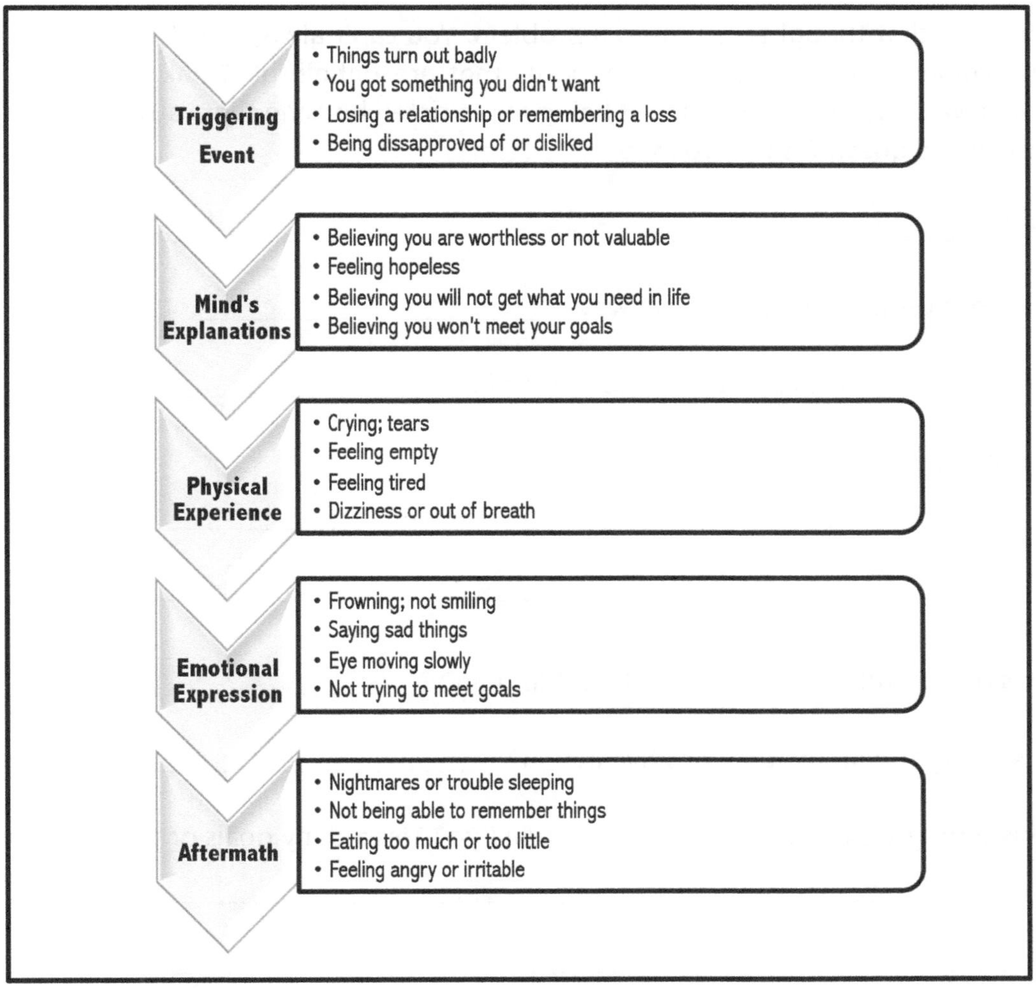

Now assess where your feelings of sadness come from and how you experience them.

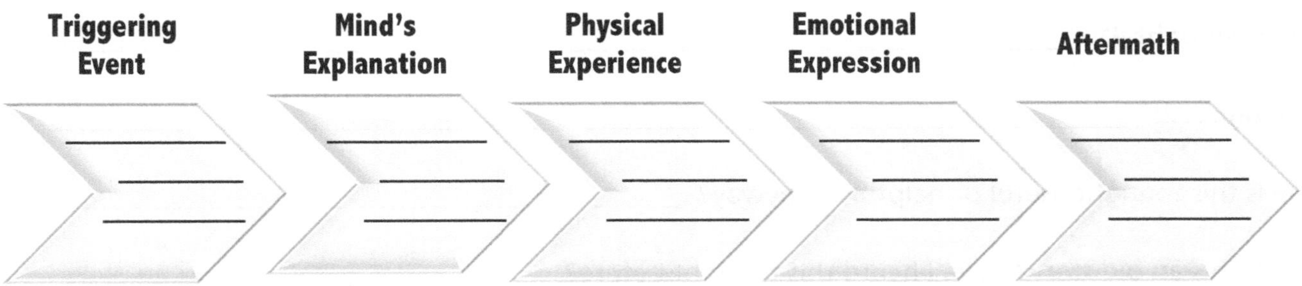

Shame and sadness can also lead to thoughts of suicide. If you are experiencing suicidal thoughts, go back to the handouts from Module 3 and review your suicide prevention plan.

Exercise: Thought Interrogation

You know by now that thoughts are often a problem. You can't always trust the first thought that comes to mind, especially thoughts that are unhelpful. Think of two thoughts you have about yourself or about being in restricted housing that cause you to feel shame or sadness. Answer the questions that follow.

Thought #1: " ______________________________ **"**

Is this thought useful or helpful in anyway? ______________________________

Is this an old story? Have I heard this thought before? ______________________________

What would I get for buying into this story?

____

____

Could this be helpful or is my mind just babbling on? ______________________________

Does this thought help me take positive action? ______________________________

If I let this thought guide my actions, where will I go? Toward my goals or toward struggle?

____

____

Does this thought help me be who I want to be? ______________________________

***New* thought #1: "** ______________________________ **"**

Thought #2: " ______________________________ **"**

Is this thought useful or helpful in anyway? ______________________________

Is this an old story? Have I heard this thought before? ______________________________

What would I get for buying into this story?

____

____

Could this be helpful or is my mind just babbling on? ______________________________

Does this thought help me take positive action? ______________________________

How do your NEW thoughts make you feel? Do they reduce shame or sadness?

If I let this thought guide my actions, where will I go? Toward my goals or toward struggle?

____

Does this thought help me be who I want to be? ______________________________

***New* thought #2:** " ____ "

Module 4
Recap

In This Module You Learned About

☑ **The difference between anger and aggression, and where they come from**
☑ **Your own level of anger and aggression**
☑ **Reducing your level of anger—as well as your feelings of fear, shame, and sadness**
☑ **Resolving conflicts with others peacefully**
☑ **The role of anger and aggression in manhood**
☑ **Feelings that are often hidden underneath anger**

Now place an ✗ mark next to the techniques that you will continue to practice and write down WHEN you will practice them, WHAT you will do, and HOW they will help you. Give your counselor permission to hold you accountable for following through with your plan.

Technique	I WILL do this (place ✗ here)	Whenever I . . .	This is how I will do it . . .	To help me cope with . . .
Be aware of events that trigger my anger				
Be aware of my physical, emotional, and cognitive cues				
Take a time out				
Use Progressive Muscle Relaxation (PMR)				
Talk to someone I trust about my emotions				
Get some exercise				

Technique	I WILL do this (place ✗ here)	Whenever I . . .	This is how I will do it . . .	To help me cope with . . .
Refocus myself on my goals				
Explore feelings that are hidden under my anger				
Use *My Aggression Log*				
Use cognitive restructuring				
Use thought stopping				
Act opposite of my emotions				
Use the conflict resolution model				
Decide when to walk away from a bad situation or roll with resistance				
Use imagery to make hurtful words meaningless				
Evaluate the evidence for my fear—how real is it?				
Talk to someone if my risk of harm is high				
Avoid making friends with people I don't know anything about				

Technique	I WILL do this (place ✗ here)	Whenever I . . .	This is how I will do it . . .	To help me cope with . . .
Be aware of the consequences or aftermath of my emotions				
Question how helpful my thoughts are to me				
Take deep breaths				

Module 5

Exploring My Mental Distress and Criminalness: Where It Comes From, What It Looks Like, and How to Recognize It

Handout #21
Defining "Mental Distress"

What Is It?

Mental distress happens when your mind is not working right. There are two factors that cause your mind to do things that are not normal for you: **(1) biology** and **(2) environment**. Biology means the stuff already inside of you, like your genetics or chemicals in your brain. When you experience a number of related psychological symptoms that cause distress, mental illness can develop. Mental illness is sometimes inherited from people in your family. You may know other family members who have a mental illness or have experienced symptoms similar to yours. There are also chemicals in your brain that send messages to other parts of your brain—these messages tell your mind how to think and act. These chemicals are called **neurotransmitters** (neuro = brain; transmitter = sending messages). When your neurotransmitters are not working correctly, the wrong messages get sent to the different parts of your brain. This is called a chemical imbalance. There are many different types of neurotransmitters in your brain; the symptoms you experience depend on which ones stop functioning properly. But, in most cases, biology isn't enough. For almost everyone, stress or other events in their environment (for example, death of a loved one, loss of a job, childhood abuse, living in poverty, or incarceration) also play a role. When your biology AND your environment are working against you, it increases your chances of having serious mental distress or a mental illness (it's no guarantee, just very likely).

Basic Facts About Mental Health and Illness

- Mental illness is a more serious form of mental distress and is usually experienced as a thought or behavior that causes stress or emotional (and even physical) pain to you or the people around you. These thoughts and behaviors may look different for different people, even if they have the same mental illness that you have.
- Mental illness is not simply a reaction to stress. What makes something a mental illness is when the thought or behavior is not typical (or abnormal) for other people in your culture. Take anxiety for example. Anxiety is normal sometimes. You may have felt anxious or nervous about coming to this restricted housing unit. That's understandable; it's an uncomfortable and sometimes scary place to be. But when your anxiety is so high that you can't eat, can't sleep, can't communicate with other people, or can't bring yourself to shower or exercise, your anxiety could be a symptom of mental illness. Those behaviors are not normal and could cause a lot of problems for you.

- A doctor or counselor who went to school to learn about mental health determines the type of mental illness or concerns that you have. What these professionals look for is a specific group of symptoms that happen at the same time. These clusters of symptoms make up a **diagnosis** (diagnosis simply means the label or name used to describe each cluster of symptoms). Diagnosis helps professionals communicate about a person's mental illness quickly and easily. It can also give people some relief that there is a name for what they are going through.
- To have a mental illness, you don't have to experience ALL of the symptoms that make up a particular diagnosis, and not everyone will express these symptoms in the same way. To make a correct diagnosis, your doctor or counselor needs very specific information about you. This is why it is important to be honest with him or her when asked about your mental health. If you lie to your doctor or counselor, he or she cannot help you get better. Your doctor or counselor has more knowledge about this stuff than you might think. If you have not told the truth to your doctor or counselor in the past, go back and tell him or her what's really going on. He or she understands that it can be difficult to talk about mental illness.
- Many people have a mental illness. Mental health problems are especially common in prisons and in disciplinary units. Nearly 16% of people who are incarcerated are believed to have a mental illness.
- You often cannot tell just by looking at a person whether he or she has a mental illness. Lots of people with mental illnesses are able to hold it together on the outside, but on the inside, they are hurting. Your cellmate or neighbor may have a mental illness, and you just don't know it.
- It is ***NOT*** your fault that you have a mental illness. But this isn't an excuse for your behavior. You are responsible for managing your symptoms so that they don't get the best of you and take you away from your goals.
- Even if you do not meet full criteria for a mental illness, you may still experience symptoms of mental distress that are worth talking about in treatment and that may relate to your behavior problems. So, don't dismiss this module just because you may not have been given a diagnosis. If you believe a disorder or group of symptoms does not apply to you, still consider what parts may hold some truth for you.

How Do I Get Over Mental Distress or Illness?

The fact is—you may never get over your mental distress or illness for good. Many people have to work for the rest of their lives to manage psychological symptoms. They don't go away forever. But this doesn't mean that you have to suffer forever. Imagine being sick with a cold (fever, chills, headache). What do you need to do to get better again? Take medicine, get lots of rest, drink plenty of water, and eat soup. Once the symptoms are gone, the cold is over. There is no need to continue taking medicine, resting, guzzling water, or eating soup. This is not true when you have mental health issues. Yes, there are things you can do to feel better, but you can never give up working on it. The good news is—the more you practice new skills, the easier your work will become. It may not even feel like work after a while.

You are going to start breaking the old habits that kept your symptoms going and develop new habits that keep your symptoms under control. And if you're wondering whether treatment programs like this one can work, the answer is YES. Many times, people also need medication to help with their symptoms (medications can correct your neurotransmitters). So it's important that you take medication if the doctor tells you to; remember, he or she is trained about this stuff. You always have the right to ask questions about your medications if you are confused. For many mental symptoms and illnesses, there is a 70%–80% chance that people will see improvements in their lives if they take the necessary steps. But you have to be an active participant. If you sit there and wait for change to happen, you will be sitting and waiting for a long time. ***YOU*** HAVE TO DO SOMETHING!

Exercise: Mental Distress Mini Survey

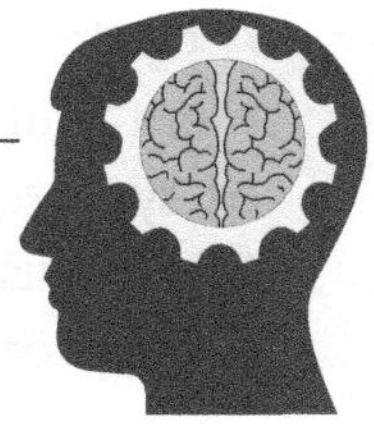

Answer the following questions. Some questions ask about mental health problems more generally, and some questions ask about your specific mental distress of illness (you can still talk about your symptoms/experiences even if you do not know your diagnosis).

1. **What did you think/know about mental distress or illness BEFORE reading this handout?**

    ____

    ____

2. **What new information did you learn about mental distress or illness by reading this handout?**

    ____

    ____

3. **Do you know anyone else (family member, friend) who has a mental illness or experiences symptoms of a mental illness? How are their symptoms similar to and/or different than yours?**

    ____

    ____

4. **What do you think causes your mental distress and illness?**

    Biological factors: ____

    Environmental factors: ____

5. **When are your symptoms at their worst?**

    ____

    ____

6. **What ways have you tried in the past to reduce your mental health symptoms? How well did they work for you?**

    ____

    ____

    ____

Handout #22
Common Diagnoses: Part I

Acute Clinical Disorders vs. Personality Disorders

Professionals who know a lot about mental illnesses and how to diagnose them typically separate them into two main categories: **(1) acute clinical disorders** and **(2) personality disorders**. Acute clinical disorders are generally thought to be less stable over time, and their symptoms are usually easier to manage than personality disorders. People with acute clinical disorders often recognize or understand that there is something not quite right with them, and they are likely to ask for help. People with personality disorders often need other people to point out their problems, and they don't like when this happens! They are less likely to ask for help on their own. Having a personality disorder can severely impact how you relate to other people and can be very damaging to your personal relationships.

What's in This Handout?

This handout discusses acute clinical disorders that are common in the general public as well as in prisons. You will learn more about personality disorders in Handout #23. Here are the disorders covered now:

Depression

- Depression is one of the most common mental disorders. About 15%–20% of people in the U.S. will experience depression in their lives.
- It causes people to have low moods in which they feel sad, blue, and down.
- It can impact your social life, your work, and your health.
- The good news is that people with depression can learn to manage their symptoms and lead happy, productive lives.

- Most people develop depression as teenagers or young adults, typically around the ages of 16 and 30.

  Some people only have symptoms a few times in their lives, but other people have more extreme symptoms that can lead to suicidal thoughts and/or hospitalization.
- Symptoms tend to come in episodes—this means that people will have symptoms for a period of time, and then their symptoms go away for a bit. These episodes may continue throughout a person's life if they do not get help. **Major depressive disorder** is characterized by several symptoms happening at the same time for two weeks or more.

Symptoms of Depression (Check Which Ones You Have Experienced)

Symptom	Example	Has something similar happened to you before?
Sad mood	"There is nothing good in my life."	
Eating a lot or a little	"The last time I was depressed, I gained over ten pounds."	
Sleeping a lot or a little	"I slept over 11 hours. When I woke up, I laid in bed for another few hours because I didn't have the energy to get up."	
Feeling tired/low energy	"The other day I skipped rec time because I didn't have the motivation to go."	
Feeling helpless, worthless, or hopeless	"Everyone is better than me; I just hold people back."	
Feeling guilty for things that aren't your fault	"Maybe if I wasn't depressed, the officer wouldn't be in such a bad mood and other inmates wouldn't be getting in so much trouble."	
Suicidal thoughts or actions	"The best thing for me to do is leave this world."	
Trouble thinking or making decisions	"One day, when I was working in the kitchen, I couldn't focus on what the other guys were saying, and I couldn't figure out how to make the dinner we were serving."	
Loss of interest in enjoyable activities	"I used to draw in my cell to reduce stress, but now I just don't feel like it anymore."	

Bipolar

- Bipolar disorder happens to about 1 in every 100 people at some point in their lives.
- Bipolar used to be called "manic depression"—this is because it has a lot in common with depression. But there is an extra part to it: the mania. Depression, as you know, causes people to be in a low or sad mood. Mania, on the other hand, causes people to be in very high moods (without using substances). Bipolar (bi = two; polar = sides) is characterized by BOTH high and low moods. People feel on top of the world for a while (sometimes as long as a week or more) and then come way back down for a while (sometimes as long as a month or more).
- Like depression, bipolar can impact your social life, your work, your health, and other important things.
- People with bipolar disorder can learn to manage their symptoms and lead happy, productive lives.
- Most people develop bipolar disorder as teenagers or young adults, typically around the ages of 16 and 30.
- Some people only have symptoms a few times in their lives, but other people have more extreme symptoms that can lead to suicidal thoughts and/or hospitalization.
- Symptoms tend to come in episodes—this means that people will have symptoms for a period of time, and then their symptoms go away for a bit. Manic episodes usually do not last as long as the depression episodes. People tend to like feeling manic but dislike feeling depressed. These episodes of mania and depression may continue throughout a person's life if they do not get help.
- Mania can be dangerous because it blocks people from seeing the consequences of their behaviors. Spending money you don't have, having sex with a lot of partners, or taking illegal drugs are examples of these. Mania can also lead to psychotic symptoms (hallucinations, delusions) that are similar to schizophrenia (see the following for more information).

Symptoms of Mania (Check Which Ones You Have Experienced)

Symptom	Example	Has something similar happened to you before?
Mania	"I'm so happy that I feel like I've never done anything wrong."	
Irritability	"I can't believe those people questioned my great ideas!"	
Unrealistic self-confidence	"I'm sure that I'm one of the smartest people alive."	
Need for less sleep	"I'm so excited for tomorrow that I only slept two hours last night."	

Symptom	Example	Has something similar happened to you before?
Talking a lot	"I felt like I was talking faster than normal, and the person I was talking to could hardly understand what I was saying."	
Racing thoughts	"I was thinking so fast that I couldn't think clearly."	
Easily distracted	"I was working on my homework, but every noise that I heard made me look up."	
Extreme over activity	"I did pushups in my cell for five hours straight just because I was feeling up for it."	
Bad judgment	"I knew this inmate would make me a lot of money on a bet, so I gave him all the money and commissary I had. I was swindled when he didn't show up with my winnings."	

Note: The symptoms of depression that go along with bipolar disorder are the same as those listed in the first table.

Schizophrenia

- About 1 in every 100 people will have schizophrenia (schizo = split; phrenia = mind) at some point in their lives.
- Symptoms of schizophrenia can get in the way of important things in your life and can make it difficult for you to tell what is real and what it not real. It may feel like you are dreaming when you are really awake. Sometimes, people have a hard time understanding when their feelings or beliefs aren't real. So even when someone tries to prove them wrong, they still think those things are real when, in fact, they are not. This makes it hard for some people to realize when they have schizophrenia.
- Schizophrenia is considered one of the most severe mental disorders, but that doesn't mean there isn't help. Many people with this disorder can be happy, healthy, and productive.
- Most people develop schizophrenia as teenagers or young adults, typically around the ages of 16 and 30.
- Some people only have symptoms a few times in their lives, but other people have more extreme symptoms that can lead to suicidal thoughts and/or hospitalization.
- Symptoms tend to come in episodes—this means that people will have symptoms for a period of time, and then their symptoms go away for a bit. These episodes may continue throughout a person's life if they do not get help.

Symptoms of Schizophrenia (Check Which Ones You Have Experienced)

Symptom	Example	Has something similar happened to you before?
Hallucinations (seeing, hearing, smelling, or feeling something that is not real)	"I hear a voice telling me that I'm not good, that I should just kill myself." "Sometimes I hear a radio playing when there isn't a radio near me."	
Delusions (extreme false beliefs)	"I am God." "The government is poisoning me."	
Confused thinking	"People keep saying that I'm using made up words." "I forgot what I was saying halfway through a sentence."	
Cognitive problems	"I couldn't understand the officer's instructions." "I don't remember what I ate for lunch today."	
Problems with other people or work	"I avoid other people because I might hurt them by accident."	
Disorganized behavior	"When I walk around, I make sure my hand is always touching the wall." "I sat perfectly still for hours on my bed."	
Lack of enjoyment or emotion	"The thought of going to the rec yard doesn't seem like fun anymore." "Another inmate called me a 'bitch' today, but I didn't seem to care one way or the other."	

Anxiety

- Remember that the type of anxiety discussed here is extreme and disproportionate to the situation. Anxiety becomes a problem when you are worrying so much about something that it causes serious impairment to your life (like work, exercise, or relationships).
- Some people worry a lot about many things (this is called generalized anxiety) or one specific thing (this is called a phobia; examples include being in public or fearing closed spaces). Anxiety disorders can also develop from a past traumatic event in which your mind keeps remembering the event and triggers you to worry about future trauma (this is called posttraumatic stress disorder [PTSD]).
- About 5% of people will experience generalized anxiety disorder in their lifetimes, about 8% of adults will experience PTSD, and up to 13% of people will experience social phobia.

- Many people with anxiety disorders can be happy, healthy, and productive.
- Most people develop anxiety disorders as teenagers or young adults, typically around the ages of 16 and 30.
- Some people only have symptoms a few times in their lives, but other people have more extreme symptoms that can lead to suicidal thoughts and/or hospitalization.
- Symptoms tend to come in episodes—this means that people will have symptoms for a period of time, and then their symptoms go away for a bit. These episodes may continue
- throughout a person's life if they do not get help.

Symptoms of Anxiety (Check Which Ones You Have Experienced)

Symptom	Example	Has something similar happened to you before?
Intense fear or worry	"If I don't get out of here, I will die." "What if I say something stupid and everyone laughs at me?"	
Physical complaints	"I get so nervous that my chest starts hurting, my hands sweat, my heart races, and I feel dizzy."	
Avoidance of social events	"I refused to participate in rec time because I didn't want other people to look at me." "I skipped a meeting with my counselor because I felt he would criticize me if I told him my problems."	
Compulsions	"I feel the need to wash my hands five times after every meal to stop something bad from happening."	
Nightmares	"I had a bad dream that my father was beating me again for not taking out the trash when I was a kid."	
Increased arousal	"I am always looking over my shoulder for danger." "I get jumpy and angry when someone calls for my attention."	

What Do These Disorders Say About Me?

You did not read about every possible acute clinical disorder out there. Just because you said you experienced some of the symptoms that make up each disorder does not mean you fit one of the diagnoses. Only your doctor or counselor can help you figure out what is going on with you. You may have a disorder that is not discussed here. If that's the case, your counselor can tell you more about your specific disorder and help you understand the symptoms you experience. Many disorders share similar symptoms. So, even if you do have another disorder, you may still experience symptoms like the ones listed in this handout. It is also common for people to have more than one diagnosis. And, it's common for people to experience what is called sub-clinical levels of a disorder—meaning that they have some symptoms but do not meet full criteria for a mental illness. So, you may not have a disorder, but may still experience symptoms that are problematic and for which you need to learn how to cope.

Exercise: Know Thy Self, Part I

Explore the **acute clinical disorders** or related symptoms that you may have. You may need to ask your counselor what, if any, your specific diagnoses are. Fill in the boxes that follow.

My acute clinical diagnoses are:

These are my most problematic symptoms:

I have been dealing with this disorder since:	My pattern of symptoms is like this:	What I didn't know about this disorder BEFORE was:	My experience with treatment in the past has been:

Handout #23
Common Diagnoses: Part II

What's in This Handout?

This handout discusses personality disorders that are particularly common in prisons. Personality disorders are only diagnosed in adults because doctors need to know that the symptoms have been around a long time. Remember that personality disorders are stable over time and become part of who a person is. These disorders are especially problematic for people's relationships with others. People with personality disorders often think, "It's not me, it's everyone else!" But the truth is, it really is YOU. Here are the disorders covered now:

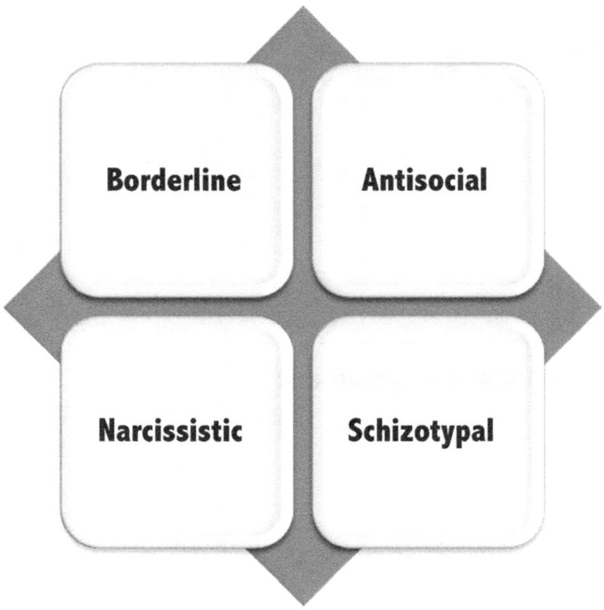

Borderline

- About 2 in every 100 people have borderline personality disorder.
- Borderline personality begins to appear in adolescence and continues into adulthood.
- The biggest issue with this disorder is unstable relationships. People with this disorder experience very rocky relationships with others, where one minute they love the other person and the next minute they hate that person.
- Your intimate relationship history will give you hints as to whether you may be borderline.
- If you are borderline, other people are likely to see you as unpredictable, short-tempered, irrational, or out of control.
- The good news is, once people become aware that they are borderline, they can learn to manage their symptoms and lead happy, productive lives.
- Borderline often gets confused with bipolar disorder, but they are not the same. In people with borderline, changes in mood or attitude come quickly, sometimes minute by minute, and they

usually happen in response to an interaction with another person. People with bipolar disorder experience slower changes in mood, staying in their manic or depressive episodes for several days (or more) at a time. Bipolar is also not as commonly triggered by interactions with other people as borderline. Ask your doctor or counselor if you are still confused by the differences between borderline and bipolar.

Symptoms of Borderline (Check Which Ones You Have Experienced)

Symptom	Example	Has something similar happened to you before?
Low self-worth	"My counselor had to cancel today. That must mean that I am a bad person."	
Pattern of unstable relationships	"My wife and I have a history of arguing. Every time she would do something I didn't like, I would threaten to leave her."	
Impulsive or reckless behavior	"I was so upset after I got fired from my job that I drove my car into a tree." "I had sex with three different people in one night because I wanted to feel loved."	
Identity problems	"I don't even know who I am anymore; sometimes I wonder what I'm doing with my life."	
Feeling empty or alone	"I have a lot of people who would call me their friend, but they don't really care about me."	
Anger outbursts or irritability	"I got so angry when my girlfriend came home late one night. I grabbed her and pushed her to the floor because I thought she was cheating on me."	

Antisocial

- In the community, about 3% of men and 1% of women have antisocial personality disorder. In prison inmates, this number is on average about 30% (men are around 40% while women are around 20%).
- Antisocial personality begins to appear in adolescence and continues into adulthood.
- The biggest issue with this disorder is a disregard for, and violation of, the rights and well-being of other people. Being antisocial does not mean that you don't like being around other people; it means that you break the moral and legal rules of society. Just like any other disorder, this is NOT an excuse for bad behavior.
- Your juvenile and adult criminal history will give you hints as to whether you may be antisocial.
- If you are antisocial, other people are likely to see you as irritable, irresponsible, manipulative, and deceptive.

- The good news is, once people become aware that they are antisocial, they can learn to manage their symptoms and lead happy, productive lives.

Symptoms of Antisocial (Check Which Ones You Have Experienced)

Symptom	Example	Has something similar happened to you before?
Failing to respect social norms or laws	"I've spent my childhood in and out of juvenile detention because I was robbing people and selling the stolen property."	
Disregard for others' safety	"I've been arrested three times for drunk driving; once, my daughter was in the car with me."	
Aggression	"I punched that motherfucker in the gut for cutting me in line at dinner."	
Lack of remorse for harm caused	"I didn't even care that she had a black eye, as long as she knows not to sleaze around behind my back."	
Failure to plan ahead or impulsivity	"I knew I would need money to pay my rent. Instead of saving up for it, I sold some dope at the last minute to get the cash."	
Lying or conning other people	"This girl was really sexy, and I wanted to take her on a date. She wouldn't go for a guy like me, so I told her I was a marketing executive."	

Narcissistic

- In the community, about 1 in every 100 people have narcissistic personality disorder. Most (50%–75%) of these people are men.
- Narcissistic personality begins to appear in adolescence and continues into adulthood.
- The biggest issues with this disorder are a grandiose sense of self (meaning that you believe you are wonderful, superior, unique, and can do no wrong), need for admiration (meaning that you want others to praise you and look up to you), and lack of empathy for other people (meaning that you don't care how you treat other people to get to the top).
- Your relationships with friends, romantic partners, and coworkers will give you hints as to whether you may be narcissistic.
- If you are narcissistic, other people are likely to see you as sensitive to criticism, entitled, demanding, and arrogant.
- The good news is, once people become aware that they are narcissistic, they can learn to manage their symptoms and lead happy, productive lives.

Symptoms of Narcissistic (Check Which Ones You Have Experienced)

Symptom	Example	Has something similar happened to you before?
Grandiose sense of self	"That report I wrote for my boss was perfect. I'm the best damn employee they've got."	
Thinking a lot about success, power, beauty, ideal love	"My ultimate goal in life is to have a multimillion-dollar home and a collection of luxury cars to show off." "Money is power."	
Believing oneself to be unique or special	"I felt I was just too smart for people to really get me; no one understood how talented I really was."	
Sense of entitlement	"I always get what I want, even if it means I have to take it from someone else. They probably didn't deserve it anyway."	
Need for attention	"I enjoy being the center of attention. In school, I was a real jokester. I wanted people to look at me and want to be me."	
Little empathy for others	"It was me and another guy up for a promotion at my last job; so I told my supervisor that this guy tried to pocket money from the company. He was fired."	
Believing others are envious of achievements	"He's just jealous of me because I could take his girl if I wanted to; I'm better looking and more successful."	

Schizotypal

- About 3% of people have schizotypal personality disorder.
- Schizotypal personality begins to appear in adolescence and continues into adulthood. A few people with this disorder will also develop schizophrenia or another psychotic disorder in their lifetime.
- The biggest issue with this disorder is poor social and interpersonal (this simply means how you relate to other people) skills. People with this disorder have difficulty forming close relationships and generally feel like they don't fit in with other people.
- Your intimate relationship history will give you hints as to whether you may be schizotypal.
- Unlike people with borderline, where relationships are chaotic and dramatic, people with schizotypal have relationships that are distant and shallow.
- If you are schizotypal, other people are likely to see you as strange, bizarre, odd, and socially awkward.
- The good news is, once people become aware that they are schizotypal, they can learn to manage their symptoms and lead happy, productive lives.

Symptoms of Schizotypal (Check Which Ones You Have Experienced)

Symptom	Example	Has something similar happened to you before?
Thinking a lot about superstitions or paranormal activities	"There was a black cat that always walked around my neighborhood. I think he knew I was up to no good." "I felt I could hear other people's thoughts"	
Unusual bodily experiences	"I think I've been to heaven before; I've felt my spirit leave my body."	
Odd thinking or speech	"Other people say that I take too long to communicate my thoughts" "I used the word 'talkable' the other day, but someone told me to say 'talkative' instead."	
Odd behavior or appearance	"I sometimes walk down the street with a shopping cart in case I find something I want to keep." "My clothes don't match most of the time."	
Suspicious or paranoid beliefs	"I wore a pair of orange-and-purple stripped socks whenever I left the house so I would feel safe."	
Fears about being around other people	"I really don't want to go to my little nephew's birthday party. What if someone tries to steal my new hat?"	
Few close friends	"I like to keep to myself because I don't fit in with a lot of other people." "My mom is really the only person who I can talk to about my problems."	

What Do These Disorders Say About Me?

You did not read about every possible personality disorder out there. Just because you said you experienced some of the symptoms that make up each disorder does not mean you fit the diagnosis. Only your doctor or counselor can help you figure out what is going on with you. You may have a disorder that is not discussed here. If that's the case, your counselor can tell you more about your specific disorder and help you understand the symptoms you experience. Many disorders share similar symptoms. So, even if you do have another disorder, you may still experience symptoms like the ones listed in this handout. It is also common for people to have features or traits of more than one personality disorder. And, it's common for people to only have features or traits but not a full-blown personality disorder. So, while you may not have one of these disorders, you may still experience related symptoms that are problematic and for which you need to learn how to cope.

Even though help is available, treating the symptoms of a personality disorder is often more challenging than treating acute clinical disorders. This is because people with personality disorders don't always realize that they are part of the problem and that they need to change some things about ***themselves***. They will often blame other people or their environment for their problems so they can make themselves feel better. In reality, the way they react to stress and the way they treat other people are the root causes of their problems.

Exercise: Know Thy Self, Part II

Explore the **personality disorders** or features that you have. You may need to ask your counselor what your specific diagnoses are. Fill in the boxes that follow.

My personality diagnoses are:

These are my most problematic symptoms:

I have been dealing with this disorder since:	**My pattern of symptoms are like this:**	**What I didn't know about this disorder BEFORE was:**	**My experience with treatment in the past has been:**

Handout #24
Stigma and Mental Illness

What Is Stigma?

You have probably been a victim of stigma and not even realized it. **Stigma** is a negative opinion or feeling that someone has about another person (or group of people) who they don't know a lot about. It happens when people don't understand something. So they base their opinion on what little information they do have. Stigmatizing beliefs can come from many sources—seeing a movie, watching the news, hearing a story, social stereotypes, or having short interactions with only a few people who belong to a particular group. All of these sources can lead to negative and, often, incorrect judgments about people. You can be stigmatized by people in the general public ("everyone with mental problems is just crazy and weird") or by your own attitudes ("having to go to therapy is embarrassing; it must mean that I'm a weak person"). Stigma can make it difficult for you to cope with your mental distress or illness, integrate back into society, hold a job, or secure housing.

What are some groups of people that might be the targets of stigma?

Which groups listed earlier do you belong to?
Give examples of how you experienced stigma as someone in this group.

Luckily, when people learn more about mental illness and meet people who have mental illnesses, their stigmas begin to go away. This is true for other stigmas as well (e.g., "criminals are always bad people," "lawyers are nothing but liars and cheats," "gays are dirty").

Responding to Stigma

So should you just accept stigma as a normal part of life? NO. You can play a role in changing how people think. Here are some ways to do this:

☑ **Educate yourself about mental symptoms and disorders**

- Learn as much about your own mental distress or illness as you can. This helps reduce your own self-stigma (thoughts that make you feel bad about your mental health problems) and helps you learn more about who you are. Knowing about your psychological issues will also help you to educate other people about your symptoms and your need for help or special accommodations. You've already started to do this with these handouts.
- Becoming part of a group can also help you learn more about different mental illnesses and symptoms. Take advantage of opportunities to talk with other inmates who have similar problems and ask to join mental health groups if they are offered on your unit once you return to the GP.

☑ **Confront other people who have incorrect thoughts about mental distress and illness**

- For example, if another inmate says that mentally ill people are violent, you can tell him that only a very small number are actually dangerous and that most mentally ill people are not a threat at all. His opinion may have come from news reports or because he is in a prison and has no other experience upon which to base his opinion.
- Don't buy into jokes about mental illness (i.e., mocking or making fun of someone for their mental problems). This only encourages stigma. Use your knowledge to educate the jokesters. Don't worry if this puts you in bad favor with those people. They're probably not going to be helpful to you in reaching your goals anyway. If it would be physically dangerous to confront someone, just walk away. The important thing is that you do not participate in behaviors that support stigma.
- You don't ever have to tell people about your mental distress or illness. You can simply be a teacher and help people learn.

☑ **Tell people about your mental distress or illness when it can help you**

- Sometimes it is better to tell people about your mental health problems. But give it some thought first. Ask yourself: **How will this benefit me?** For example, let's say Todd has a job as a salesman that requires him to go door-to-door. The problem is that Todd has social anxiety. He gets nervous talking to other people, and that hurts his sales performance. Todd tells his boss about this problem and asks for one hour off each week so he can attend counseling and learn to cope with his anxiety. In this case, Todd told his boss because he needed special accommodations to be better at this job.
- Don't be afraid to let correctional staff know about your personal mental health problems if it will help you. Sometimes, staff do not have a clear understanding about mental illness and often mistake odd or bizarre mental health symptoms for disciplinary or behavioral problems, thus leading to more time in restricted housing. Remember—mental distress or illness is not an excuse! Calmly talking with staff about your symptoms and your goals may show them that you are serious about getting better. Thus, they will be more likely to understand and help you rather than lock you up in segregation. But if you don't follow through with the help you are given, they will see this as manipulation and will be less likely to help you again. So be honest the first time!

Stigma is a barrier to your health and well-being, but you CAN do things to soften the impact for yourself and other people with mental health problems.

Exercise: Stopping Stigma

Think of four different times that you experienced stigma because of your mental distress or illness. Talk about your response at the time. Then come up with a better way to respond based on the points discussed earlier. Be specific!

Event #1

- **Response then:**
- **Better response:**

Event #2

- **Response then:**
- **Better response:**

Event #3

- **Response then:**
- **Better response:**

Event #4

- **Response then:**
- **Better response:**

Handout #25

Defining "Criminalness"

What Is It?

Crime is about breaking a law for which you could be punished. That's why you are in prison. You broke a state or federal law, and your time here is your punishment. **Criminalness** is more than crime or thinking about crime; it is any behavior that shows irresponsibility and does not consider the rights, well-being, or welfare of other people or yourself. Some types of criminalness cannot be punished by the courts, but, nonetheless, have consequences for you and those around you. Criminalness is offensive, whether it is legal or not.

Criminalness Meter

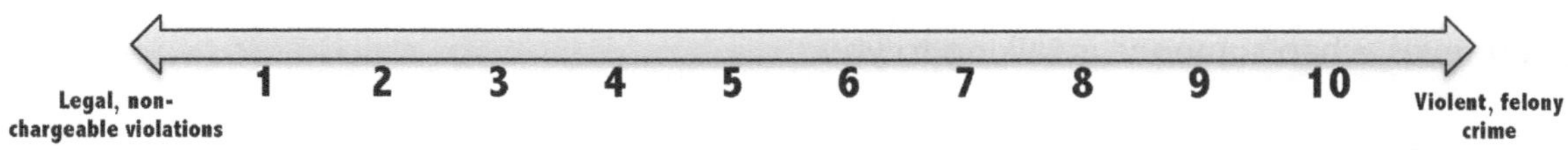

What types of behaviors would fall under "criminalness"?

Now rate yourself on the Criminalness Meter—where are you?

As an offender, you are higher on criminalness than nonoffenders (yes—other people think this way *sometimes* too). The very fact that you engaged in crime and continue to have disciplinary problems makes you an irresponsible adult who is not acting as a meaningful member of your community (whether that community is in the real world or in the general prison population).

Here Are Some Other Examples of Criminalness. Rate Where Each Behavior Would Fall on the Criminalness Meter

Cheating at a game of poker __________

Robbing a thrift shop owner at gunpoint __________

Driving while drunk or high __________

Calling in sick for work when you aren't really sick __________

Making sexual comments to a woman about her body __________

Killing someone as initiation into a gang __________

Spitting in an officer's face __________

Lying to your counselor about why you didn't do your homework __________

Rolling your eyes when someone is talking to you __________

Hiding drug supplies or hooch in your cell __________

Why Is Criminalness a Bad Thing?

Criminalness, no matter where it lies on the meter, is negative because it puts you on a pathway of trouble. While minor forms of criminalness are normal and happen to everyday people, the more often you think and behave this way, the further up you will slide on the meter. More criminalness helps you justify criminal behavior or think crime is ok. You will likely never get off the Criminalness Meter completely. That would be unrealistic—you're only human. But you need to work hard at bringing your criminalness down to a point where it is not your primary way of thinking and behaving. Monitoring your criminalness will help keep you out of trouble and out of segregation.

Exercise: Criminalness Mini Survey

Answer the following questions about your own criminalness. The things you say here will remain private, and you don't have to share specific details. This is to give you a sense of how serious your criminalness is.

1. **List the FELONIES (more severe crimes) you have been FOUND GUILTY of:**

   ____

   ____

2. **List the FELONIES you have gotten away with:**

3. **List the MISDEMEANORS (less severe crimes) you have been CONVICTED of:**

4. **List the MISDEMEANORS you have gotten away with:**

5. **List examples of things you have done in the past that violated the rights or well-being of others, but were not against the law (that is, you could *not* be charge with a crime, but the behavior was still irresponsible and offensive).**

Now that you have a more complete picture of your criminalness, rate yourself again on the Criminalness Meter:

Criminalness Meter

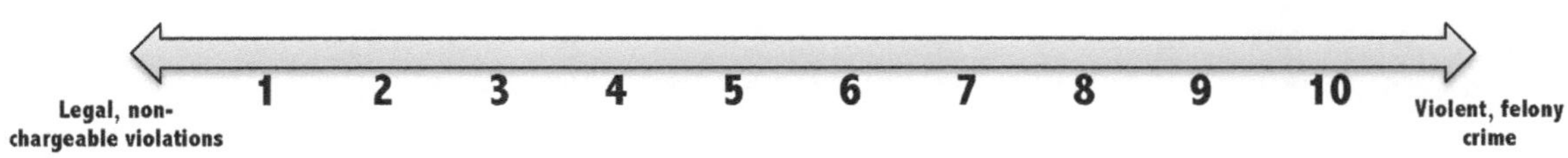

Did your rating change from the first time you did this?

- ☐ **I rated myself higher**
- ☐ **I rated myself lower**
- ☐ **I rated myself the same**

Quick Tips for Reducing Criminalness

1. **Seek out supportive people when you need help, like other rule-abiding inmates, your counselor, doctor, or staff.**
2. **Develop a plan of action for when you think about something offensive or criminal—what will you do?** (Use thought stopping, cognitive restructuring, or acting opposite; see handout #14.)
3. **Refocus on your goals—remember what you need to do to get out and stay out of this unit.**
4. **Take medications as prescribed. They can help with symptoms like aggression or paranoia.**
5. **Avoid using drugs or alcohol. They lead to impulsivity and poor decision-making**

Handout #26
Signs of Criminalness

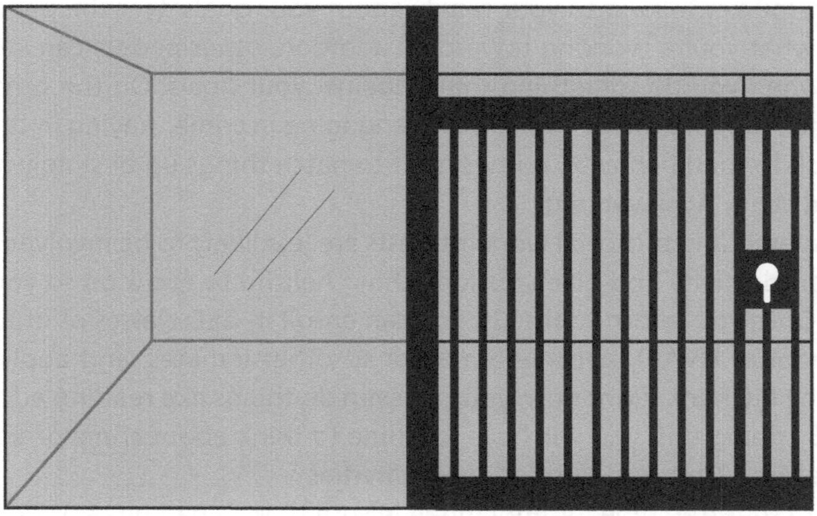

There are several factors that put people at risk for high criminalness and continued criminal behavior. A return to criminal conduct is called **criminal recidivism** (think of "recidivism" as a return—it could be a return to jail, prison, or to restricted housing). Criminal recidivism is a big problem; about 70% of all offenders commit more crimes once released from a correctional facility. This is also true of disciplinary housing units; many inmates who leave come back later on. This is because they don't manage their mental health symptoms or their criminalness. Earlier you learned about the symptoms of your mental illness. In this handout, you will learn about the symptoms of your criminalness. Having an awareness of these symptoms lets you recognize them later on and implement a plan to stop them from causing problems and distracting you from your goals. You will learn how to create this plan in another handout.

Risk Factors for Criminalness and Criminal Recidivism

These factors have been identified by researchers as the most likely to lead to higher levels of criminalness and further involvement in crime or rule-violating behaviors.

1. **Criminal Thinking**
   There are different ways of thinking about your world and the people in it. Criminals are more likely to think in ways that support negative behaviors than the average person. As you can guess, criminal thinking is very common in prisons. But it's this kind of thinking that keeps you in trouble. Your counselor will assess you on your go-to styles of criminal thinking. Once you know yours, you can challenge them with more helpful ways of thinking.

2. **Criminal Associates**
Criminals who talk to and hang around other criminals are at a high risk of committing crime. This is a problem in prisons, because *everyone* is a criminal. So who *can* you associate with? Find those model inmates who are following the rules. They exist! You will read more about this topic later.
3. **Family or Relationship Problems**
You don't get a lot of family contact while in prison. So there may not be a lot you can do here. But if you have family members on the outside who are supportive and willing to help you with your goals, use this resource. Talking to your family about your goals over the phone or in letters helps you remember what you're working toward. In addition, other people can keep you in check and challenge you when you do something that's against your goals. On the other hand, if you have family who do not support you or who are also engaging in crime, staying in touch with them could increase your risk for bad behavior. Is it worth it to patch things up or simply move on?
4. **Poor School and Work Achievement**
People with academic and prosocial work interests are less likely to be involved in crime. School and work increase productivity and give you something helpful to focus on so you are not temped to behave poorly. Once you return to the GP, you can enroll in GED classes or other training programs (like barber school or HVAC), become a mentor to other inmates, and apply for jobs within the facility (like in the kitchen). Right now, you can even do things like reading educational books from the book cart. By doing this, you will have less time to think about crime or acting out.
5. **Lack of Prosocial Free Time and Recreational Activities**
You heard before that free time, or unplanned leisure time, is bad news. When you get bored, you try to stir up some excitement. That excitement gets you into trouble. Just like school and work, staying active and using your spare time wisely will keep you occupied. This will give you less time to think about breaking the rules. You have already identified some things you can do on the unit to stay busy. And remember, don't skip rec time!
6. **Substance Abuse**
Using drugs leads to high criminalness and crime in several ways. First, using drugs or alcoholic substances is against the law—both inside and outside the prison walls. So being caught with drugs will likely send you back to segregated housing. Second, using these substances reduces your ability to think clearly or make good decisions. They make you more impulsive and cause you to lose sight of your goals. Go to AA or NA if this is a problem for you.
7. **Failing to Cope With Mental Illness**
Uncontrolled symptoms of your mental illness places you at a greater risk for crime and rule-violating behaviors. This is because, as you have seen, mental illness that is not treated can lead to bad decisions, impulsivity, anger, and aggression, suicidal intent, or a loss of interest in accomplishing healthy goals. All of these things can lead to behaviors that threaten your safety or the safety of others, resulting in more time spent in restricted housing. So take your medications as prescribed and continue working hard in this program (even when things feel difficult).

Exercise: Criminalness Checklist

Listed next are some common symptoms of criminalness. These are signs that you may be inching up the Criminalness Meter and that you are closer to rule-breaking behaviors. Place a ✓ mark next to the ones that fit for you. Then come up with a few more on your own. Finally, on a scale of 1–10 rate how much of a problem you think each risk factor is for you (1 = not a risk factor; 10 = a very serious risk factor).

Symptom	I have experienced this . . .
Criminal Thinking	
I think impulsively without considering what will happen later.	
People are out to get me or take advantage of me.	
Everyone else does bad things. I'm just the one who gets caught.	
I get a rush or high when I commit a crime or do something bad.	
I have thoughts of breaking the rules (hitting another person, using drugs, taking something that doesn't belong to me).	
Other signs of my criminal thinking:	**My Rating:** ________
Criminal Associates	
Most of my friends have been convicted of a crime.	
People I hang out with talk about doing drugs or breaking the rules.	
I have more in common with criminals than with people who don't do crime.	
I seem to wind up where all the bad guys are hanging out.	
My family likes to party and have a good time; most of them have also been to prison.	
Other signs that I spend time with criminal associates:	**My Rating:** ________

Family and Relationship Problems	
I usually argue and yell when I have an issue with someone.	
I have kids by several women.	
I don't need anyone to be happy.	
I don't have a lot of contact with my family (kids, parents, brothers/sisters).	
I feel uncomfortable in social situations.	
Other signs of family and relationship problems:	**My Rating:** ________

Poor School and Work Achievement	
I have no job training or real work skills.	
I never finished high school.	
There is no point in getting an education.	
I get money by doing illegal things, like selling dope or booking.	
I wouldn't be caught dead working for this facility.	
Other signs of poor school and work achievement:	**My Rating:** ________

Lack of Prosocial Leisure and Recreational Activities	
I don't like being around other people.	
I often skip rec time in the yard.	
I listen to music during most of my free time.	
I feel bored a lot.	
Acting out helps me pass the time away.	
Other signs that I'm lacking prosocial leisure and recreational activities:	**My Rating:** ________

Substance Abuse	
Drug treatment can't help me.	
I really miss getting high.	
I like to make hooch in my cell.	
If another inmate can get me drugs, I will take them.	
Alcohol or drugs helped me relax.	
Other signs of substance abuse:	**My Rating:** ________
Failing to Cope With Mental Illness	
I feel depressed a lot.	
I keep to myself and don't want to be bothered.	
I make decisions based on what mood I'm in.	
Anger is one way that I like to deal with my problems.	
I don't think treatment programs can help me.	
Other signs that I'm not coping with mental illness:	**My Rating:** ________

PICTS Supplemental Handout: Understanding Your Criminal Thinking Styles

Offenders think differently than nonoffenders. You think like other criminals and, as a result, you are high on criminalness. Criminal thinking does not mean that you think about crime all the time. Rather, you have a set of core thoughts, attitudes, and beliefs that support criminalness and rule-breaking behavior. Next is a list of the eight styles of thinking that are likely to place you at high risk for criminal recidivism and returning to restricted housing.

1. **Mollification** reflects a tendency to blame others or one's situation (e.g., family problems, poverty, the "man") for their criminalness. Mollification is rooted in rationalizing and minimizing your behavior, including both past and current criminalness. If you blame others or your situation for your criminalness, you are engaging in mollification. Typical examples include "I wouldn't have to commit crime if black men were treated fairly"; "the 'man' is keeping me down"; "this system is against me"; "if staff would quit harassing me, I wouldn't have to break the rules"; or "if other people would just leave me alone, I wouldn't have to act crazy." Offenders are prone to use mollification to avoid accepting responsibility for their behavior or to avoid the guilt of irresponsible actions. This is true with regard to recovery for both criminalness and mental illness.
2. **Cutoff** refers to a style of thought that supports acting impulsively to pursue what you want regardless of the outcome for you or others. Offenders do what they want, when they want, and how they want. Offenders are typically not patient and do not like waiting for what they want. Statements such as "to hell with it," "this is not worth my time," or "fuck it" indicate the offender's refusal to do what is right. Drugs and alcohol are commonly used to eliminate those things that lead people to behave responsibly (e.g., "I drank a few beers for courage to confront my boss," "a joint helps me relax and makes my medications work better"). When you engage in criminalness or do not manage your mental illness because it is hard work or is more enjoyable than acting responsibly, cutoff is taking over your thought process.
3. **Entitlement** reflects a sense of ownership, privilege, and uniqueness that is used by offenders as a means of giving themselves permission to break the law, harm others, or avoid other responsible behavior. Being mentally ill, for example, does not entitle you to privileges; you still have to work at things just like non-mentally ill people. Offenders high on entitlement view themselves as superior individuals and maintain the belief that they can do anything they want to do. Entitlement also reveals a style of thought whereby if the offender wants something, it is his to have. For example, a person with this thinking error might say, "If I want something that belongs to someone else, I'm going to take it. If he's man enough to stop me, then it's not mine to have. If he's not man enough to stop me, then he didn't deserve it in the first place." Most people do not think along these lines. Regarding entitlement, it is the taking/owning of new objects that is enjoyable. The pleasure of possession gets old rather quickly for those high on entitlement. They crave the opportunity to take/own new objects (e.g., new cars, women)
4. **Power orientation** refers to the craving of power and seeking control. To achieve control, offenders will often engage in outward displays of aggression in order to manipulate others. This is commonly seen when offenders put someone else down in order to feel good about themselves. Rather than focusing on being responsible for how they feel about themselves, these individuals put others down in order to make themselves feel better in the moment. Other times, someone might yell at a boss or a loved one and blame it on his or her mental illness, when in reality, the behavior was a power play. That is, the person exerted him or herself physically or verbally in order to maintain a sense of power and control. This is done to avoid negative feelings about oneself. Someone high on power orientation may respond to a coworker being praised by a supervisor with "so what, that wasn't a difficult task anyway. Anyone could have done a good job with that one," or "you know that task really wasn't very important, right?"
5. **Sentimentality** is the belief that doing something good or nice makes one a good person and overrides (or erases) the bad (criminalness) that one has done. These offenders fail to recognize the scope of harm they cause others. For example, burglary of a home doesn't only result in loss of property, but the victims feel a sense of violation, fear, and loss of trust in others. Doing an occasional good deed (e.g., helping an elderly person with a flat tire even though it wasn't convenient

for you, doing work for free for a person in need, cleaning the house after an outburst) does not erase or make up for the bad things one has done. People engage in this line of thinking to avoid feeling bad about their past behaviors and to avoid recognizing the scope of harm that is caused by their criminalness or mental illness when not properly managed.

6. **Superoptimism** is the belief that you will be able to avoid negative outcomes of your criminalness or mental illness. The notion that you can get away with it this one time, are too smart to get caught again are better able to manage your symptoms without medication or don't really need docs or medication anymore are all examples of superoptimism. Just like in the past, if you engage in superoptimism and continue with your criminalness or fail to manage your mental illness, you will eventually get caught or relapse and have to face the consequences. Offenders do not get caught for all crimes, but an overwhelming majority of offenders eventually get caught and face the consequences of their behaviors. Similarly, persons with mental illness must focus on managing their illness or they will relapse. To think otherwise is superoptimism. It will derail your efforts toward recovery.
7. **Cognitive indolence** is a lazy way of thinking and dealing with problems. This style of thinking is noted for the tendency to take short cuts and look for the easy way around problems. Rather than taking a prosocial approach and effectively working through problems, offenders with this type of thinking style tend to take short cuts, including breaking the law and relapsing. Examples include selling dope to make a quick buck during a time of financial need, smoking a joint to relax when faced with life stressors, or skipping a therapy session because it's an inconvenience. These offenders are typically seen as lazy and will go to great effort to avoid work, conflict, or a hard time. In fact, it is not uncommon for these offenders to work harder at getting out of something than they would work if they simply solved the problem (that is, these individuals will work harder to get out of work than they would if they just did the necessary work).
8. **Discontinuity** is the tendency to lose sight of your personal goals. Offenders often get sidetracked by things that are immediately pleasing or reinforcing and lose focus on the benefits of long-term goals. In other words, these offenders get sidetracked from a responsible and prosocial life and commit criminalness without thought of the long-term consequences. Oftentimes, these offenders will say things like "I got sidetracked," or "I got distracted" from my goals and got caught up in the heat of the moment." Similarly, you may hear an offender say, "I didn't like my meds and the side effects were too bad, so I quit taking them." This loss of focus results in some immediate gratification but has significant long-term consequences with regard to recovery. To be effective, you must learn to maintain focus on your long-term goals and learn to delay gratification.

After You Take the PICTS, Your Counselor Will Help You Complete the Following Questions

My Top Three Go-To Styles of Criminal Thinking Are

1. ______________________________

2. ______________________________

3. ______________________________

My Criminal Thinking Tends to Be More . . .

- ☐ **Unplanned, impulsive, and spontaneous (reactive)**
- ☐ **Planned, organized, and purposeful (proactive)**

My Scores on the PICTS Make Sense for Me (Y/N?): __________

Why or why not? ____

Here's an example of when I used each thinking style (even if you didn't score high on all styles, you have probably used them all at some point):

Mollification: ____

Cutoff: ____

Entitlement: ____

Power Orientation: ____

Sentimentality: ____

Superoptimism: ____

Cognitive Idolence: ____

Discontinuity: ____

Handout #27
The Road to Recovery

What Is Recovery?

Recovery can mean a lot of different things depending on the problem you are trying to recover from. Recovering from the flu, for example, means that you are working to stop your symptoms completely; you take medications, eat soup, and rest easy so you can be cured of the disease. Recovery from mental symptoms or illness and criminalness is different. You are not working to cure it or make it go away forever. It is about *controlling parts of your life that are not good for you or lead you to trouble*. You must ALWAYS work toward recovery; if you stop, you will likely go back to where you started in the first place. This is true even if you are starting to feel better. Feeling better does not mean you stop working on your recovery; it just means that you are doing all the right things and that you must *continue* to do those things. Don't stop! Your goals will help you figure out what recovery means for you. For example, if Sally's goal is to have more close and supportive relationships with other people, then recovery for her is when she is able to find and hold on to those kinds of relationships. Recovery is an ongoing journey.

Why Travel the Road to Recovery?

Recovery is not easy. This road has many bumps and detours along the way. So you may be asking yourself if it's worth the trouble. It may not seem like it at first because you will be challenged and asked to do things that are uncomfortable, and maybe even, scary. But as you learn new ways to cope with your psychological symptoms and your signs of criminalness, you will

1. **Be in a better mood and feel happier,**
2. **Have stronger and more meaningful relationships with other people,**
3. **Get into trouble less often, and**
4. **Reduce your risk of being the target of violence by other inmates.**

So don't stop when things get tough. Sometimes you have to feel worse to feel better. This is part of the process. And even when you feel solid in your recovery (like you can tackle any problem head-on), there are always obstacles to watch out for. You're never completely safe from the things that put your recovery at risk (such as bad influences or drugs); this is why you must always work toward recovery. It is your responsibility to learn how to prevent the negative effects of these risk factors (remember the yellow and red zones from your mental traffic light; see Handout #1) when you do come across them.

What Kinds of People Are Good at Their Recovery?

Some people are more likely than others to do well in their recovery. Here are some characteristics that help people meet their recovery goals:

☑ **Believing that goals—whether big or small—are very important.** Make it a priority to achieve your goals. Don't be embarrassed, ashamed, or afraid of your goals. They're yours, so own them.

☑ **Writing down goals to keep you on track.** Having goals written down somewhere serves as a constant reminder. You can look at them when you need a boost. You can also write down some motivational statements to keep you going.

☑ **Keeping in mind what is really important to you, like staying out of segregation.** Reminding yourself about the good things that you could get by changing pushes you to move forward.

☑ **Becoming involved in a treatment or self-help group**. This may not be available to you now, but once you get back into the GP, see what's out there and get involved. Talking to other people with similar problems makes you feel more comfortable talking about your own mental health problems. The more you talk about it, the more you learn about yourself. Groups also help you improve your social skills and give you the chance to help others in need.

☑ **Staying active, like working out (don't skip rec time!).** Physical activity makes your body produce natural chemicals that make you feel good.

☑ **Finding social supports—people who are following the rules and doing prosocial things.** Support systems can include family members, doctors, counselors, and model inmates, as well as your lawyer, a religious person, or anyone else you trust. Share your symptoms and goals with these people so they can keep an eye on you. Sometimes other people are able to notice things you can't see. Give them permission to tell you when you're getting distracted from your goals.

☑ **Being aware of your warning signs (yellow) and triggers (red)—things that threaten your recovery.** Knowing what these risk factors are helps you to avoid them in the future or prepare to handle them better when you can't avoid them. What makes you angry? Sad? Violent? Out of control? There is more information about this in Handout #28.

☑ **Using creativity to express yourself.** Sometimes you may feel that no one understands you or that you can't put how you really feel into words. Instead of letting it bottle up and explode later, get creative! Act it out, write a poem, or draw scribbles and doodles. This will help you get your emotions out there and will give you some guidance for talking about it later.

☑ **Following through with your treatment plan!** This is SO important. Treatment is no help at all if you don't continue to use the skills you learn. Make a plan. Decide for yourself what you need to do on your road to recovery, such as what risks do you need to take, what challenges should you be aware of, how will you deal with those challenges when they come up, and who can you count on to help you? Stick to it! This is something you can have control over.

Exercise: Cruising Down Recovery Road

You just read about some simple ways people can begin to play an active role in their recovery. Brainstorm how you can improve your chances of a smoother road to recovery, starting right now. What can you do NOW, while in restricted housing, and what can you continue to do LATER when you leave? Again, focus on what you have, not on what you don't have.

Strategy	What I Can Do NOW	What I Can Do LATER
Make goals a priority		
Stay on track with goals		
Keep in mind what's important		
Get involved in treatment group		
Stay active		
Find social supports		
Be aware of warning signs and triggers		
Use creativity		
Follow through with your plan		

Handout #28
Watching for Warnings and Tackling the Triggers

As you read earlier, recovery is hard sometimes. There are lots of things that can get in your way, slow you down, or make you take a wrong turn. Luckily, if you're aware of these things, you can plan for them. Then you will be prepared and will have a better shot at winning out. But even when you're working hard in your recovery, there is a chance that you will take a few steps back or be misdirected. This is called a **relapse**. Relapsing means that you've slipped up and fallen back into the old thinking and old behavior that got you into trouble or keeps you stuck in mental distress or illness. While relapsing is not encouraged, it does happen. If you relapse, it's important to see it as a learning experience and not as an excuse to give up on your goals. What can you learn from the relapse so that you can avoid another one in the future? Maybe you missed one of your warning signs or triggers.

Why Do People Relapse?

Relapse is more likely to happen if you do the following:

1. **Hang out with other rule-breaking inmates**
2. **Don't take your medications as prescribed**
3. **Don't seek help from other people when you need it**
4. **Refuse help from people who offer it to you**
5. **Don't use your free time wisely**
6. **Refuse to take responsibility for yourself**
7. **Don't control your mental health symptoms**
8. **Don't control your criminalness**
9. **Use drugs or alcohol**

How Can I Stop Relapse?

Usually, relapses don't just happen overnight; they take a while to unfold. This is a good thing because it gives you some time to recognize that you are at risk for relapse. Once you see that you are at risk, you can take action right away. So what you need to do is trace the steps that will lead to your relapse if you stop working on your recovery. That is, what people, places, environments, behaviors, feelings, or thoughts will likely come *before* your relapse? These are the things you need to avoid or learn to deal with if you encounter them. Think back to your history—what path originally led you to the behaviors you've been trying to change now? The earlier you can catch your risk, the more likely you will be to prevent it from becoming a full relapse. Remember the story from Handout #13. It's easier to escape a shark attack if you are in the shallow part of the ocean as opposed to the deep part.

Here's an example of what the path to relapse may look like:

Warning Sign

You start to feel like life isn't fair

You make excuses to stay in your cell because you don't want to be around other people

Trigger

Another inmate bumps into you in the rec yard

An inmate on your pod calls you "a crazy son of a bitch"

Relapse

You get into a physical altercation

You return to restricted housing

Triggers come directly before a relapse. Think of a trigger on a gun—if you pull it, the action happens immediately. Warning signs come before the trigger. In other words, warning signs are like the shallow part of the ocean; triggers are the deeper part. So it is easier to stop relapse at the warning signs but not impossible at the triggers. It's also important to know that everyone has different warning signs and triggers. For example, a beer commercial showing sexy women and a fun party might be a trigger for one man, who walks immediately to the corner store and relapses with a 12-pack. For another man, this commercial may be a warning sign that gets him to think about how relaxing a cold beer would be right now. For yet another man, this commercial may be neither a warning sign nor a trigger.

Practicing the Mental Traffic Light

Here's your chance to use your mental traffic light. Evaluate people, places, environments, thoughts, feelings, and behaviors. **GREEN** = good for your recovery. **YELLOW** = warning sign that you're headed into relapse. **RED** = trigger that relapse is next. Label the things in your life with these colors. Think about warning signs and triggers for your mental distress AND your criminalness.

Here are some other examples of possible warning signs and triggers (circle the ones you have experienced before):

Mental Distress	Criminalness
Getting "fed up" with medication side effects	*Using drugs or making hooch*
Starting to think people are against you	*Thinking you're "the shit"*
Having no energy to do things	*Feeling like others have it better than you*
Not getting along with other people	*Arguing with other inmates or officers*
Having thoughts that don't make any sense	*Talking with law-breaking inmates*
Feeling sad, depressed, or suicidal	*Saying "screw it" to treatment*
Feeling overly excited or not needing sleep	*Blaming other people for your problems*
Not participating in your treatment	*Being bored*
Avoiding people	*Using anger to deal with problems*
Having difficulty sleeping	*Being passive-aggressive or putting others down*

Exercise: Reversing Relapse

Write down your warning signs and triggers. Then remind yourself what the relapse behavior would be (that is, the behavior you are trying to avoid or stop).

MENTAL ILLNESS

Warning Signs

Triggers

Relapse

CRIMINALNESS

Warning Signs

Triggers

Relapse

Module 5
Recap

In This Module You Learned About

- ☑ **Mental distress and illness—how it develops and what it looks like**
- ☑ **Stigma and how to reduce it**
- ☑ **Criminalness—what it is and how to recognize it**
- ☑ **Your go-to criminal thinking styles that support criminalness**
- ☑ **The process of recovery from mental illness and criminalness**
- ☑ **Your warning signs and triggers for relapse**

Now place an ✗ mark next to the techniques that you will continue to practice and write down WHEN you will practice them, WHAT you will do, and HOW they will help you. Give your counselor permission to hold you accountable for following through with your plan.

Technique	I WILL do this (place ✗ here)	Whenever I . . .	This is how I will do it . . .	To help me cope with . . .
Learn more about my mental health symptoms and illness(es)				
Tell others when they have incorrect beliefs about mental illness				
Tell people about my own symptoms of mental illness				
Learn more about my criminalness				
Hang around other inmates who follow the rules				
Talk to trustworthy people when I need help				
Take my medications as prescribed; they are meant to help me				

Technique	I WILL do this (place ✗ here)	Whenever I . . .	This is how I will do it . . .	To help me cope with . . .
Keep track of when I use my criminal thinking styles				
Stop my criminalness or criminal thoughts when they happen				
Increase my work or school achievement				
Keep in contact with family who are on board with my goals, if possible				
Avoid using drugs, alcohol, tobacco				
Motivate myself to follow through with my treatment plan				
Use my mental traffic light				
Stay busy and active				
Be creative				
Get involved in other treatment opportunities				
Remind myself about my goals				
Talk about my goals with other people				

Module 6

Managing My Mental Distress and Criminalness: Improving Functioning and Preventing Relapse

Handout #29
Awareness of Automatic Thoughts

Your mind sometimes tells you things that are not helpful to you. The way you think about yourself, other people, or situations can affect how you feel (that is, what your mood is), how you behave, and where you go. This should sound familiar to you because it's part of **THE Circle of Change**. You were also asked to be more aware of your thoughts as they relate to anger, fear, shame, sadness, and criminalness—remember cognitive restructuring, thought stopping, and acting opposite? Now you will learn more about how your thinking can get in the way of your recovery. You will then learn how to recognize your problematic thinking and come up with more helpful ways of looking at different situations. This will help you stay on track with your goals. Until now, it's felt almost as if your mind has used you like a puppet on strings. But it's time to cut those strings and take back control!

What Are Automatic Thoughts?

The word **automatic** means instinctive—like a reflex. Things that are automatic happen very quickly, often without you realizing they are happening. So automatic thoughts are your go-to thoughts; they are what immediately come to mind when you think about yourself, a particular person, or situation. Your automatic thoughts can be driven by your criminalness or by your mental distress and illness. Here are two different examples:

> *Brandy is pulled over by a police officer for speeding. She was driving 85 miles per hour in a 65 mile per hour zone, clearly over the legal limit. Brandy is also driving under a suspended license. As the officer approaches Brandy's car, she begins thinking to herself, "That fucking jackass is about to slam me with another ticket! These dirty cops never leave me alone! All they want is power and money."*

What were Brandy's automatic thoughts?

____

____

How might these thoughts make her feel?

____

How might these thoughts cause her to act?

____

Are her thoughts driven by criminalness or mental distress?

____

What OTHER thoughts would be more helpful?

____

____

Travis is an inmate who regularly attends NA meetings on his pod. He likes to sit in the same chair during every meeting because it makes him feel more comfortable. Everyone at the meeting knows this about Travis. A new member joins NA and sits in Travis's chair. Travis immediately begins to think that the new group member is plotting against him and trying to steal his good ideas.

What were Travis's automatic thoughts?

____

____

How might these thoughts make him feel?

____

How might these thoughts cause him to act?

____

Are his thoughts driven by criminalness or mental distress?

____

What OTHER thoughts would be more helpful?

____

____

Can I Change My Automatic Thoughts?

Yes, you can! But be warned; it will not be easy. Your thoughts become automatic because you have taught your brain to think a certain way. For example, if you usually think negatively about yourself or your situation, you are likely to continue thinking that way in the future. Your brain then comes to learn that negative thinking is the go-to response. You get yourself caught up in a destructive cycle. Now you have to re-train your brain. Re-training your brain means improving your mind's ability to think clearly and accurately. Changing your thoughts will put you in a better mood and help you stay out of trouble. Again, use your mental traffic light to evaluate how helpful or not helpful your thoughts are (see Thought Interrogation exercise from Handout #20 for some ideas). If your thoughts are green, keep them going! If they are red or yellow, go back and consider other possible thoughts.

Feelings as Clues

Because thoughts can often happen without you knowing it, pay attention to how you begin to feel. Your emotions can be clues to how you are thinking about something around you. The key is to stop these feelings before they become too intense. Let's look at an example.

> *Randy is at the infirmary waiting for the doctor to examine a rash on his arm. The doctor comes in, asks a few short questions, quickly gives Randy a special lotion, and sends him back to the unit. Randy begins to feel frustrated. He recognizes that this frustration is a yellow warning sign for him, and he decides to evaluate his thoughts. Randy realizes that he thought the doctor was purposefully being rude and that the doctor must not really care about his patients. These thoughts explain Randy's negative feelings! So to prevent his frustration from becoming a problem (for example, causing him to go into a deep depression or having an angry outburst), Randy thinks of more helpful thoughts. Perhaps the doctor had a lot of other patients to attend to with more serious symptoms. Or maybe the doctor didn't need any more information to successfully treat Randy. Or maybe another inmate pissed him off. After all, he's only human! These new thoughts don't necessarily take away Randy's frustration entirely or let the doctor off the hook, but they help reduce the intensity of Randy's feelings and prevent him from behaving poorly.*

What Should I Do About All These Thoughts?

You may think that thinking positively is the answer to negative moods and behaviors. But this is not always the case. First, many people find it difficult to simply think positive thoughts all the time. Second, thinking only positive thoughts when you have a strong emotion may cause you to miss important signals that something is wrong. What you want to do is start looking at a problem from many different angles, including positive, negative, and neutral. Developing a number of perspectives helps you find more accurate solutions. The first step in this process is learning to be aware of the connections between your thoughts, your feelings, and your actions. Once you are aware, you can start to investigate how true or false your thoughts really are (see Handout #30 next).

Exercise: Making the Connection

For each of the events that follow, write down what your automatic thoughts might be, how these thoughts might make you feel, and what you might have done as a result of how you felt. Then talk about how your responses support your criminalness and/or mental distress or illness.

Event #1	Thoughts	Feelings	Actions
You are waiting for security to unlock the doors to the mess hall. It's taking a long time and you are hungry.			

How are your earlier answers related to your . . .

Criminalness? ______________________________

Mental Distress? ______________________________

Event #2	Thoughts	Feelings	Actions
You are in your cell trying to sleep and all you can hear is your neighbor screaming and kicking his door.			

How are your earlier answers related to your . . .

Criminalness? ______________________________

Mental Distress? ______________________________

Event #3	Thoughts	Feelings	Actions
You're back in the community, and your parole officer decides to give you a random drug test.			

How are your earlier answers related to your . . .

Criminalness?________________________________

Mental Distress? ________________________________

Event #4	Thoughts	Feelings	Actions
Write down your own example here:			

How are your earlier answers related to your . . .

Criminalness?________________________________

Mental Distress? ________________________________

Handout #30

Altering Automatic Thoughts

You've already had some practice altering problematic thoughts that lead to trouble. But because changing your automatic thoughts is so difficult, you need more practice. And this time, you are concerned about all kinds of thoughts that lead to lots of different emotions (anger, sadness, fear, depression, anxiety, paranoia, etc.) and behaviors (aggression, social isolation, panic attacks, criminal activity, staying awake all night, refusing medication, etc.).

Why Should I Change My Problem Thoughts?

Everyone has automatic thoughts, not just offenders or people who have mental illnesses. But not everyone acts out of line because of their automatic thoughts. In fact, it's very natural to feel annoyed if someone bumps into you. Most people, though, would not let this bother them to the point of aggression, depression, or any other intense emotion or behavior. For you to reach your personal goals (and to work toward recovery), you must begin to confront your automatic thoughts that lead to negative feelings and behaving in harmful ways (that is, harm you cause yourself when you lose sight of your personal goals).

How will changing YOUR problematic thoughts be helpful to you?

____

____

____

____

____

How Do I Change My Problem Thoughts?

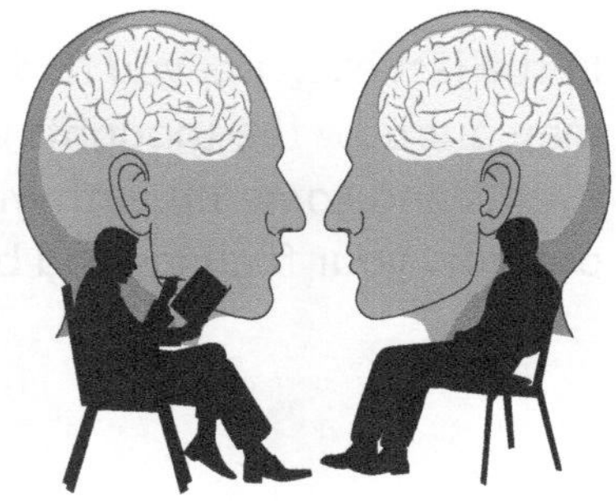

It's not easy! The first step is recognizing your thoughts (see Handout #29 for a review). The next step is to challenge them. Question them. Interrogate them. Put them on the spot. Look for pieces of evidence that support or do not support your thoughts. Have a little debate with yourself either in your head or on a piece of paper. Some thoughts are true, but many thoughts are not very true. Your job is to decide how truthful (that is, how accurate) your thinking is. Sometimes additional information is needed to figure out the extent to which your thoughts are true.

Here are some questions you can ask yourself when evaluating the accuracy of your thoughts. To be the most effective, Use ALL of them:

1. **Is this thought useful or helpful to me? Does it help me reach my goals? Does it help me take positive action? Use your mental traffic light!**
2. **Is this thought familiar? Has my mind told me this before? If so, how did things turn out before?**
3. **What would I get for buying into this thought? That is, if my thought is true, what is the *worst* thing that could happen? What is the *best* thing that could happen? What is *likely* to happen?**
4. **What is the evidence for this thought? What information do I have in favor of my idea? What information do I have that is against my idea?** (Remember, there may be evidence in both directions, just like a trial you might see in a courtroom. But you are looking for the side of the argument that is the ***most*** accurate.)
5. **What will happen if I let this automatic thought impact my feelings and behavior? What will happen to my feelings and behavior if I change this thought?**
6. **Is there a different explanation for what's going on? Are there other ways of looking at the situation?**
7. **What should I do about this? What do I want to do about this?**
8. **What would I tell a friend if he or she were in the same situation?**

When you have an automatic thought that stirs up negative feelings, check your answers to these questions. Then rate how truthful your original thought was.

Thought Accuracy Meter

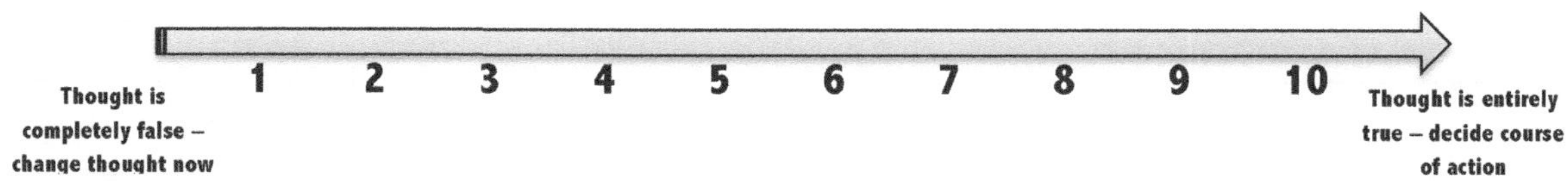

As a general rule, any rating below about a ten suggests the possibility that you need to change or alter the thought (at least to some degree). You want to be thinking as clearly as possible, so if there is any room on the meter to move up, consider how you can do so!

Exercise: Making the Connection—Remix

In the last exercise, you had to come up with automatic thoughts to a negative situation and map out how the thoughts would affect your feelings and behaviors. Now use the same four events and come up with more accurate thoughts using the eight questions noted earlier. Then map out how your feelings and behaviors may be different and more helpful.

Event #1 → **Thoughts** → **Feelings** → **Actions**

You are waiting for security to unlock the doors to the mess hall. It's taking a long time and you are hungry.

In what ways are your new thoughts more helpful in coping with your . . .

Criminalness: ____

Mental Distress or Illness: ____

Event #2 → **Thoughts** → **Feelings** → **Actions**

You are in your cell trying to sleep and all you can hear is your neighbor screaming and kicking his door.

In what ways are your new thoughts more helpful in coping with your . . .

Criminalness: ____

Mental Distress or Illness: ____

Event #3	Thoughts	Feelings	Actions
You're back in the community, and your parole officer decides to give you a random drug test.			

In what ways are your new thoughts more helpful in coping with your . . .

Criminalness: ______________________________

Mental Distress or Illness: ______________________________

Event #4	Thoughts	Feelings	Actions
Write down your own example here:			

In what ways are your new thoughts more helpful in coping with your . . .

Criminalness: ______________________________

Mental Distress or Illness: ______________________________

Before you see your counselor again, go through the ENTIRE process using a brand-new event that you recently experienced (one you haven't talked about before):

Write down your automatic thoughts

Event #5 → **Thoughts**

Evaluate your thoughts: ____________________

Now, come up with new thoughts

Rate your automatic thoughts using the Thought Accuracy Meter: __________

Thoughts → **Feelings** → **Actions**

How was it helpful to stop and evaluate your thoughts?

____

____

Progress Checkpoint

Change is hard! It takes time, dedication, and patience. But that's what you need to do to reach your goals. Sports teams have to practice hard and play hard to win, and so do you! Let's take a moment to celebrate what you've done so far to make positive changes and to reach your goals.

Make a list of things that were difficult for you, or things that you did not want to do but did them anyway because you knew you had to.

1. **Example:** Completed handouts that I did not want to complete.
2. **Example:** Talked to my counselor about problems I am having following the rules.
3.
4.
5.
6.
7.
8.
9.
10.

Handout #31
Signs of Stress

Dealing with your mental distress or illness and criminalness means more than being aware of and challenging your problematic thoughts. People with mental health problems and people who are high on criminalness have a hard time responding to stress. **Stress** is a feeling of pressure, strain, or tension. Stress can be good for you or bad for you. It can come from a negative event or situation (like losing a job, being incarcerated) or from a positive event or situation (being released from prison, starting a new relationship). Stress happens to everyone, but it's all about how you deal with it that matters. For example, it's normal to feel stressed out about being in restricted housing because it is not a pleasant or fun place to be. But if your mental illness or criminalness gets in the way of your ability to cope with stress, you will feel out of control, and your symptoms will get worse. You will move away from your goals and be at risk for relapse. So stress is a red light for both your mental distress and your criminalness. You need to learn better ways of dealing with stress.

What happens to you when you feel stressed? What are your thoughts like?
How does your body react?

____

____

____

____

____

Here are some signs of stress. Check the ones that apply to you:

_____ headaches
_____ sweating
_____ increased heart rate
_____ back pain
_____ change in appetite
_____ difficulty falling asleep
_____ increased need for sleep

_____ trembling or shaking
_____ digestion problems
_____ forgetfulness
_____ prone to accidents
_____ stomachaches
_____ dry mouth
_____ problems concentrating

_____ anger over minor things
_____ anxious
_____ feeling restless or "keyed up"
_____ tearful
_____ feeling like you need something to take the edge off

Other signs: ____________________

These signs of stress are your yellow lights. They help stop you from going into full-blown, red light stress. Being able to successfully reduce your stress is a green light for your recovery.

Bigger life events (i.e., being incarcerated, homelessness, hospitalization, money problems) and daily hassles (small stresses that happen every day, such as being in a crowded place, arguing with a loved one, feeling rushed or hurried) can both cause stress. Again, it is how you manage these events and hassles that count. Part of being able to deal with stress is not only about knowing what stress looks like for you (see the signs you checked earlier) but also about knowing what kinds of events and hassles cause you stress in the first place.

Exercise: Under Pressure

Here are some examples of life events and daily hassles that you may have encountered while in DS or in prison generally. Check the ones you have experienced and then list other stressors that you have personally experienced.

✓ Mark Here	Stressor	How does this stressor make me think, feel, and act?
	Incarceration	
	Being the victim of a crime	
	Quitting smoking or using drugs	
	Divorce or separation from a romantic partner	
	Medical illness	
	Moving cell blocks or units	
	Entering a treatment program	
	Not having enough privacy	
	Things being out of order	
	Noisy environment	
	Having to do unpleasant chores or tasks	
	Interacting with people who are rude, controlling, or scary	
	Being bored in your cell	
	Living in a dangerous place	

✓ Mark Here	Stressor	How does this stressor make me think, feel, and act?
	Personal example #1	
	Personal example #2	
	Personal example #3	
	Personal example #4	
	Personal example #5	
	Personal example #6	

Handout #32
Stopping Stress the Green Light Way

All right, so now you know about what leads to your stress and how you react to stress. But what can you do about it? This part is very important for your recovery! The better you get at lessening your stress, the more you increase your chances of reaching your personal goals. You are responsible for actively coping with stress. Don't wait for someone else to tell you to do it.

What Can I Do to Deal With My Stress?

These actions may help stop you from getting stressed out and moving away from your goals. Try them all at least once.

- ☑ **Being aware of situations that cause you stress.** Check this one off because you've already started doing this. Knowing about these situations ahead of time allows you to plan out different ways for handling the situation when it comes up again. You can better prepare for it. Or do your best to avoid the situation altogether.
- ☑ **Do things you like to do (whenever possible).** To the best of your ability, do activities that you enjoy, such as writing, drawing, reading, or meditating. Go back to your activities log for help. But make sure that these activities don't get in the way of other important responsibilities, such as doing your homework for this program or attending progress meetings with staff.
- ☑ **Relax.** You live in a very high-stress environment right now, so relaxing may sound near impossible. But give it a go anyway. Go back to Handouts #7 and #8 and review the PMR steps and guided imagery. These strategies can help you calm down.
- ☑ **Build a social support system**. This is not a new idea; you've heard this already. But again, find people who will listen to you when you're stressed and help you work through your problems. These people could be your counselor, other inmates who are doing well, family members who you can write to or call on the phone, a treatment group, or a religious/spiritual leader. Do not ask for help from people who will put you down or criticize you, who get into trouble or break the rules, or who are not focused on their own recovery. This will only make your stress worse.
- ☑ **Take care of your health.** When your body is healthy, you have more strength to deal with stress. So don't skip meals (even if you don't like the food), don't skip recreation time (even if you are given a short amount of time or a small space), don't skip your medications if needed, don't skip shower time, and keep a regular sleep schedule.
- ☑ **Talk about your feelings somehow.** Most people in prison don't like to talk about their feelings. Although holding in feelings is the common code among inmates (you might have said, "It's nobody's business" or "I'm going to do my own time"), it is very stressful to keep things bottled in. It's like blowing up a balloon. If you keep filling it with hot air, it will soon burst, and all the air will come gushing out—quickly and out of control. Talk to your social support network. Or if you're not comfortable yet talking about your feelings or don't know how to talk about your feelings,

get creative (write them down or draw them out). Other inmates may try to make you feel bad or stupid for talking about your feelings but remember where they are!

☑ **Know that you will make mistakes and be ok with that.** You are human. You will mess up every now and then; that's all part of the process. So don't get too bent out of shape. The important part is that you LEARN from the mistake so you can avoid it in the future. Don't just say, "Oh well!" and forget about it. Trace your steps. How did you get to the mistake? What should you do differently next time? Mistakes could be failing to take your medications as prescribed, engaging in criminalness (but let's hope not illegal stuff), or not working in your treatment program. Commit to doing better the next time around.

Exercise: Keeping Your Inner Peace

First, talk about how you typically handle stressful situations (think back to the events and hassles you listed in Handout #31). Then decide which of the actions described earlier you will commit to doing. State what you will do specifically (for example, don't just write "relax," say what you will do to relax) to keep the peace within you.

Old Actions	New Actions
☐ ______________	☐ ______________
☐ ______________	☐ ______________
☐ ______________	☐ ______________
☐ ______________	☐ ______________
☐ ______________	☐ ______________
☐ ______________	☐ ______________
☐ ______________	☐ ______________

Place a ✓ next to the old actions that may still be helpful. You can keep these.

Place an ✗ next to the old actions that were not helpful. Commit to stopping these.

Place a ✓ next to the new actions you are willing to commit to.

Handout #33
Learning to Cope With Cognitive Problems

Remember that the word "cognitive" means what or how you think. But the thought problems described in this handout are not about inaccurate ways of thinking about yourself or your situation. These thought problems have to do with your inability to focus, concentrate, or attend to what's going on around you. Cognitive problems can be a symptom of many different mental health disorders, including depression, anxiety, bipolar, and schizophrenia. If you are easily distracted, lose focus on tasks, or have trouble paying attention to what other people are saying to you, then you likely have cognitive problems.

The words "concentration" and "attention" mean having the ability to focus on one specific thing (for example, your homework, reading these handouts, listening to someone talk) for an extended period of time. If you have a hard time doing that, these strategies might be helpful for you. Commit to trying each one by saying out loud, "I will do this!"

Strategies to Try

1. Minimize distractions to the best of your ability such that there is only one thing to concentrate on. For example, if you are trying to concentrate on your homework, make sure the radio and TV are off. If it's noisy where you are and you cannot move, try a meditation technique (PMR, deep breathing, guided imagery, positive self-talk) to help you block out distractions and refocus.
2. Nicely ask the person who is talking to you to slow down or repeat things if you missed what he/she said or did not follow along the first time. So you could ask, "I'm sorry, but could you repeat that for me? I just want to make sure I understand." Most people will not mind doing this for you.
3. Check to make sure you understand what someone is saying to you by summarizing what you heard. For example, you can say something like, "Let me see if I'm following you; are you saying ________?"
4. Break down activities or tasks into smaller parts and take frequent breaks. For example, if you have trouble with these handouts, read a few sentences and then stop. Take a few deep breaths and then read a few more sentences. You can do this with other things you need to do too.
5. A similar strategy is to start out an activity by spending a brief time on the activity and gradually increasing the amount of time you spend. For example, if you are having difficulty paying attention when reading, you could start by reading a few sentences of an article in a newspaper or a magazine. When you feel comfortable with that, you could try reading a few paragraphs. After that, you could select a short article and read it entirely. Then you could gradually build up to reading chapters in a book. The important thing is to progress at a pace that is comfortable for you.
6. When you can, ask someone to join you in an activity that requires attention, such as a board game, card game, a jigsaw puzzle, or doing work for a support group. Many people find that doing something with others helps them to focus better.

Exercise: Recovery Rescue—Part I

Read the following story and write down how you can offer help to this person using the strategies discussed earlier.

Calvin has been diagnosed with major depressive disorder. His mental illness sometimes causes him to think negatively about himself or the situations that he experiences. His depression also puts him in a sad mood most of the time. Sometimes Calvin's sad mood and negative thoughts distract him and prevent him from focusing on what's going on. Yesterday, the correctional officers decided to do a surprise cell search because it was rumored that an inmate on the pod had drug contraband. The officers came to Calvin's cell and told him that his cell was being searched. They then asked him to cuff up, wait for his cell door to open, and step out toward the right of his cell where he would be detained and strip searched by another officer. Calvin was again distracted by his thoughts and did not understand what the officer said. Calvin didn't do anything about these thoughts. So he went through the whole procedure feeling nervous, scared, and confused. Then another incident happened today. Calvin was sitting in his cell trying to complete his homework, but he kept losing focus. He would look away every time someone or something on the pod made a loud noise. He also worried that his counselor was going to get on his case about his homework because he felt he was too stupid to do a good job. Calvin got frustrated and stopped doing his homework altogether.

1. **What cognitive problems does Calvin have as a result of his depression?**

2. **What do you think will or could happen in the long run if Calvin does NOT work on his cognitive problems?**

3. **If Calvin asked you for help in the situations he recently experienced, what would you suggest he do about his cognitive problems?**

4. **What would have been different if Calvin followed your advice?**

5. **How can YOU relate to Calvin? That is, what do you have in common with him?**

Handout #34
Learning to Cope With Negative Moods

Negative moods and feelings happen to all kinds of people, but they can be a big problem for people with mental health symptoms and illnesses, such as depression, anxiety, bipolar, and schizophrenia, among others. For these people, their moods frequently get in the way of their daily activities and their ability to achieve goals. If you often feel worried, scared, nervous, sad, hopeless, or tired and you don't show a lot of emotion or prefer to be alone, this handout is designed to offer you some help.

Commit to trying each strategy by saying out loud, "I will do this!"

Strategies to Try for Anxiety

People who have anxiety feel worried, nervous, afraid, or tense. They think a lot about what could go wrong in a situation and often feel that they don't have the skills to deal with things. It may feel like your mind won't shut off. People worry about many different things; some people worry about being in social situations; some people worry about germs or heights; some people worry about almost everything. As you read before, sometimes there are physical signs of anxiety, such as a headache, racing heart, sweating, or breathing problems. Many people will do very extreme things to avoid the stuff that makes them anxious. But here are some tips.

1. Talk with someone in your support system to let him or her know about your feelings.
2. Use relaxation techniques, such as deep breathing, PMR, or guided imagery to stay calm (see extra handouts).
3. Identify situations that tend to make you anxious and make a plan to do something about them. For example, if you are anxious about an upcoming progress meeting on your pod, practice how you will act and what you may say to staff. Rehearse it like a play or movie.

What situations make you nervous?

____

____

____

____

____

4. If it is safe to do so, gradually expose yourself to situations that make you feel anxious. For example, if someone is anxious about talking to other inmates on the pod, he might start by sitting alone in the common area and seeing how other people get along. After becoming more comfortable with that, he might try introducing himself to one or two people. The idea is to feel comfortable before moving on to the next step.

Strategies to Try for Depression

When people are depressed, they often feel bad about themselves, stop doing things they enjoy, sleep too much or not enough, have little energy, don't eat right, or have trouble making good decisions. People with very severe depression may think about hurting themselves or ending their lives. If this happens to you, go back and read your suicide prevention plan. Here are some strategies to help with your depression.

1. Set goals for daily activities. Start with one or two activities and gradually build up to a full schedule. Review your activities log. And remember—don't skip meals or rec time!
2. Identify things that you still enjoy (for example, reading, drawing, or writing) and build your strengths in those areas. Tell yourself what your strengths are!

What strengths do you have? What are you good at?

3. Schedule something pleasant (like relaxation, reading, or a TV show) to do each day, even if it's a small thing. This will give you something to look forward to.
4. Talk to someone in your support system to let him or her know how you are feeling. Sometimes they have good ideas you can try. Also, finding other people with similar problems as you can help you feel like you're not alone.
5. When you can, ask people to join you in activities. You may be more likely to do your plans when someone else is involved.
6. If you're not eating well, start by eating small portions of food and taking your time.
7. Practice relaxation (PMR, deep breathing, guided imagery) on a regular basis.
8. Remind yourself of all the things you have accomplished toward your goals and don't focus on past mistakes.
9. Use positive self-talk, even if you don't 100% believe in what you're saying right away. The more you pump yourself up, the more you will really start to believe in yourself and your abilities.

Strategies to Try for Loss of Interest

Some people lose interest in activities when they feel worried or sad. And it's hard to stay active when you don't feel like it. But as you know, more activity is good for you because it helps you deal with your situation better and reach your goals. Remember that you have to DO something to change. So it's important that you improve this area. Here are some ways you can begin to do that.

1. Be patient with yourself. Remember that change is hard, but it will happen slowly.
2. Start with an activity that you used to enjoy. Check your activity log for some ideas. Think of something brief that you could do that is related to that activity. For example, if you used to enjoy exercising, you could try doing a few pushups (5–10 reps) in your cell. Be attentive to what you experience as you work out. How do your muscles feel? Do you feel more relaxed after doing this?

   As you get more comfortable with brief activities, gradually plan longer activities. For example, after doing a few pushups, you could try doing a few more reps or take advantage of the time you have in the rec yard.

3. Check out new interests, such as computers; arts and crafts; reading about different topics, such as the news, science, or pop culture (remember to pick topics that are prosocial, not violent); telling jokes; listening to music; writing; yoga; observing nature; singing; word games; trivia; puzzles; or many other things. When you get back into the GP, explore what else there is to do and learn about. This opportunity for greater privileges can give you something to look forward to and a reason to keep at your goals.

   Be willing to try something a few times to get familiar with it. Don't give up the first time you try something new. The more familiar and comfortable you feel with an activity, the more likely you will enjoy it. If you still don't like the activity, then move on to something else.

Strategies to Try for Poor Emotional Expression

If other people tell you that they cannot read your facial expressions or that it is hard to tell what you are thinking or feeling by the expression on your face or your tone of voice, you may have a problem expressing your emotions. This can create misunderstandings. For example, when you are interested in something, other people may think you are bored or not paying attention. The following strategies may help you avoid this kind of misunderstanding.

1. Say out loud what you are feeling or thinking. Make clear comments about your reactions to conversations or activities.
2. When trying to say how you feel, make "I" statements, such as the following: "I am enjoying talking to you today." "I was a little nervous about playing basketball today, but I'm happy I did because it was fun." "I liked that movie. It was funny." Or, "I'm feeling a little discouraged today."

Strategies to Try for Social Withdrawal

Everyone needs time alone, and you are told to spend lots of time alone in your cell as part of being in restricted housing. But if you find that you are purposefully withdrawing from people and avoiding contact with others even when you get the chance to do so, it may create problems for you and for your relationships. The following strategies may be helpful in coping with social withdrawal.

1. Join a support group like AA/NA or attend a spiritual meeting or a therapy group if one is available to you.
2. Explore jobs at the facility (for example, in the kitchen) or volunteer work that involves contact with other people.
3. Schedule contact with someone every day, even if it is for a short time. This could be something as simple as saying "thank you" to the staff member who brings you your meal.
4. If you find it stressful to be with people, practice relaxation techniques (see extra handouts) before and/or after you talk with them.
5. If it's too stressful to have personal contact, write letters or call people on your phone list when you get the chance and talk for at least a few minutes.
6. Make a list of people in your support system you feel most comfortable with, like your counselor. Talk to these people when you are starting to withdraw. If possible, make a plan to meet with them.
7. Sometimes it's more comfortable to spend time with people when you are engaging in an activity together. When you can, try planning activities with someone, such as playing a card game on the pod, putting together a puzzle, or playing in the rec yard.

Exercise: Recovery Rescue—Part II

Read the following story and write down how you can offer help to this person using the strategies discussed earlier.

Luke has been diagnosed with posttraumatic stress disorder (PTSD)—a type of anxiety disorder that is caused by some very bad things that once happened to Luke. Luke used to live in a dangerous neighborhood. While there, he saw two of his cousins get shot to death on the streets. Also, he suffered several gunshot wounds himself. As a result of this trauma, Luke is always afraid of being hurt again. He worries a lot about his safety and feels helpless about his ability to protect himself. Sometimes the terror gets so bad that he thinks about killing himself to make it go away. Luke is housed on a general population pod within the prison, but he does not like to talk to many people. He usually keeps to himself and stays in his cell, even when he is allowed to be in the common area. He doesn't eat or sleep very well either; he barely picks at his meals and both the noises on the unit and the worried thoughts in his head keep him awake all night. Luke is also scared to use the shower area and the rec yard. Sometimes he will refuse to shower because he believes bad things will happen to him there. Luke has a counselor who tries to work with him on his problems, but Luke often confuses the counselor. The counselor doesn't know if Luke is interested in getting help or if he is even paying attention to their conversations at all. Luke never shows any emotion during their meetings (even though he actually likes being in therapy) and often seems bored. The counselor is thinking about stopping treatment with Luke until he seems ready to move forward.

1. **What mood problems does Luke have as a result of his PTSD?**

2. **What do you think will or could happen in the long run if Luke does NOT work on his mood problems?**

____

____

3. **If Luke asked you for help in the situations he recently experienced, what would you suggest he do about his mood problems?**

____

____

4. **What would have been different if Luke followed your advice?**

____

____

5. **How can YOU relate to Luke? That is, what do you have in common with him?**

____

____

Handout #35
Learning to Cope With Psychotic Symptoms

You remember from Handout #22 that psychotic symptoms often happen with mental illnesses, such as bipolar disorder and schizophrenia. Two psychotic symptoms are hallucinations and delusions. Hallucinations are sensations (hearing, touch, smell, taste, sight) that are not real; you may experience them even though nothing is really there. This can make life confusing because you cannot tell what is real and what it not real. Delusions, on the other hand, are strong ideas that are not real or even impossible, such as believing that aliens are putting thoughts into your head. So if other people often tell you that they cannot see, hear, smell, taste, or touch the same things can, or if other people tell you that your beliefs are "crazy" or strange, then this handout could be helpful to you.

Commit to trying each strategy by saying out loud, "I will do this!"

Strategies to Try for Hallucinations

Again, hallucinations are "false perceptions"; your mind is playing tricks on you. Hallucinations sometimes come in episodes, meaning that they go away for some time and then come back again. If your hallucinations come in episodes like this, then the return of hallucinations is a warning sign of relapse. For other people, their hallucinations do not go away between episodes. If you experience hallucinations on a regular basis, you can still learn to manage your symptoms. But if the hallucinations get worse (for example, voices tell you to do harmful things), then you should talk to a doctor or your counselor. Here are some things you can try to control your hallucinations.

1. Distract yourself by doing something that uses your attention, such as having a conversation with someone, reading, or exercising. Some people who hear voices hum to themselves or listen to music to drown out the voices.
2. Check out your experiences with someone you trust. For example, one man who thought he heard voices outside his window asked his brother to listen and give an opinion.
3. Use positive self-talk. Some people tell themselves things like, "I'm not going to listen to these voices." "I'm not going to let these voices get to me." Or, "I'm just going to stay cool, and the situation will pass."
4. Don't take your hallucinations seriously or as absolute truths. Instead, try to see your hallucinations as your mind's way of telling you that you need to start paying closer attention to your thoughts, feelings, and needs. This gives you a better understanding about why the hallucinations are happening to you. For example, one woman heard voices telling her not to go outside. Instead of listening to the voices, she took the command as a sign that she was afraid of something. She then started to think about where her fear was coming from and challenged it. So look for a symbolic meaning not an exact meaning.
5. If you can't figure out helpful meanings for your hallucinations, just ignore them as much as possible. Some people say that it helps to focus on other things instead.

6. Put the hallucinations "in the background." Some people acknowledge what they are hearing or seeing but don't pay any further attention to it. For example, they might tell themselves, "There's that critical voice again. I'm just going to let it happen and go about my business. I'm not going to let it bother me or affect what I'm doing."
7. Use relaxation techniques. Oftentimes, hearing or seeing hallucinations will get worse when people are under stress. Doing some deep breathing or PMR reduces the stress and lessens the intensity of the hallucination.
8. If the voices start to tell you to do something to hurt yourself or someone else, and you think you might act on this, talk to a doctor or counselor immediately! If you can't reach your counselor, tell a staff member on duty. If you do need to involve staff members, it may be helpful to share your mental illness with them so that they understand that the hallucination is a symptom. If you don't do this and only tell them that you may hurt yourself (or whatever you are thinking about doing), then they will handle the situation much differently. Consequently, you could find yourself with a disciplinary sanction.

Strategies to Try for Delusions

Sometimes people have beliefs that are firmly held even when there is no clear evidence to support them. For example, they may start to believe that the FBI is monitoring their phone calls, even though there is no evidence of this. Or they may believe that people are talking about them or staring at them. Delusions sometimes come in episodes, meaning that they go away for some time and then come back again. If your delusions come in episodes like this, then their return is a warning sign of relapse. For other people, these beliefs do not go away. If you experience delusions on a regular basis, you can still learn to manage your symptoms. But if the delusions get worse or more bizarre, then you should talk to a doctor or your counselor. Here are some things you can try to control your delusions.

1. Distract yourself from the disturbing belief by doing something that takes your mental attention, such as doing a puzzle or adding up rows of numbers. You can also try one of your relaxation techniques, such as deep breathing, PMR, or guided imagery.
2. Check out your beliefs by talking to someone you trust. For example, you might ask your counselor to help you look at the evidence for and against your belief. Ask for his or her point of view. If your beliefs cause you to worry about safety, for example, you might ask, "What is the evidence that supports that I am in danger, and what is the evidence that does not support that I am in danger?" This is very similar to cognitive restructuring and changing automatic thoughts (see Handouts #29 and #30).
3. Distract yourself with a physical activity, such as doing a few pushups.
4. Keep in mind that you should contact your doctor or counselor if you become so convinced of your belief that you are thinking of acting on it. For example, if you become convinced that someone means you harm, you might start thinking of defending yourself, which could possibly lead you to harm someone else. If you can't reach your counselor, tell a staff member on duty. If you do need to involve staff members, it may be helpful to share your mental illness with them so that they understand that the delusion is a symptom. If you don't do this and only tell them that you may hurt someone (or whatever you are thinking about doing), then they will handle the situation much differently and you could find yourself with a disciplinary sanction.

Exercise: Recovery Rescue—Part III

Read the following story and write down how you can offer help to this person using the strategies discussed earlier.

Andy started hearing voices when he was about 20 years old. The first voice he ever heard was friendly; it would just make comments about what Andy was doing throughout the day, such as "he is going for a walk." But after a while, the voices got mean and would tell Andy that he was a bad person. They would call him a failure and laugh at him. Andy started using heroin to deal with the voices and to shut them up. Andy also sold large amounts of heroin, which resulted in his incarceration. In prison, Andy still hears the voices sometimes. When Andy is stressed out, his symptoms get worse, and the voices will warn him of dangers that aren't really there. They say things like, "Don't go out there; you're going to die," or "Make a shank and hurt yourself." Andy is at a point where he thinks others are plotting to kill him. Whenever he is in the common area with other inmates, he always thinks they are looking at him and talking bad about him. This agitates Andy. He sometimes has angry outbursts where he will yell and scream at the people he believes are planning to cause him harm. Other inmates and staff members don't know what to do about Andy because he is sometimes very unpredictable.

1. **What psychotic symptoms does Andy have as a result of his schizophrenia?**

2. **What do you think will or could happen in the long run if Andy does NOT work on his psychotic symptoms?**

3. **If Andy asked you for help in the situations he recently experienced, what would you suggest he do about his psychotic symptoms?**

4. **What would have been different if Andy followed your advice?**

5. **How can YOU relate to Andy? That is, what do you have in common with him?**

Handout #36
Learning to Cope With Interpersonal Problems

Remember that interpersonal problems mean that you have difficulty talking to or interacting with other people; these are problems related to your social relationships. Such relationships may be between you and family or friends outside the prison walls, your counselor, facility staff, your lawyer, other inmates, doctors, or anyone else. Interpersonal problems are very common in people who have personality disorders, such as borderline, antisocial, narcissistic, and schizotypal (see Handout #23). If you tend to have rocky or unstable relationships, don't get along well with others, or find that you don't fit in well with others, this handout may be helpful for you.

Commit to trying each strategy by saying out loud, "I will do this!"

Strategies to Try

1. Deal with interpersonal problems ahead of time. Think about upcoming social situations that are likely to make you feel anxious or awkward. Imagine the situation clearly in your mind and rehearse how you will handle the situation. Ask yourself these questions:
   - What will you say?
   - What is the other person likely to say?
   - What is likely to happen?
   - What would you want to happen?
   - How would you like the other person to feel about you when the interaction is over?
   - How would you like to feel about yourself when the interaction is over?
   - What can you do to make the interaction better?

   This way, you will be prepared when a similar situation comes up.

2. Remember your assertiveness and conflict resolution skills from Handout #15. Don't be aggressive or passive; this won't get you what you really want or need. You can still be respectful even if you disagree with someone.
3. Think about your own goals, values, and beliefs. Keeping these in mind will help you act in ways that make you feel proud—including dealing with other people.
4. Be aware of your common criminal thinking styles, as many of these styles involve blaming other people (inmates, staff, doctors) for things or putting other people down ("That job was easy. . . . Any idiot could have done that."). People don't like this very much, so it doesn't help you make good relationships.
5. Practice good communication skills. Give someone some information about you before you ask something of him or her. For example, you can say something like, "Hi, my name is _____. What's your name?" Here you gave the person your name before asking for his or hers. That sounds much better than saying, "Who are you?" But don't always talk about yourself!

6. Be aware of your body language. Don't stand in a threatening manner; don't clench your fists, cross your arms, or stand over people. Especially in prison, this type of body language can lead to trouble.
7. Prepare topics of conversation and use them when you need to start a conversation or keep a conversation going. But don't use topics that get people all worked up like politics, religion, abortion, gay rights, etc. This doesn't leave a very good impression, because it pushes people's buttons. When you get to know a person better, then you can talk about deeper issues.

What topics could you talk about in a conversation?

____

____

____

____

8. Sometimes, people are worried about how good they will be in social situations. For example, they might think, "They won't like me"; "I won't do it right"; "I'll probably fall apart." People can also worry about asking others for something (i.e., to be treated differently in a relationship, to ask for more information about their medications). These people may think things like, "If they say 'no,' it will kill me"; "I have to know that a person will say 'yes' before I ask them to do something"; "If I make a request, I will seem like a weak person"; "I don't like when people are upset with me." And yet some people are worried about how to say "no" when others ask for something (for example, if someone asks you to do something you don't want to do). They might think, "Saying 'no' is selfish"; "I can't say 'no' because this person is more powerful than I am"; "They won't like me anymore if I don't do this."

   You guessed it. . . . Challenging automatic thoughts and using positive self-talk can help you here too.

Think of some thoughts that challenge the ones listed earlier:

____

____

____

____

____

9. Use "I" statements to express your feelings and opinions. Don't assume people know how you feel. Instead, tell the person exactly what you're reacting to. Hinting at the problem or beating around the bush only confuses people.
10. When making a request, use phrases such as, "I would like" or "I don't want" instead of saying, "you should" or "I need." For example, saying something like, "I need you to tell me about the side effects of these medications" will sound pushy and demanding. Rather, you might say, "I would like more information about the side effects of the medication I'm taking." This way, you still get what you wanted but keep a healthy relationship. And be confident when asking! Even if someone says "no," it doesn't mean that you shouldn't have asked.
11. If you want to say "no" to someone, be firm and confident (use eye contact, don't stammer or whisper, or say "I'm not sure"). Having a clear reason for saying "no" may help you express your opinion or emotions.
12. If you can't come to an agreement with someone (either because you don't want to fulfill their request, or because they don't want to fulfill yours), you can try to negotiate or make a compromise. Offer alternative solutions to the problem or reduce your request. Focus on what will work to solve the issue. You may even turn the tables by saying, "What do you think we should do here?"
13. Don't respond when people try to verbally threaten or attack you. Don't let that distract you from making your point. Walk away if you have to.
14. Practice interpersonal interactions. It's the only way to get better at reacting and responding to other people. For example, while talking with someone, change the subject. You could also try asking your counselor for a favor, respectfully disagree with someone's opinion, or ask a person to stop doing something that bothers you.
15. Don't be afraid to use a little humor. Smile. Be lighthearted. But make sure you don't use offending humor that would upset people, like anything related to race, homosexuality, mental illness, etc.

Exercise: Recovery Rescue—Part IV

Read the following story and write down how you can offer help to this person using the strategies discussed earlier.

Stephen was recently diagnosed with borderline personality disorder. He has a long history of bad relationships that quickly go from love to hate. He got married at an early age. Stephen and his wife argued a lot. As a result, he would often move in and out of their home depending on how bad things got until they finally divorced. He married again not long after that, and the same pattern unfolded. Stephen gets jealous easily and needs a lot of attention to feel loved. But he never spoke about his jealousy problems or need for attention. He felt that his romantic partners should just know when something was wrong with him. It made him feel weak and stupid to have to tell people about his emotions. Stephen is incarcerated for domestic violence. He got so upset with his current wife for having lunch with a male coworker to discuss a possible promotion that he let his anger get out of control. He beat her, breaking several ribs and causing bruises all over her body. His wife filed for divorce. Stephen is now in a treatment group for inmates with domestic violence convictions. The other group members don't like Stephen because he's very frustrating and confusing. One minute he's praising the other group members and the counselor for their hard work (usually when Stephen is the focus of attention), and the next minute he is on a tangent about how much of an idiot everyone is (usually when he is not the center of attention). He never seems to share any deeper emotions or clearly communicate how he's feeling. Stephen makes other people feel like they need to walk on eggshells. He keeps coming to the group, but he is afraid to ask the other members for help with his real problems.

1. **What interpersonal problems does Stephen have as a result of his borderline personality?**

   ____

   ____

2. **What do you think will or could happen in the long run if Stephen does NOT work on his interpersonal problems?**

   ____

   ____

3. **If Stephen asked you for help in the situations he recently experienced, what would you suggest he do about his interpersonal problems?**

   ____

   ____

4. **What would have been different if Stephen followed your advice?**

   ____

   ____

5. **How can YOU relate to Stephen? That is, what do you have in common with him?**

   ____

   ____

Handout #37
Learning to Cope With Criminalness

As you know, criminalness distracts you from achieving your goals. It means any way of thinking or behaving that violates the rights or well-being of other people . . . including yourself. Criminalness can include anything from less serious offenses, such as cheating at a card game, cutting someone off in line, or calling someone a bad name to more serious offenses, such as hiding contraband, fighting with someone, or sexual assault. Being high on criminalness means you are not taking responsibility for yourself and, consequently, not working toward your goals. If you find that you don't like to follow the rules, are getting into trouble frequently (e.g., disciplinary write-ups, more time in "the hole"), or are arguing a lot with other people, then this handout is designed to help you.

Commit to trying each strategy by saying out loud, "I will do this!"

Strategies to Try for Boredom or Restlessness

When people get bored and restless, they look for things to do. Sometimes, this often means people will create their own excitement by doing nonproductive or rule-breaking things. When you feel bored or restless, it is time to get busy, but busy in ways that will actually help you achieve your goals.

1. Exercise when you can. Do pushups or go to the rec yard when you can. Make sure you break a sweat. Get to the point of exhaustion. You should be tired afterward. You will release your built-up energy and will exhaust all physical restlessness. A positive side effect is that you will feel healthier.
2. Try a new hobby like drawing, writing, reading, singing/rapping, or arts and crafts (make something of your own!). Check your activities log for things you can do now.
3. Call on your social support network for help. You may not have a lot of chances to do this while in restricted housing, but when you can, find other people to talk to or engage in some other social activity, such as playing basketball in the rec or putting together a puzzle. Remember to find other inmates who are following the rules. You will learn more about this in the next module.
4. Look for opportunities to work or volunteer your time in meaningful ways. For example, when you get back into the GP, check into what's available. You may be able to run an AA or NA meeting, participate in group therapy, help a religious or spiritual leader, enroll in classes, or apply for a job in the facility (kitchen duties, laundry, maintenance). Using your time this way will also look good on your record.

Strategies to Try for Self-Injurious Behavior (SIB)

Some people find that harming themselves (e.g., cutting, burning, scarring) is a way to release built-up pain and frustration. Many mental health professionals view harming oneself as a psychiatric symptom. But as you've heard before, it can also be a sign of criminalness. Remember that some people use SIB to manipulate other people or their situation because it can give them special rewards, such as attention. And inmates use SIB to manipulate people so often that prison staff usually see it as a behavioral problem. Consequently, you may be sanctioned for it. Although injuring yourself is not criminal, it is an irresponsible, nonhelpful way of dealing with emotional pain. If you find that hurting yourself relieves emotional pain, you need to develop alternate coping strategies. Some of these strategies may be helpful.

1. Again, try a good, hard exercise. Working your body to the max can feel painful, but it is a much healthier way of releasing your emotional pain.
2. Use the relaxation exercises you previously learned.
3. Talk with someone who cares about you and that you can confide in (these people should be identified in your suicide prevention plan). Talk to your counselor or write letters to people who support you.
4. Put in a sick call to meet with your doctor or counselor. If it's an emergency, talk to a staff member on duty. If you do need to involve staff members, it may be helpful to share your mental illness with them so that they understand that your SIB is a symptom not an attempt to manipulate them. If you don't do this, then they will handle the situation much differently, and you could find yourself with a disciplinary sanction.
5. If you must engage in behavior that physically hurts in order for you to "feel," choose less harmful options. For example, rather than cutting or burning yourself, try the following:
   - Squeezing your fist tightly and then releasing
   - Taking a very cold shower
   - Eating something aversive (but that you can actually eat) like pepper.
   - Wear a rubber band you can snap on your wrist

Strategies to Try for Poor Motivation to Do Good Things

Sometimes people don't have the desire or energy to do "the right thing," to be responsible, or to be prosocial. It is hard work being responsible. Essentially, you don't get to do what you want, when you want, and how you want to do things all the time. When you are losing the motivation to stay away from crime or rule violations, and you find that you are less and less motivated to be responsible, you need to take immediate steps to increase your motivation to remain responsible as you work toward your goals.

1. Take time to review the personal goals you have developed in this program. Think about the importance of these goals and why you have them in the first place, and use this as motivation to stay responsible.
2. Visit (if you can) and talk with other people you admire and respect about what is important in life. This could be your counselor, family member or friend you can write to, or model inmates who are following the rules and doing well for themselves. If you can't talk or visit, think about the people you look up to. What do they do right in their lives? What good things do they have because of it? What can you learn from their behaviors?
3. Attend a religious or spiritual service and remind yourself that there are more important things in life than your own wants and desires.

4. Remind yourself how bad and terrible being in restricted housing really is and that you don't want to come back here. Look at how other inmates' criminalness keeps them stuck here and take note of what they get for behaving that way. Tell yourself that you won't be like them; you can reach your goals.
5. Create a small list of necessary things you must get done to remain responsible that particular day. Keep the list realistic and focus on getting those things done. For example, you might include eating all meals, using your rec time, or keeping your cool when an officer asks you to do something. When your motivation returns, you will be able to increase your focus beyond the day-to-day items.
6. Commit to doing one nice thing for someone else before you do anything for yourself. The mere act of being friendly or helping another person is prosocial and reinforces a responsible lifestyle. For example, you might say "thank you" when a staff member escorts you to the rec area. Plus, you will hopefully be reminded of how good it feels to do nice things for others rather than always focusing on yourself.
7. Contact your doctor or counselor and ask for help with your recovery. Just being able to recognize your criminalness and knowing when to ask for help is a step toward achieving your goals and doing what's right.

Exercise: Recovery Rescue—Part V

Read the following story and write down how you can offer help to this person using the strategies discussed earlier.

Jarrod has a diagnosis of bipolar disorder, so he goes through periods of really low moods (depression) and really high moods (mania). Jarrod is taking medication for his mental illness and has been working with a counselor in the prison, whom he meets with briefly one time a week. He started out with a lot of motivation and drive for getting better. He was sick of feeling so bad about himself during his depression, and he didn't want to get in trouble anymore because of his mania. When Jarrod is depressed, he likes to stay in his cell alone. He is also easily frustrated and will refuse to comply with officers' orders. When Jarrod is manic, he will cut himself with the edge of a piece of paper until he bleeds. Jarrod's mania also gives him a lot of energy that he doesn't know what to do with, so he tries to find ways to stir up some excitement. The last time Jarrod was manic, he went into the rec yard during a thunderstorm, rolled around on the wet ground, and argued with staff members when they told him to come inside. He also got bored and started banging on the sink in his cell until it broke. With treatment, Jarrod has been able to manage his symptoms, but lately, he has been finding that it is very difficult to keep doing this. Change is harder than he thought, and he doesn't feel like doing the homework his counselor gave him. He started missing the feeling of being manic and cheeked his meds this morning. He's getting restless and is beginning to think there is no real point to changing his behaviors. He is starting to believe that maybe it's not even possible for him to change.

1. **Describe Jarrod's criminalness associated with his bipolar disorder.**

____

____

2. **What do you think will or could happen in the long run if Jarrod does NOT work on his criminalness?**

____

____

3. **If Jarrod asked you for help in the situations he recently experienced, what would you suggest he do about his criminalness?**

____

____

4. **What would have been different if Jarrod followed your advice?**

____

____

5. **How can YOU relate to Jarrod? That is, what do you have in common with him?**

____

____

Handout #38
Sticking With Your Medications

Why Do I Take Medications?

You learned earlier that mental distress and disorders are partially caused by biology. Your brain has neurotransmitters that help communicate messages between different parts of it. Sometimes these chemicals get a little disorganized and become imbalanced, so your brain doesn't get the appropriate messages anymore. It's kind of like losing the signal on your TV set, and the images don't come in clear. These wrong messages result in certain symptoms (depression, anxiety, hallucinations, delusions, loss of focus). This is where some medications can be helpful because they try to put your neurotransmitters back in order so that they communicate the right messages again. As a result, you can think more clearly. If you are taking medications for mental health symptoms, it is probably because a lot of what you are experiencing has to do with these imbalanced neurotransmitters.

Why Should I Keep Taking My Medications?

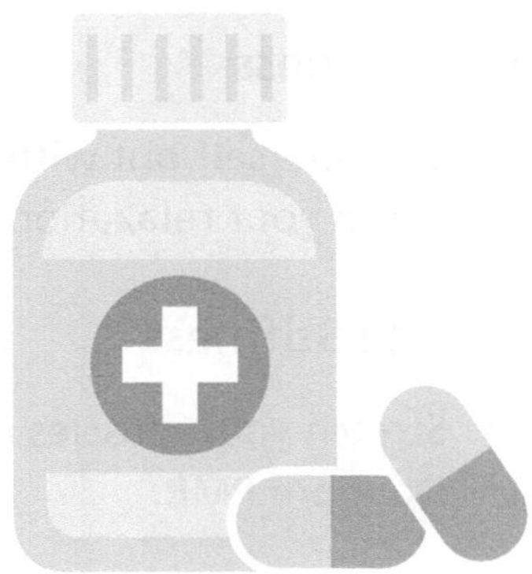

People with serious mental health symptoms and illnesses must take medications to help reset the chemicals in their brains. The more consistently a person takes his or her medications, the better the result. People with these symptoms can't simply take their medications whenever they feel like it and expect to reduce their symptoms. This would be like a person with diabetes who chooses to take his or her insulin some days, but not others. Although medication alone is not likely to result in your recovery, it is an important part. For example, antidepressants (used to treat symptoms of depression) can help a person feel motivated enough to actually participate in treatment and do the required work. Therefore, *to recover and successfully reach your goals, you must have an effective medication treatment plan and stick to that plan.* Taking your medications along with practicing the skills you learned in this module will substantially increase your chances of doing well and staying out of restricted housing.

What About Side Effects?

The bad part about taking medications is that they almost always involve some negative side effects. This is true no matter what the reason or condition for which you are taking medications. To have the best outcomes with your medications, it is important to know what side effects your medications can have and to tell your doctor what side effects you experience. Before each time you visit or check-in with the doctor, you should take a personal survey and make a list of your experiences and reactions to the medications that you have taken since your last doctor visit.

Next is an example of what you might say to your doctor:

I am taking ___________ to treat my depression, but it does not seem to be working, as I still feel ___________ and ___________. I wonder if the dosage should be increased or if there is something else you can give me to help with my depression?

And here are some common side effects and tips for dealing with them:

Drowsiness

- ☑ Take a brief nap during the day, but don't sleep all day.
- ☑ Take advantage of time outside; be mindful of what you see, notice the feeling of the air, and the sun on your face.
- ☑ Ask your doctor about changing your medication to the evening.
- ☑ Stand during activities (e.g., therapy sessions, pod meetings); you may need to explain to staff members why you are standing so that they do not see it as a safety threat.

Weight Gain

- ☑ Eat healthy foods that are available to you, such as fruits and vegetables.
- ☑ Limit how much sugary or fatty foods you eat, such as soda and candy (when you get commissary, for example, use it to buy food low in fat or calories).
- ☑ Exercise regularly; don't skip rec time!

Restlessness

- ☑ Tire yourself out with exercise; do pushups in your cell, for example.
- ☑ Go to your relaxation techniques like deep breathing, PMR, or guided imagery.

Muscle Stiffness

- ☑ Stretch your muscles regularly.
- ☑ Do more PMR.

Dizziness

- ☑ Try not to stand up too quickly from sitting or lying down; when you get up in the morning, for example, rise slowly.
- ☑ Ask the doctor if there are other medications you can take to reduce this effect.

Blurry Vision

- ☑ Ask to have your eyes checked, as your problem may not be related to the medication.
- ☑ Ask if you can have eye drops to increase the moisture in your eyes.
- ☑ Ask if you can try a pair of reading glasses.

Dry Mouth

- ☑ Make sure you always have water to sip on.
- ☑ Don't let yourself get dehydrated; drink plenty of liquids.

☑ Suck on ice cubes.
☑ Ask the doctor for special mouthwash designed to reduce dry mouth.

Shakiness or Tremors

☑ Don't fill cups or glasses of fluids to the very top.
☑ Ask the doctor if there are other medications you can take to reduce this effect.
☑ Use your stress management techniques, including deep breathing or PMR.

Constipation

☑ Drink lots of water every day (six to eight glasses).
☑ Try to eat foods that have a lot of fiber in them, such as whole grains, bran cereals, vegetables, and fruits.
☑ Keep exercising when you can.
☑ Ask the doctor if there are other medications you can take to reduce this effect.

Sensitivity to the Sun

☑ When you do get more time outdoors, try to stay in the shade as much as possible.
☑ Keep your shirt on when outside to protect yourself from the sun's UV rays.
☑ Whenever possible, exercise outside in the morning or evenings when the sun isn't as hot.

Red, Yellow, and Green of Medication Compliance

Time to use your mental traffic light again! Just as you do with everything else, you must evaluate your thoughts, feelings, and behaviors related to your medication use. There are clues you can look for to help you recognize when you are doing well with your medication treatment plan and when you are headed toward relapse.

GREEN LIGHT = Monitor

A helpful treatment regimen includes monitoring your side effects and taking your medications as prescribed. Remember to review your experiences and reactions since your last doctor visit and plan to tell your doctor about any negative side effects. Don't argue, fight, or refuse medications when staff gives them to you. If you have questions, just ask. You have a right to know what they are giving you, why they are giving it to you, and what experiences you can expect to have.

YELLOW LIGHT = Identify early warning signs of noncompliance

Noncompliance occurs when you stop taking or refuse your medications. Early warning signs of medication noncompliance include ***thoughts***, ***feelings***, or ***beliefs*** that you no longer need your medication or that you can function as well (or better) without your medications. Examples of early warning signs include thinking you are better off with your symptoms than the side effects, thinking your symptoms weren't really all that bad before, thinking you've "out grown" your illness, or believing the side effects are "not worth it."

RED LIGHT = Stop triggers of noncompliance

Triggers are events or situations that have led to your noncompliance in the past. Everyone has different triggers, so you must learn to recognize your triggers. Triggers to medication noncompliance include not discussing your side effects with your doctor and other mental health care professionals, cheeking or selling your medications, or using alcohol or drugs. Triggers here are actual behaviors that you do (or don't do) in response to taking (or not taking) your meds properly.

What YELLOW warning signs and RED triggers do you need to look out for regarding your medication compliance?

Yellow: ______________________________

____

Red: ______________________________

____

Exercise: Mapping My Meds

Fill out the table that follows so you know exactly what medications you are taking, why you are taking them, and what the risks and benefits of taking them are. ***Note*** : You may need to **ASK** your doctor or counselor for some of this information.

Medication I take:	I take this to treat symptoms of my . . .	This medication gives me these benefits:	This medication gives me these side effects:	If I didn't take this medication anymore, I would feel . . .
1				
2				
3				
4				
5				

Module 6
Recap

In This Module You Learned About

☑ **Automatic thoughts—how to be aware and challenge them**
☑ **Recognizing signs of stress and how to reduce it**
☑ **Different strategies for dealing with your specific symptoms, including cognitive problems, negative moods, psychotic symptoms, interpersonal problems, and criminalness**
☑ **Medications for mental health symptoms—why you are taking them, how to monitor your side effects, and how to look for signs of noncompliance**

Now place an ✗ mark next to the techniques that you will continue to practice and write down WHEN you will practice them, WHAT you will do, and HOW they will help you. Give your counselor permission to hold you accountable for following through with your plan.

Technique	**I WILL do this (place ✗ here)**	**Whenever I . . .**	**This is how I will do it . . .**	**To help me cope with . . .**
Pay attention to my negative feelings as clues to my thoughts				
Challenge automatic thoughts that are causing me problems				
Record automatic thoughts that are causing me problems				
Celebrate my accomplishments				
Be aware of my signs of stress				
Use Progressive Muscle Relaxation (PMR)				
Do breathing exercises				

Technique	I WILL do this (place ✗ here)	Whenever I . . .	This is how I will do it . . .	To help me cope with . . .
Use guided imagery				
Use positive self-talk				
Take care of my physical health				
Work on my cognitive problems (concentration)				
Work on my anxiety				
Work on my depression				
Work on my poor emotional expression				
Work on my social withdrawal				
Work on my psychotic symptoms				
Work on my loss of interest in things				
Work on my interpersonal problems				
Work on my boredom and restlessness				
Increase my motivation to do good things				

Technique	I WILL do this (place ✗ here)	Whenever I . . .	This is how I will do it . . .	To help me cope with . . .
Reduce my self-injurious behaviors				
Learn more about the medications I'm taking for my mental distress				
Keep track of my side effects				
Be aware of my warning signs and triggers for stopping my medication				
Talk to my doctor about my medications and how they make me feel				
Talk to people in my social support network about how I'm feeling				

Module 7

Seeking Supportive Allies: Finding Helpful Others Among the Crowd

Handout #39

Separating the Good From the Bad

Remember **THE Circle of Change**? Part of that circle was your environment. And part of your environment is the people you are around. Review the diagram in the box that follows:

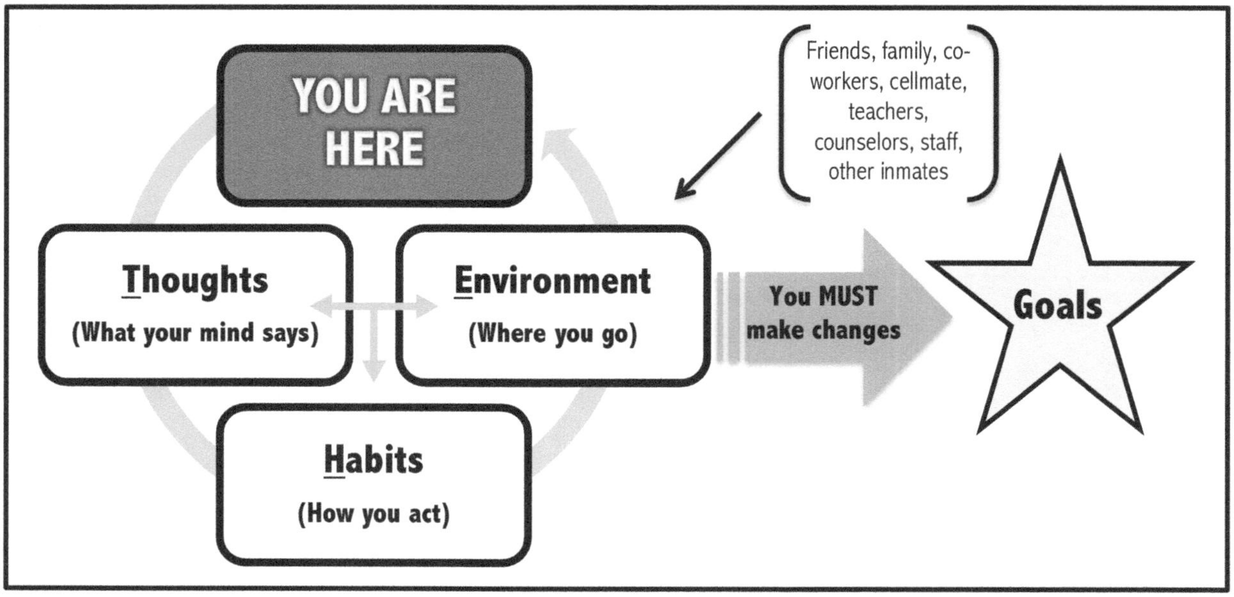

Like most people, you probably like to think that you are your own person and that you can make your own decisions and act without the influence of other people. But this is not true. We often act a lot like the people we hang around with. We share similar beliefs and do similar things. Imagine being at a neighborhood party where everyone is drinking beer, smoking, and having a great time. How would you feel going to that party and not drinking beer? You are likely to feel out of place, strange, awkward, or unwanted. So you are more likely to drink and smoke too. If you think that other people do not or cannot impact how you think and act, you could be in trouble for relapse! Many people make the mistake of believing that they can say "no" when a yellow- or red-light event comes up without help. (Think back to your criminal thinking style. Is "superoptimism" one of yours? If so, beware of this!)

Here's an example:

Howie is 22 years old, and this is his first time in prison. On the outside, he didn't have many friends and kept to himself. He found excitement in robbing houses and stores in nice neighborhoods. He was arrested one night after holding a shop clerk at gunpoint and then driving away in a stolen vehicle. In prison, Howie is smaller in size than a lot of the other guys and doesn't talk very much. When he first got to prison, he felt alone and scared. His fears got worse when other inmates started bullying him and threatening to hurt him. Howie was even beaten up in the rec yard on several occasions by stronger inmates. One time, he suffered three broken ribs. This event was very shameful for Howie, and he stopped using his rec time, preferring to stay in his cell by himself instead. About a month ago, an inmate named Mitchell started talking to Howie. He told Howie about this group of guys who could help protect him from danger. Mitchell said he just wanted to be friends with Howie because he seemed so lonely. Everything was great at first. Howie could go out into the rec yard again because Mitchell and his buddies were always close by. And now Howie had people to sit with in the mess hall. He didn't feel alone anymore, he felt safe. But after a few weeks, things started to change. Howie was talking to Mitchell about a new treatment program he was starting, and Mitchell says, "Man, you don't need that shit; you got us! We'll help you out, dog. In fact, I need you to do something for me. We're about to take out some motherfuckers who screwed us over on a bet. We can't let them get away with that!" Mitchell went over the details of what he wanted Howie to do. It didn't seem right, but Mitchell told Howie that he's "in too far to back out" and that he would be "as good as dead" if he did. Mitchell reminded Howie that his crew supported him when he was in a bad spot, so Howie felt he had to carry out the plan to keep his friends happy. Howie got caught by staff assaulting another inmate and was sent to the hole. He could also be facing another criminal charge.

How did Howie's new friends influence his THOUGHTS?

____

____

____

How did Howie's new friends influence his HABITS (how he acts)?

____

____

How did Howie's new friends influence his ENVIRONMENT (where he is now)?

____

____

If you think you can work on your recovery alone, you could also be in trouble. Finding the right people—people who are doing well and have similar goals as you—will help you stay on track. Consider this: is it easier to stick to a workout routine by yourself or with a partner? Most people will say it is easier with a partner because someone else is counting on them to show up! This works for your recovery also. But first, think about the people you were hanging around in the past. This will help you figure out who you should be hanging around and who you should avoid in the future.

Who did you hang out with before coming to prison?
What did you DO with these people?

Who did you hang out with before coming to this restricted housing unit?
What did you DO with these people?

How have these people led you to where you are now?

It's time for you to start changing WHO you are spending your time with in this facility so you can get out and stay out of this unit. This is where you can again to use your mental traffic light to decide who will be helpful for your goals (green light) and who will not be helpful for your goals (yellow and red lights).

Exercise: Getting the Good Guys, Banning the Bad Boys

How can you tell if someone is going to help you? How can you tell if someone is NOT going to help you? Think about the qualities, features, or characteristics that distinguish these two types of people. Keep these in mind when you evaluate the people in your life. Remember: Good guys have good goals (and will support you with yours). Think about the "good guys" and "bad boys" you'll find in prison.

____

____

____

____

____

____

____

Good Guys **What do they look like, how do they act, what do they do/say, where do they go?**	**Bad Boys** **What do they look like, how do they act, what do they do/say, where do they go?**

Now, circle the things you wrote down in each column that could also describe you (how you think, what you say and do, where you go). Which side has more circles?

____

Handout #40
Moving Away From Antisocial Associates

Why Do People Have Antisocial Associates in the First Place?

Remember that antisocial associates (friends, family, coworkers) are people you hang around with who are not doing positive things with their lives. They get into trouble with the law, have a lot of disciplinary problems, are offensive to other people, and generally don't care how their behaviors affect other people. So why do people hang out with antisocial associates? There must be some benefits. You might have these kinds of people in your life because you feel comfortable around them, because you can relate to them, because they seem like the "in-group" (especially in prison), or because they give you a sense of who you are (that is, you can be someone specific, and people know who you are as this person).

What benefits have you experienced from being around antisocial people or by being antisocial yourself?

____

____

____

____

____

Here's More Information About Why People Seek Out Antisocial Associates

1. **BELONGING**—We want to feel that we belong and do not want to feel left out. We want to feel like we are part of a group. The more we want to be *accepted*, the more likely we are to do whatever it takes to belong, even if that means belonging with the wrong crowd.
2. **SECURITY**—We want to be around others who share similar values and attitudes because they provide a sense of security and safety. We want to feel protected and being part of a group often gives us this feeling.
3. **SENSE OF PURPOSE**—The benefits of criminal or antisocial behavior often include money, excitement, or status (power, authority, control over others). These things can boost our self-confidence and give us a sense of accomplishment. When we are around other people who are also committing crime or not following the rules, it makes antisocial behavior seem ok. It may seem even

normal because it's accepted. But ultimately, the standard of what's acceptable gets lower, and our behaviors move further along the Criminalness Meter. In other words, antisocial others encourage these criminal benefits and give your behaviors meaning. As a result, we continue them.

4. **MENTORING**—We see the benefits of others' behaviors, such as money, excitement, or status. We often envy our friends' lifestyles, so we imitate what they are doing. In other words, we see the benefits of what they do, and we try the same things to get the same benefits. But remember that antisocial associates often think of the immediate benefits and not the long-term consequences. Fast money and wild parties may seem like a great time, but they can get people into big trouble down the road. Pissing off the staff may get you a tough reputation among other inmates but will likely land you in segregation . . . or worse.

Now, Here Are Some Tips for Avoiding the Pull of Antisocial Associates

Commit to trying these by saying out loud, "I will do this!"

1. Remember your identity pre-prison. Think about the positive qualities that made you who you were before you got to prison. Don't get too tangled up with your prison identity (that is, who you are as an inmate here); this one is not real. It will also help you to remember your goals and think about the person you WANT to be in the future. Anyone who makes you feel more comfortable with your prison identity than with your real (or desired) identity should be avoided.

   Think about some positive qualities you had outside of these walls:

   ____

   ____

2. Keep busy! Fill your schedule with activities, such as doing puzzles, reading, attending treatment groups or classes, going to spiritual services, working, exercising, or taking advantage of other programs that are available to you. By staying active, you won't have much time to be bored. So when someone asks you to do something that could get you into trouble, you have an excuse to say "no." Although some activities are not available right now because of your housing status, start thinking now about how you can fill your schedule with positive, prosocial activities.
3. Learn as much as you can about a person before you hang out with him. This will help you evaluate whether or not he is a red/yellow light or a green light for your personal goals. Does he have a bad reputation? Is he in a gang? Does he bully other inmates? Is he often in trouble with staff? Does he disrespect staff? Is he currently in the hole? Does he have contraband? What does he do in his free time? Have you heard him say things that are in line with criminal thinking like "Fuck it"; "Treatment is bullshit"; "I don't owe society nothing!"; or "I'm going to do what I want, and nobody who can do anything about it"?
4. Use cognitive restructuring, thought stopping, or positive self-talk to help you move away from antisocial associates. Tell yourself that you don't need those types of people bringing you down. Tell yourself that the immediate benefits, such as belonging to a group, aren't worth the long-term consequences of getting into trouble. Or, tell yourself that you are more likely to stay out of segregation or prison if you can learn to avoid these people now. There are lots of other thoughts you could tell yourself.
5. Avoid places where antisocial people hang out. Don't be in the same area with people who are known to cause trouble. Instead, go to another part of the rec yard or sit at a table farther away from them. Surround yourself with people who have similar goals as you. Find some common

ground with these inmates. You can also get a feeling of belonging with prosocial people. This is where a treatment group would be helpful. If you're in a cell or cellblock where a lot of dangerous or criminal activity is going on, ask if you can be moved (but this will depend on availability of extra space).

6. Make it part of your treatment plan to find positive social supports. As you know, this will help you stay in line with your goals and give you a better chance for recovery. Tell your counselor and other staff about your plan so they can hold you accountable.
7. Keep in touch with positive people on the outside, like family, good friends, children, neighbors. Call or write letters when you can. These are the people you should imitate—people who are being responsible for themselves, going to work/school, obeying the law, and treating others with respect.
8. Think about whether you would want a loved one to hang around these people. If the answer is "no," then they probably aren't good for you either! For example, if your son or daughter, mother, girlfriend were in your position, who would you want them to associate with?

What Do Model Inmates Do?

While you are in prison, your best bet is to seek out model inmates—inmates who are working on positive goals. How can you spot them among the crowd? You should have thought of some of these qualities in the exercise in Handout #40 (under "Good Guys"), but here are a few more ways to pick out well-behaved inmates:

- ✓ Stay in contact with family.
- ✓ Remain involved in treatment
- ✓ Don't pick on or bully other inmates (maybe even stand up for them)
- ✓ Have few misconducts/disciplinary reports
- ✓ Control their anger and remain calm under stress
- ✓ More likely to be older, have less serious convictions, or have a lower custody status
- ✓ Volunteer, have jobs, eat all meals, and use rec time
- ✓ Spend less time alone, just "hanging around," or feeling bored
- ✓ Involved in religious or spiritual activities
- ✓ Place few sick call requests
- ✓ Take responsibility for actions
- ✓ Respect staff (not cussing, spitting, or resisting orders)

How do you measure up? Which of these qualities do you have?

Why Move Away From Antisocial Associates?

Are these kinds of people really all that bad? Yes! Remember that they influence how you think, how you feel, how you act, and the places you go or situations you find yourself in. But they also influence your chances of staying out of segregation and out of prison once you are released. Antisocial or criminal associates are a risk factor for returning to crime. Don't buy it yet? Research has shown that if you hang around just ONE other person who is engaging in crime or rule-breaking behaviors, your chances of doing the same thing dramatically increase.

Look at these facts from inmates who were released from prison:

Number of Criminal Friends	Likelihood of Returning to Prison
0	**23%**
1	**44%**
2	**47%**
3	**47%**
4	**50%**

(1–4:) Not much of a difference here!

So it's not how many antisocial associates you hang around; it's if you hang around *any* at all!

Exercise: Be Aware of Your Surroundings

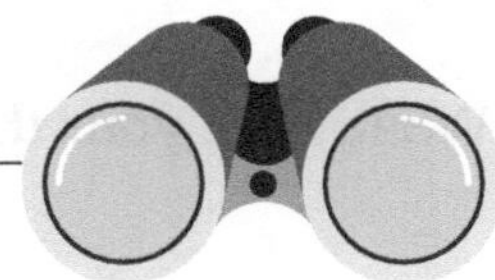

Take an inventory of the people and places you should avoid and the people and places you should seek out while you are incarcerated.

Avoid	Seek Out
Places **where I might find** ***antisocial*** **people:**	***Places*** **where I might find** ***prosocial*** **people:**
People **I know who are** ***antisocial*** **(these could be people you used to hang around or people you know who have a bad reputation—use initials):**	***People*** **I know who are** ***prosocial*** **(these could be people who can help you or people you know who have stayed out of trouble—use initials):**

Handout #41
Making the First Move

New situations can make people feel nervous, anxious, or afraid. This is because we often worry about how other people will see us, if we will fit in, if we will say or do something stupid, or if others will hurt us (abandon us, threaten us, or physically harm us).

Think back to when you first came to prison or when you first came to segregated housing.

What were your thoughts?

____

How did you feel?

____

How did your body respond (e.g., shaky, sweating, fast heart rate)?

____

____

How did this impact your mental health and/or criminalness?

____

____

Now think about your fears or anxieties regarding going back to the GP.

What are your thoughts?

____

How do you feel?

____

How is your body responding (e.g., shaky, sweating, fast heart rate)?

____

____

How does this impact your mental health and/or criminalness?

____

____

Remember to use your new skills to challenge any automatic thoughts you have about being in new social situations, such as returning to GP. By challenging these thoughts, you will improve your mood and your actions.

Social Skills and Communication

One reason why some people get anxious in new social situations where they are meeting new people is because they don't have very good social and communication skills. These skills have become a lost art, but if you can learn them, they can take you a long way. Think about how many times you have been in a conversation with someone and things got weird! Maybe the other person didn't look you in the eye when talking to you, maybe she answered questions with one-word responses, or maybe he shared too much personal information. Being able to communicate builds self-confidence in social situations and reduces anxiety. Next, you're going to read about some easy steps for meeting prosocial people who can help you with your goals.

Ready, Introduce, Talk, Exit (RITE)—Think of RITE as a ritual or routine for communicating.

1. **Ready**—This is the step where you prepare yourself for the conversation.
   - Start to think positively. See yourself meeting new people and making a good impression. Positive thoughts such as "this is good for me" or "I can do this" are essential.
   - Get your "game face on." Smile. Have an open posture with your arms relaxed. Approaching people with your arms crossed or folded is threatening. If you feel awkward with your hands at your sides, put your hands in your pocket.
   - Remember that shyness can be interpreted by others as arrogance or disinterest. Showing fear can also cause you trouble, because antisocial people feed off of fear. So it's better to be open to conversations with people and feel confident doing so.
   - Don't forget that there are other people in this facility who are nervous and talking with them might put them at ease. If you relieve their anxiety, and they feel good, this leaves them with a good impression of you.
2. **Introduce Yourself**—This is the step where you make the first move and start the conversation.
   - Don't wait for someone to come to you; just go to him or her.

- Look for someone who is not involved in conversation. He or she may be having some social anxiety too.
- Give something before you ask for something. For example, it's more polite and less threatening to say, "My name is ______. What's yours?" than to say, "Who are you?" Here you are giving your name before you ask for the other person's name.
- If you don't catch someone's name the first time, ask the person to repeat it. People are usually not offended by this if you ask politely. It shows that you are interested in remembering who they are. Saying the other person's name in the conversation will also help you remember it.
- Shaking hands is always acceptable when you meet someone for the first time.
- Smile, keep positive thoughts, and look the person in the eyes (but don't stare!).

3. **Small Talk**—This is the step where you keep the conversation going.
    - You assume the burden of conversation. This means that you are ready to talk even if the other person isn't.
    - Have several "go-to" topics in your head that you can use to get a conversation started or to keep one going. The best topics are ones that most people know something about. That's why most people talk about the weather because it is a common experience. Your "go-to" topics should be general and something you know about (e.g., something current in sports or world news).
    - You should never have a strong opinion on a topic; just act like an interested observer. When you're meeting someone for the first time, you don't want to overwhelm them! So don't talk about things like politics or religion. Neutral topics are always best—like a recent natural disaster. Once you get to know a person better, then you can have more meaningful conversations.
    - Never agree with strong negative statements about others. Politely nodding your head means you agree with the statement in the other peoples' eyes. You can politely say, "I have never seen/heard of that before," or "That has not been my experience." You don't want to get mixed up in someone else's drama or problems.
    - If the person you are talking to does not know anything about topic number 1 then go to your next "go-to" topic.
4. **Wrap Up and Exit**—This is the step where you evaluate how the conversation is going and end it appropriately.
    - Figure out how the conversation is going. You don't want to waste your own or someone else's time. If the other person looks bored or disinterested, notice it and politely excuse yourself. If you want to move on, you can also excuse yourself by saying something like "all right, well, I'll let you go. It was nice talking with you."
    - If the conversation is going well, leave with an opening like "all right, man, well it was good meeting you. Maybe I'll see you on the courts tomorrow."

These four steps can be helpful in a number of situations besides meeting new friends. You can use these steps when applying for a job or going in front of the parole board. People will be impressed with your skills. And if you ever get stuck in a social situation, just think about how you would like to feel after the conversation is over. Or if you were the other person, how would you like to be spoken to or treated while in a conversation?

Exercise: Conversation Corner

Start thinking about what you could say at each step of the RITE model.

1. Positive Thoughts before Conversation (what you tell yourself)	**2. Statements to Introduce Yourself** (saying "hi")	**3. Go-to Conversation Starters** (specific topics)	**4. Statements to Exit the Conversation** (saying "bye")

Handout #42
Avoiding Prison Gangs as Social Supports

What Is a Prison Gang?

A prison gang is a close-knit group of disruptive inmates who share a common connection or affiliation. This connection could be based on race, ethnicity, a particular belief system (religion, politics, etc.), or geographic location (where people come from). These gangs have several purposes, including (1) providing protection and caretaking, (2) unity and fellowship, and (3) profit-making criminal activity (for example, gambling, loan-sharking, trading contraband, contract murder, and prostitution). Prison gangs have a hierarchy of command; in other words, people hold varying ranks of power or authority within the gang. These gangs also work through a code of conduct, meaning that there are certain expectations and rules to follow. Not following these rules could get you into trouble, hurt, or even killed.

Gangs are violent social networks. They use violence as a way to bond with each other, defend themselves, establish social status, obtain money or things of value, or control others.

What Is the Purpose of Prison Gangs?

Prison gangs are so common because they serve a purpose. They benefit people in some ways. Here are some of the ways prison gangs seem attractive and helpful to people:

1. Gangs help people cope with highly stressful living conditions where people must go without certain freedoms, such as independence, safety, and security, sexual contact, and romantic relationships. Prison gangs are a way for people to feel safe and to get access to contraband.
2. Gangs can help people feel comfortable because their ways of life in the prison are familiar. That is, the rules, attitudes, beliefs, and behaviors that gangs follow inside the prison walls are similar to the rules, attitudes, beliefs, and behaviors that people followed outside the prison walls. Handling problems with violence is a way of life for some people. You read about this in Handout #12.

What has been your experience with gangs?

____

____

____

____

____

Don't Be Fooled . . .

Prison gangs may seem like a good option if you are feeling lonely or scared, but the problems caused by gangs ***far*** outweigh their benefits. Here are some of the ways prison gangs can harm people:

1. Gang members are at greater risk of getting disciplinary reports, more time in segregation, additional criminal convictions, and, possibly, more time in prison. Getting in trouble so much distracts you from your personal goals. As a prison gang member, you may not even be allowed to participate in certain programs that would help you reach your goals because of your violent tendencies or rule-breaking behaviors.
2. Gang members are also at greater risk of being the victims of violence. In fact, gang membership is just as strongly related to being a victim of crime as it is to being a perpetrator of crime. Inmates who are in prison gangs are four times more likely than inmates who are not in prison gangs to be victimized. This is because gangs are not well liked by other inmates or other prison gangs. If your gang puts out a murder hit on another gang, that gang is going to seek revenge and retaliate. Getting caught in the middle of gang wars can get you seriously hurt or killed. So even though people turn to gangs for protection, they actually put you in more harm!
3. Gang membership is not good for your mental health or criminalness. Although being in a gang may seem secure and safe at first, you soon need to constantly watch your back for danger. This can increase anxiety, fear, depression, paranoia, and other mental health symptoms. In addition, gang activities are usually illegal, thus automatically putting you high on the Criminalness Meter. The gang mentality encourages criminal thinking and makes criminal conduct seem ok and normal.
4. Gangs threaten the overall safety of the prison facility. Prison gang activity leads to a breakdown of safety and security controls. Gangs create a lot of disorder and violent misconduct that reduce staff's ability to properly manage the prison population, making prison an even more dangerous and chaotic place to be. This leads to increased assaults on both staff and inmates.

Stay away from prison gangs! Once you get involved in one, you may never be able to get out. The people you meet in a gang are not your friends; they will put your life on the line to save their own. You are disposable and replaceable to them.

Exercise: The Gang Game

What are the common prison gangs in your institution? What are their attitudes and behaviors like? Where have these attitudes and behaviors landed them?

Gang Name	Attitudes and Behaviors	Consequences of Attitudes and Behaviors

Gang Name	Attitudes and Behaviors	Consequences of Attitudes and Behaviors

Avoid these gangs. Figure out where they hang out and don't go to those places whenever possible. But be careful when finding out information about gangs; you don't want anyone to think you are interested in becoming a member. It may be best to ask your counselor or a trusted staff person for help.

Some Other Things to Keep in Mind to Keep Away From Gangs

- ☑ ***Never forget your personal goals.*** **Being in a gang is completely opposite of your goals.**
- ☑ **Remember that real men don't need violence to solve their problems; real men use better ways (even though these better ways may seem harder at first) to get what they need and want in life.**
- ☑ **There are other inmates in this facility who want to better their lives too and have goals for doing so. These inmates can give you the same sense of belonging, safety, and comfort that a gang would, without the added dangers. Find out where they are (see Handout #41).**
- ☑ **Use cognitive restructuring, thought stopping, and positive self-talk to tell yourself that you don't need gangs to help you feel better. You are above all that. You are learning more helpful ways of surviving in prison that will benefit you for a long time.**

Handout #43
Don't Befriend the Bully

Bullying Isn't Just for Kids

When you think of the word "**bullying,**" what comes to mind? Many people will think of school bullies who give the little kids swirlies in the bathroom and take their lunch money. Bullying may seem like a childish thing to do, but it is a big problem in jails and prisons. Unfortunately, adults bully and get bullied too. It isn't just for children anymore. Bullying may be direct violence (physical abuse, assault), indirect aggression (talking down to you, spreading rumors), or nonconsensual sexual violence (rape, molestation, fondling).

Why Do Inmates Bully?

There are a number of reasons why an inmate might bully someone. Here are a few:

- To gain social status as a "tough guy," to be seen as strong, power, or superior, or to keep up with the "dog eat dog" world of prison. However, research shows that they are not always respected by other inmates!
- To get material objects or things of value (money, food). They usually don't have good problem-solving skills, so bullying is the best way they know how to get what they want.
- To feel pleasure and excitement; they feed off the thrill of scaring other people.
- To deal with the lack of stimulation (limits activities and social contacts) in prisons.

How to Spot a Bully

Bullies can be hard to spot sometimes. This is because they often hide their intention by being friendly, or they might start out with less serious forms of bullying that you may not pick up on right away (such as gossiping behind your back). Here are some warning signs that you might be dealing with a prison bully:

- Bullies often groom their victims, meaning that they manipulate their victims over time. For example, they may befriend you first by saying that they share some of your interests. They try to reel you in and get you to trust them before they take advantage of you. Victims are usually unaware that they are being groomed!
- Bullies create an imbalance of power between themselves and their victims. Again, they may achieve this slowly over time. If you don't feel like an equal when you are around this person (e.g.,

they make all the decisions, boss you around, use your belongings, call you mean names, make you feel less than), then you may be a victim of bullying.

- Bullies are often younger (under 35 years old), have been convicted of more violent offenses than their victims, have drug or alcohol problems, are not involved in treatment programs, are more physically aggressive, have a larger and stronger physical appearance than their victims, are more "at home" in the prison environment, and express procriminal attitudes (that is, beliefs that support criminal activity and reject rule-following behaviors). They may also be members of gangs.

Remember that it only takes one time—one act of aggression—to be considered bullying!

How to Avoid Being a Victim

There are some ways that you can avoid being a victim of bullying. This involves knowing yourself and being aware of the situations you put yourself in.

- Your mental health problems put you at higher risk for bullying. Bullies target people they see as being weak. Even though mental distress and illness is not a weakness (it is a chemical imbalance triggered by stressful events), many inmates who bully will see your symptoms as a sign that you are easily controllable. Therefore, it is essential that you manage your mental health symptoms: use the techniques that you have learned to reduce your depression, anxiety, fear, and psychotic symptoms so that you do not attract bullies.
- Walk and stand with confidence. Again, if you look weak and timid, someone will try to take advantage of that. Portray an image of strength and courage (try the technique of acting opposite if you have trouble feeling confident). But be careful not to appear too arrogant or as if you are more important than others; this will make people angry and make you potentially a target for violence.
- Be aware of inmates who try to corner you or lead you to an area out of staff view. If you find yourself in an isolated area with another inmate, leave the area right away and notify staff.
- **Nothing is FREE in prison!** If someone offers you something for free, they expect to be repaid. Do not indebt yourself to ***anyone*** for ***anything***, including food, drugs, or reading material!
- You are more likely to be a victim of bullying if you are younger; smaller in physical size; white; gay; a first-time offender; have "feminine" characteristics, such as long hair or a high voice; are smart or intellectual; lack street-smarts; are "passive" (see Handout #15); or have been convicted of a sexual offense. You may not be able to do much to change these characteristics, but they can help you become more aware of you risk for bullying.
- Do not provoke known bullies. Don't try to "win out" over them or give them "a taste of their own medicine." They will eventually get in trouble for their behaviors. Provoking bullies will only make the situation worse and possibly get you into trouble as well. When bullies are really getting to you, use some of the strategies you have learned, such as positive self-talk, cognitive restructuring, thought stopping, or relaxation techniques (PMR, deep breathing, guided imagery) to block them out.

It's important to avoid being the victim of bullying because you can experience a number of negative effects, including increased suicide risk and self-injury, worsening mental health problems, and continued victimization by other inmates.

Exercise: Bully or Buddy?

Can you tell when someone is bullying you and when someone is really trying to be a friend? In an effort to find positive social supports—people who will help you reach your goals—you must weed out the people who are only trying to play nice so they can take advantage of you. Read the following stories and determine which ones are bullied relationships and which ones are buddy relationships.

This is William's first time in prison. He's a 21-year-old heroin user and dealer. William is thin and frail looking (mostly from using too much dope); he's white and has long stringy hair. He keeps to himself a lot and never makes much eye contact with other people. Some of the other inmates in William's cellblock call him "weird," "a fag," and "a loser." One day in the common area, another inmate named Sully starts talking to William. Sully's been incarcerated for aggravated robbery. This is his second time in prison, so he knows the ropes. Sully seems to know his away around the institution. He knows people, especially those who will do things for him. Sully tells William that he used to be just like him, scared, hopeless, and at the bottom of the barrel. Sully offers to help William with his problems. Soon, the name-calling stops from the inmates in the cellblock, and William is relieved; he feels safe. Sully seemed like a cool guy, he even brought William a sports magazine to look at. But a few weeks later, Sully and William walk to a corner in the rec yard away from everyone else, and Sully tries to touch William inappropriately. When William backs away, Sully says, "No one takes from me without giving back."

Are Sully and William buddies or bull and victim?

What information in the story supports your answer?

What effect will this relationship have on William?

Shawn has bipolar disorder, where he experiences cycles of high moods and low moods. He's only ever been on probation once for stealing a watch from a department store. This time, he's been incarcerated for burglarizing a home and stealing high-priced valuables. Shawn has the urge to steal most often when he is manic. Doing something exciting like that is what helps him cope with his high moods. In prison, he manages his mania by jumping on his cell bed and hitting the walls.

Shawn has been sent to the hole several times for damaging property in the facility. Dave also has bipolar disorder and notices that Shawn has been getting into trouble a lot for his behaviors. When Shawn returns to the general population, Dave approaches him. He tells Shawn that he shares some of the same symptoms, that he's been going to a treatment group, and that he's been taking medications. Dave tells Shawn that he's "sick of this shit" and wants to get out of prison so he can make a real life for himself. Shawn asks Dave for the name of the group so he can place a sick call request and enroll. After a few weeks, Shawn begins attending the group, and he and Dave work on their assignments together.

Are Shawn and Dave buddies or bully and victim?

____

What information in the story supports your answer?

____

____

____

What effect will this relationship have on Shawn?

____

____

Marcel is good at getting things done. He's been in and out of prisons for the last 15 years. He knows a lot of people on the outside who are willing to take risks for him. Marcel has a reputation in the facility as a "baron," meaning that he can get people whatever they want for a price—drugs, weapons, magazines, food, just about anything. Marcel has received disciplinary reports a few times for having contraband, but that hasn't stopped him. Working with Marcel is great; he's friendly, delivers on time, and he doesn't ask for the money up front. But Marcel makes a lot of money doing this because he charges customers a high interest rate. If an inmate can't pay up, Marcel knows people to take care of that too. Eric is a petty thief and an addict. He has a long criminal history starting as a juvenile. He's been incarcerated this time for aggravated assault—a theft gone wrong. Eric is not the most street savvy guy (he keeps getting caught!). He's starting to feel withdrawal from meth and seeks Marcel's help. Marcel gets Eric what he needs but charges him twice what it would cost him on the streets. Eric is desperate so he doesn't care. After a while, Eric becomes a primary customer and begins racking up debt with Marcel. Marcel hasn't made a big fuss about the money . . . yet.

Are Eric and Marcel buddies or bully and victim?

____

What information in the story supports your answer?

____

____

____

What effect will this relationship have on Eric?

____

____

Module 7
Recap

In This Module You Learned About

- ☑ **Antisocial associates—how they influence you, why people hang around them, and how to avoid them**
- ☑ **Social and communication skills**
- ☑ **Prison gangs—benefits and consequences**
- ☑ **Bullying—how to spot one and how to avoid being a victim**

Now place an ✗ mark next to the techniques that you will continue to practice and write down WHEN you will practice them, WHAT you will do, and HOW they will help you. Give your counselor permission to hold you accountable for following through with your plan.

Technique	I WILL do this (place ✗ here)	Whenever I . . .	This is how I will do it . . .	To help me cope with . . .
Use my mental traffic light to evaluate people				
Remember my pre-prison identity				
Stay active				
Use cognitive restructuring				
Use positive self-talk				
Use thought stopping				
Avoid places where antisocial people are likely to hang out				

Technique	I WILL do this (place ✗ here)	Whenever I . . .	This is how I will do it . . .	To help me cope with . . .
Keep in touch with positive people outside the prison				
Seek out prosocial people in prison				
Use the RITE model for effective communication				
Manage my mental health symptoms				
Walk with confidence				
Act opposite				
Use relaxation techniques				

Module 8

Integrating "Us" and "Them": Improving Inmate-Staff Relations

Handout #44

Keeping Order Among Disorder

The Role of Correctional Staff

Most staff members in a prison are correctional officers. The number-one priority of correctional officers is to ensure safety by enforcing the rules. They are like police officers for the prison. They also supervise, and sometimes counsel, inmates. Many correctional officers had other jobs before this. This includes teacher, counselor, parole or probation worker, welfare or social worker, firefighter, nurse, clergyman, emergency medical technician, air traffic controller, business supervisor or manager, car or insurance salesperson, security guard, law enforcement agent, or park ranger.

How Is Correctional Staff Trained?

Safety is always first. Staff is trained to keep themselves, inmates, and visitors safe from harm. If they feel they are in danger, they will do whatever it takes to stop that danger, including shooting to kill. Talking with you and working together to solve a problem is not an option when there is a threat of violence. Most correctional staff members do not typically get training on the mental health needs of inmates. But the good news is that more prisons are starting to add this piece to their training programs. Research shows that even short classes (lasting just a few hours) on the mental health needs of inmates are helpful for reducing staff and inmate conflicts (the use of force by staff and battery by bodily waste goes down). You can always help staff understand your problems by respectfully informing them about the symptoms you specifically experience and what you are doing to manage them (see Handout #24).

Staff Burnout

Inmates are a tough group to deal with on a daily basis! Inmates tend to have a long history of conflicts with authority, and they see correctional staff as part of "the man" or "the system." They think staff members are "out to get them" or "screw them over."

What is your attitude toward the staff at your prison?

____

____

____

____

____

What criminal thinking styles are your earlier attitudes similar to?

The fact is simple: staff member go through a lot every day to keep people safe. Imagine being yelled at, disrespected, talked down to, and hated, dealing with the threat of being spit on, kicked, stabbed, or having bodily waste thrown at you. And that's all in a day's work! What would you do in that situation? How would you feel when you left work each day? How long do you think you could last in a job like that? Correctional staff members get tired of dealing with this kind of stuff; they get emotionally and physically exhausted. There's only so much one human can take! Many staff members are overworked because of prison overcrowding (something that is out of their control). Studies show that prison staff members are more stressed than police officers! The government understands that this is a stressful job and even offers early retirement for prison staff.

People who work in prisons are at a high risk for suicide. They are also at high risk for serious health problems. For example, inmates who throw bodily waste can spread disease and infection that can then spread to other inmates whom staff members comes in contact with. Staff members have spouses, children, parents, and friends who need them to be healthy outside of work.

Prison as an Organization

Think of a prison as an organization, like a business with bosses and workers. Businesses run best when everyone works together to solve problems. Take an example like the airline company, Southwest. Southwest is known worldwide for being a highly successful company because its employees are treated fairly and, in turn, they work very hard and take pride in the airline. And the harder employees work, the more perks they get from the company. In this same way, prisons also run better when people are respectful and fair. To get this type of treatment, you must give it too. You are more likely to have less stress while incarcerated if you simply follow the rules and don't put up a fight when officers are trying to enforce the rules. They do this for everyone's safety, including yours. The more well-behaved you are, the more privileges you will earn. Also, remember that staff members often do not make the rules and, just like you, they answer to a higher authority, such as their supervisors, the prison warden, and government officials.

Exercise: In Their Shoes

Could you cut it as a correctional officer? Read the situations that follow and decide which response officers are trained to use. Place a ✓ mark next to the choice you think is best. These are actually part of an exam correctional officers have taken as part of their training.

Situation 1: You are a correctional officer assigned to a cellblock. You have been assigned to this cellblock several times, and one of the inmates in the cellblock seems to never violate any of the rules and always does what he is asked to do. He has a good reputation as not being a troublemaker and has a good daytime assignment that could be taken away if he were to violate a rule. One day, he asks if you would take and mail a letter that he has written to his mother, who is dying of cancer and whom he has not seen since he was incarcerated five years ago. Which of the following should you do?

- ☐ Leave your duty post without permission and without backup so you can immediately inform the supervisor on duty of the request.
- ☐ Refuse to take the letter.
- ☐ Take the letter and promise the offender that you will mail it, but really plan on giving it to your supervisor instead.
- ☐ Counsel the offender on why he should not make such a request because you do not want to see him lose his assignment.

Explain your answer here:

Situation 2: You work at a correctional facility and are equipped with a firearm and a radio. While making a security round through one of the 75-man dorms, you observe Inmate John Doe, who is 6′2″ and 250 lb, strike Inmate Joe Smith (who is of similar size) in the head with what appears to be a lock in a sock. Inmate Smith falls to the ground, gets back up, and charges Inmate Doe. The remaining inmates immediately surround the two fighting inmates and begin yelling and cheering them on, ignoring your commands to move and blocking your observation of the fight. Which of the following should you do?

- ☐ Use your radio to call for backup and use deadly force to stop the fighting.
- ☐ Remain under your security station until you receive backup from other officers on duty arrives.
- ☐ Try to ask the inmates who are involved in the fight to describe how the fight happened and figure out a way to calmly resolve the issue.
- ☐ Take the sock lock from Inmate John Doe and show it to your supervisor as proof of the event.

Explain your answer here:

Situation 3: You are a correctional officer assigned to the supply warehouse. You are responsible for inmates who work in the warehouse. There are other noncorrectional employees who also work in the warehouse. One day, you notice that an employee who has only worked there for two days returns from his lunch hour and sneaks what appears to be a sack lunch from a local fast-food place to an inmate. Which of the following should you do?

☐ Immediately notify your supervisor.
☐ Tell the inmate to give you the sack.
☐ Tell the employee that this is against the rules.
☐ Watch the inmate to see what he will pull out of the sack.

Explain your answer here:

____

____

Situation 4: While assigned to one of the GP dorms, you observe that an inmate has picked up a mop and started striking the television set and windows in the dayroom. As he strikes the TV, he states, "I'm tired of all this mother fucking noise." You call for backup but have not entered the wing yet. You call the inmate over the intercom system in the dorm and order him to stop his actions. He refuses and says, "I will quit when I take out this TV." The inmate is 5'10", approximately 185 lb. You are a male, approximately 5'9", 190 lb and have a chemical agent (like pepper spray). There are approximately 50 other inmates in the area. Which of the following should you do?

☐ Tell another inmate to help you calm this inmate down because he might listen better to his peer than to you.
☐ Spray the inmate in the eyes with the pepper spray and physically constrain him.
☐ Pull out your firearm and use deadly force to take down the inmate.
☐ Try to intimidate the inmate by telling him to "shut up" and then grab the mop from out of the inmates' hands.

Explain your answer here:

____

____

Handout #45
The Nature of Inmate-Staff Relations

It's (Not) Cool to Hate

In prison, inmates usually see it as a cool thing to disrespect staff and to disobey the rules. Model inmates are often seen as "weak" or "suck-ups." The mind-set is typically that staff members are "on the other side" or "against" inmates. In other words, there is an "us vs. them" mentality that leads to conflicts and assaults on the staff. Some inmates take joy from harassing staff members and like to play mind games to see how much stuff they can get away with. But remember that when staff members are stressed and burnt out, they're going to have a much harder time treating you nicely, thereby increasing your stress and making your mental distress and criminalness worse.

Think about the criminal thinking style of power orientation. Was this one of your common errors? If so, you may want to pay attention to how you interact with staff members. Do you tend to undermine or undercut them? Talk down to them? Tell them that they are worthless, stupid, or motherfuckers? Do you like to argue with the staff to gain control? These behaviors place you at high risk for disciplinary reports and more time in segregation. Being in a tug-of-war with the staff never ends well for anyone. You will either get in trouble or be seriously hurt.

It's also important to remember that criminal attitudes are a risk factor for future crime. So if you think things like "officers are more corrupt than half the inmates in here," then you are likely high on this risk factor. What do these thoughts do for you? Are they helpful? Usually, the answer is "no." Having a bad attitude toward authority decreases your desire to follow the rules. Not following the rules will land you in hot water. Try acting opposite to reverse some of your negative attitudes toward the people in positions to enforce the rules of the facility and keep everyone safe.

Mixed Expectations

Staff members often feel divided between what their bosses want and what the inmates want. Supervisors have the expectation that correctional officers and other staff members will show responsibility and leadership over the inmates they oversee. But inmates have the expectation that staff members will establish good relationships with them, more like a "buddy" feel. Many staff members have a hard time balancing both—keeping in good favor with their bosses and the inmates they deal with every day. This can cause stress and conflict. Inmates see staff members' need to be responsible leaders as being at odds with being buddies (have you ever thought, "He won't let me do this because he doesn't like me"?). Staff members should still be respectful, but they are not meant to be your friends. Understand that their job of keeping order always comes first.

Dealing With the Power-Hungry Officer

But staff members are not free from this power struggle either. A very famous study back in the 1970s at Stanford University showed how easy it is for people to step into the role of superior and subordinate. The researchers in this study set up a fake prison in the basement of the psychology building and selected college students to play either a prison guard or a prisoner. Within days, the study was stopped because the students started to take their roles too seriously. Guards were abusing their power, and prisoners were rebelling. (Keep in mind that these students were also not properly trained as correctional officers.) It quickly became an "us vs. them" environment. So even ordinary people fall victim to this social divide that prison can create. Once the students were out of that study, they realized that what they did was wrong. Some inmates (and some staff members) unfortunately never get to this point.

So what can YOU do if a staff member is too controlling, too authoritative, or likes to show off his or her power?

How do you act toward staff members like this?

____

____

____

____

Many inmates may resist orders, get in officers' faces, spit on them, be assaultive, or throw bodily waste. They think that if an officer or staff member is nasty to them, they should be nasty back. This may seem tempting, like it's the fair thing to do. But fair or not, fighting back will get you into trouble. Staff members have more on their side than you do. It's like gambling in Las Vegas; the odds always favor the house. It's not worth it, even if the officer is really a jerk. Here are some strategies that you are familiar with:

- Check to see what role you played in the situation—Are you resisting orders, or did you give the officer some other reason to treat you the way you've been treated? Did your behavior deserve the actions of the officer? Remember that the officer's role is to make sure safety comes first.
- Use cognitive restructuring—For example, tell yourself that the officer's behavior probably has nothing to do with you. He or she has a stressful job, and this may be the way he or she knows how to cope with it. Think about the consequences of letting your anger get the best of you.
- Use thought stopping—Stop yourself from thinking about "getting even" or seeking revenge on the officer.
- Act opposite—Pretend to be polite and friendly, even if that's not how you feel at the moment (but make sure you don't come off like a smartass!)
- Use positive self-talk—Tell yourself that you can handle the situation. The officer isn't allowed to hurt you unless you pose a danger to him or her, or another inmate. Tell yourself that you have the ability to calm down and follow the officer's instructions.
- Use your conflict resolution skills—Be assertive (but respectful) and try to talk to the officer about how his or her attitude toward you is making you feel or how it's contributing to your mental health symptoms. This may come as a surprise to staff members because most inmates won't take the time to express their feelings.

- Don't react other than to do what you're asked—Sometimes people who seek power do it to get a reaction (like fear or aggression), and when they no longer get a reaction, they stop. So don't react as if you're scared or ready to fight; this may be what they want. Just follow the basic order you were given, whether it's to cuff up or wait in the hall while your cell is being searched.
- If a staff member is truly targeting you, you may file a complaint with the facility. Check what the procedures are for doing this at your prison.

Remember that most staff members are not like this. In fact, studies have shown that, even though the public and policy-makers strongly support punishment for inmates, most correctional officers do not share this view and actually support rehabilitation and treatment programs for inmates. So they're on your side!

Exercise: Attitude Check

Your counselor will give you the results of an assessment used to determine your beliefs about authority. Higher scores on these attitudes may suggest more conflict with the staff. Answer the questions that follow.

My Scores

1. **Law:** ______
2. **Police:** ______
3. **Courts:** ______
4. **Tolerance for Law Violations:** ______
   (How ok are you with people breaking the rules?)
5. **Identification with Criminal Others:** ______
   (How much do you have in common with other criminals?)

Compared to people not in prison, I am high on these attitudes:

1. ________ **4.** ________

2. ________ **5.** ________

3. ________

Did you expect this result? ________

Why or why not?

____

What evidence from your past supports your attitudes toward authority (think about your past relationships with teachers and parents, or the fact that you are in prison)?

____

____

____

____

Talk about how these attitudes could lead you to more rule-breaking behavior:

____

____

____

____

List 2 thoughts about laws/rules, the court, and the people who are in charge of supervising you and keeping you safe that will *help* you stay out of trouble:

The Law:

____

____

The Courts:

____

____

Police/Correctional Officers:

____

____

List 2 thoughts about breaking laws/rules and other people who break laws/rules that will *help* you stay out of trouble:

Tolerance for Law Violations:

____

____

Criminal Others:

____

____

Do you think your scores will be lower now?

Module 8
Recap

In This Module You Learned About

- ☑ **The role of correctional staff members and how they are trained**
- ☑ **The nature of inmate and staff relationships**
- ☑ **Your own attitudes toward authority**
- ☑ **How to follow staff members' requests even when you don't want to**

Now place an ✗ mark next to the techniques that you will continue to practice and write down WHEN you will practice them, WHAT you will do, and HOW they will help you. Give your counselor permission to hold you accountable for following through with your plan.

Technique	I WILL do this (place ✗ here)	Whenever I . . .	This is how I will do it . . .	To help me cope with . . .
Assess my own role in conflicts with staff members				
Use cognitive restructuring				
Use thought stopping				
Use acting opposite				
Use positive self-talk				
Use conflict resolution skills				
Don't give a reaction				

Technique	I WILL do this (place ✗ here)	Whenever I . . .	This is how I will do it . . .	To help me cope with . . .
Protect my rights and well-being as an inmate				
Recognize what the staff's job is				
Keep my goals in mind				
Remind myself about the importance of rules in prison				
Use PMR or deep breathing				
Be aware of my attitudes toward authority				
Be aware of my attitudes toward people who break the rules				

Module 9

Road Map to Recovery: Creating Your Relapse Prevention Plan

_______________'s

Road Map to Recovery

This relapse prevention plan is made up of everything that you have learned so far in this program. You will need to go back and review all the handouts you completed. This plan works as a reminder of all your hard work as well as a quick reference for when times get tough. You now have the skills to *get out and stay out* of segregation.

Quick Reference

My Goals Are:

______________________ ______________________

______________________ ______________________

My Mental Health Diagnoses Are:

______________________ ______________________

______________________ ______________________

My Common Criminal Thinking Styles Are:

______________________ ______________________

______________________ ______________________

My Biggest Warning Signs Are:

______________________ ______________________

______________________ ______________________

My Biggest Triggers Are:

______________________ ______________________

______________________ ______________________

1. Where I've Been

A famous writer once said, "Where you come from is part of where you are going." Looking at the past helps us see what needs to change for a better future. Remind yourself about the problems that led you to prison and to restricted housing.

Before coming to prison, I . . .

Had These Thoughts:	Acted This Way:	Went to These Places:	Hung Around These People:

Before coming to segregation, I . . .

Had These Thoughts:	Acted This Way:	Went to These Places:	Hung Around These People:
____________	____________	____________	____________
____________	____________	____________	____________
____________	____________	____________	____________
____________	____________	____________	____________
____________	____________	____________	____________

2. Going for the Goal

List the goals you set for yourself at the beginning of this program:

Goal #1

Goal #2

Goal #3

Goal #4

Now think of two NEW goals that you have come up with over the course of this program:

Goal #5

Goal #6

Goals Progress Check

- Was **GOAL #1** met? ______

  If ***YES***:

  How did you reach it?________________________________

  ____

  What do you need to do to keep the goal? ________________________________

  ____

  If ***NO***:

  What barriers got in your way? ________________________________

  ____

  What else can you try to reach this goal? ________________________________

  ____

- Was **GOAL #2** met? ______

If ***YES***:

How did you reach it?____

____

What do you need to do to keep the goal? ______________________________

____

If ***NO***:

What barriers got in your way? ______________________________

____

What else can you try to reach this goal? ______________________________

____

- Was **GOAL #3** met? ______

If ***YES***:

How did you reach it?____

____

What do you need to do to keep the goal? ______________________________

____

If ***NO***:

What barriers got in your way? ______________________________

____

What else can you try to reach this goal? ______________________________

____

- Was **GOAL #4** met? ______

  If ***YES***:

  How did you reach it?______________________________

  ____

  What do you need to do to keep the goal? ______________________________

  ____

  If ***NO***:

  What barriers got in your way? ______________________________

  ____

  What else can you try to reach this goal? ______________________________

  ____

- Was **GOAL #5** met? ______

  If ***YES***:

  How did you reach it?______________________________

  ____

  What do you need to do to keep the goal? ______________________________

  ____

  If ***NO***:

  What barriers got in your way? ______________________________

  ____

  What else can you try to reach this goal? ______________________________

  ____

- Was **GOAL #6** met? ______

If ***YES***:

How did you reach it? ____

____

What do you need to do to keep the goal? ____

____

If ***NO***:

What barriers got in your way? ____

____

What else can you try to reach this goal? ____

____

3. Always Alert

As you have learned, you must always be aware of your thoughts, feelings, behaviors, and places/environments. The way you think, feel, act; where you go; and who you hang out with can lead you to trouble or to recovery. Never forget your mental traffic light to evaluate situations that are good (green), ones that are risky (yellow), and others that are just plain bad (red). Remind yourself what to look out for.

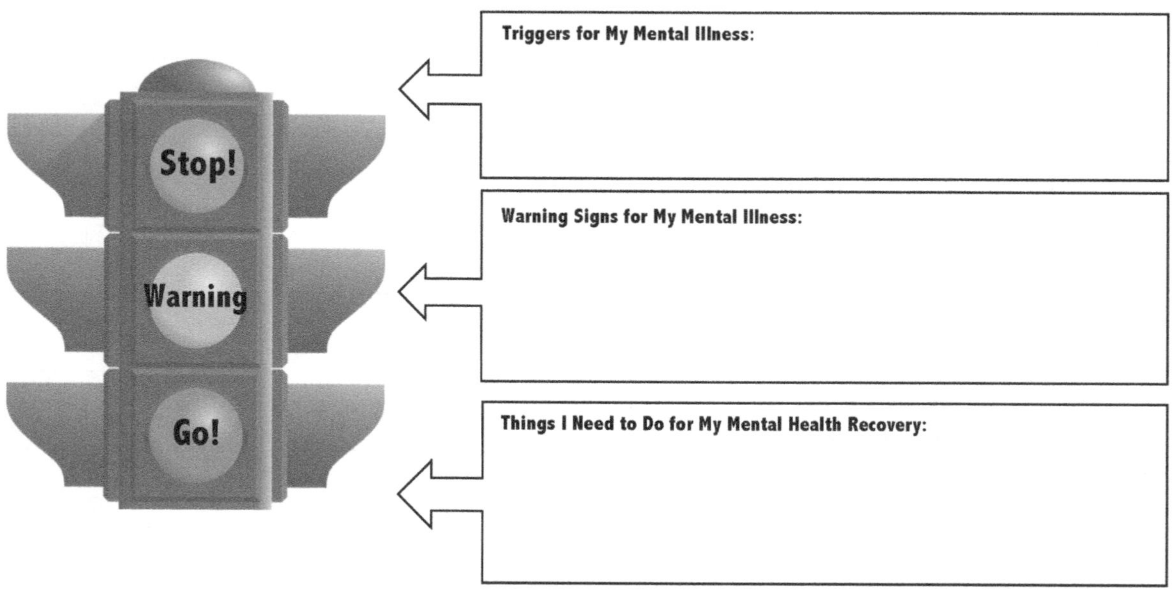

Triggers for My Criminalness:

Warning Signs for My Criminalness:

Things I Need to Do for My Crimanlness Recovery:

4. Playing Favorites

List your top-ten favorite strategies that you learned. Pick the ones that worked BEST for you. Commit to using them when you need help.

This is the strategy I like:	This is the problem it helps me with:
#1	
#2	
#3	
#4	
#5	
#6	
#7	
#8	
#9	
#10	

5. Quick Thinker

Knowing ahead of time which phrases help to calm you down takes away the effort of having to think of them in the moment when your mind is already trying to sweep you away. Write down the thoughts that have helped stop your emotions from getting the best of you.

This is a thought I like:	I will say this whenever I start to feel . . .
#1	
#2	
#3	
#4	
#5	
#6	
#7	
#8	
#9	
#10	
#11	
#12	

6. People Picking

You learned that the people you hang around could make or break you. Bad people (red lights) pull you down; good people (green lights) pull you up. Remind yourself who these people are.

People who will *bring me down*	Where will I find them?
#1	
#2	Avoid
#3	Avoid
#4	Avoid
#5	

People who will *pull me up*	Where will I find them?
#1	Go
#2	
#3	Go
#4	
#5	Go

Share THIS plan with THESE people!

When getting ready to meet or talk to helpful people . . .

How should you prepare yourself mentally (what can you tell yourself)?

____

____

How should you introduce yourself?

____

____

What should you do with your body (hands, arms, eyes)?

____

____

What can you talk about?

____

____

How will you end the conversation?

____

____

7. Busy, Busy, Busy

Keeping busy keeps you out of trouble. List the activities that you like the best **AND** activities (including other classes, volunteer opportunities, and *treatment* programs) that you can look for when you go back to the GP.

Activities I can do NOW that I like BEST	This activity helps me because . . .
#1	
#2	
#3	
#4	
#5	

Activities I can do LATER (in general pop)	This activity will help me because . . .	This is how I can start this activity . . .
#1		
#2		
#3		
#4		
#5		

8. Medication Management

Remember that taking your medications is important for your recovery. But make sure you keep track of your side effects and talk to the doctor at your facility.

These are the medications I am taking:

____

____

My medications help with these symptoms:

____

____

____

____

☐ **I will continue to complete my Medication Monitoring Card and share this with my doctor** (place a ✓ in the box)

My Letter of Progress

Write a formal letter to your unit officers, counselor, caseworker, warden, or whoever is in charge of your release from restricted housing. This letter should talk about your goals and the steps you have taken (and will continue to take) toward your recovery. This is your chance to show off your hard work. Refer back to your relapse prevention plan for help.

Today's Date: ____________

Dear ____________________:

Sincerely,

My signature above certifies that I will continue to work on my recovery in the ways stated in this letter.

Index

Note: Page numbers in italics indicate a figure and page numbers in bold indicate a table on the corresponding page.

Acceptance and Commitment Therapy 3
acute clinical disorders 107–113
administrative segregation (AS) 3
aggression 70–71, 81–84
anger: acceptance of 49–50; aggression and 70–71; assertiveness 81–84; assessment of 72–75; breaking cycle of 74–75; cognitive restructuring 76–77; as habit 73; meaning behind 88–89; as problematic 72–73; thought stopping 77–80
Anger Management and Assertiveness Training (SAMHSA) 3
antisocial associates 192–195
antisocial personality disorder 115–116
anxiety 111–112, 163–164
assertiveness 81–84
assessment: of anger 72–75; *Stepping Up, Stepping Out* program 14–18, **18**; of suicide risk 61
attention, defined 160
Attitude Check 24
automatic thoughts: ability to change 145–146, 149–154; altering of 149–154; awareness of 144–148; dealing with 146–148; defined 144–145; feelings as cues to 146; reason to change 149

bad (less productive) goals 12
belonging, feelings of 192
best behavior 47–48
bipolar disorder 109–110
borderline personality disorder 114–115
boredom, strategies against 175
brain, chemical imbalance in 104
Brief Situational Confidence Questionnaire (BSCQ) 15
bullies/bullying 203–207

Changing Lives and Changing Outcomes program 3, 9
chemical imbalance in brain 104
clinical disorders 107–113
cognitive indolence 133
cognitive problems 160–162
cognitive restructuring 76–77
concentration, defined 160
conflict resolution model 82
correctional staff: burnout by 212–213; inmate-staff relations 216–219; keeping order among disorder 212–215; mixed expectations of 216; power-hungry officers 216–218; prison organization 213; role of 212; training of 212
Creating Your Suicide Prevention Plan handout 19
criminal associates 128
criminalness: assessment measures 15; defined 123–126; examples of 124; learning to cope with 175–178; nature of 124–125; PICTS handout 131–134; recovering from 135–137; relapse into 138–140; responsibility for 9–10; risk factors for 127–131; signs of 127–134; tips for reducing 126; warning signs and triggers 138–140; *see also* Exploring My Mental Distress and Criminalness: Where It Comes From, What It Looks Like, and How to Recognize It; Managing My Mental Distress and Criminalness: Improving Functioning and Preventing Relapse
criminal recidivism 127–131
Criminal Sentiments Scale-Modified (CSS-M) 15, 23–24
criminal thinking 127
criminogenic risk factors 6
cutoff, defined 132

delusions 169
depression 107–108, 164
Depression, Hopelessness, Suicide Screening (DHS) 15, 19
Diagnostic and Statistical Manual Fifth Edition (DSM-5) Self-Rated Level 1 Cross-Cutting Symptom Measure 15

Dialectical Behavior techniques 22
disciplinary segregation (DS) 3
discontinuity, defined 133
Dropping the Anchor exercise 50

entitlement, defined 132
evidence-based interventions 7
Exploring My Mental Distress and Criminalness: Where It Comes From, What It Looks Like, and How to Recognize It: antisocial personality disorder 115–116; anxiety 111–112; bipolar disorder 109–110; borderline personality disorder 114–115; common diagnoses 114–119; criminalness 123–140; depression 107–108; introduction to 4; mental distress, defined 104–106; narcissistic personality disorder 116–117; program outline 21–22, 30–31; recap of 141–142; recovering from 135–137; schizophrenia 110–111; schizotypal personality disorder 117–118; stigma over mental illness 120–122; warning signs and triggers 138–140
Extra Relaxation Techniques 23

false perceptions 168–169
false suicidal intent 65–66
family problems and criminalness 128
fear 90–94
feelings, as cues to automatic thoughts 146

general population (GP) inmates 4–5, 7, 60
good behavior 47–48
good (productive) goals 11–12, 37–38
Green Light to Goals 35–36, 158–159, 181
guided imagery 54–56

hallucinations 168–169
hearing sense 54–56
hope, role of 10–11

initial prison experiences 196–199
Inmate Score Report Template 16
inner peace 159
Integrating "Us" and "Them": Improving Inmate-Staff Relations: inmate-staff relations 216–219; introduction to 4; keeping order among disorder 212–215; program outline 23–24, 31; recap of 220–221
interpersonal problems 171–174
In Their Shoes handout 24

Letter of Progress 24, 236–237
Linehan's Dialectical Behavior Therapy 3
loss of interest 165

Maine Department of Corrections 7
Managing My Mental Distress and Criminalness: Improving Functioning and Preventing Relapse: automatic thoughts 144–154; cognitive problems 160–162; interpersonal problems 171–174; introduction to 4; medication 179–182; negative moods and 163–167; program outline 22–23, 31; psychotic symptoms 168–170; recap of 183–185; stress and 155–158
Measure of Criminal Attitudes and Associates (MCAA) 15
medication 179–182, 235
Medication Adherence Rating Scale (MARS) 15
Medication Monitoring Card handout 23
mental distress, defined 104–106
mental health/illness: assessment measures 15; criminalness and 128; facts about 104–105; responsibility for problems 9–10
Mental Traffic Light 18–19
mentoring 193
Missouri Department of Corrections (MDOC) 7, 13
model inmates 194
module content quizzes 16–17
mollification, defined 132
morbid rumination 63
Mueser's Illness Management and Recovery 3
My Automatic Log handout 22
My Letter of Progress handout 24, 236–237

narcissistic personality disorder 116–117
negative moods 163–167
neurotransmitters 104

occupying mind and body 45–46

passive-aggression 85–88
perceived burdensomeness 62
personal goals, setting 37–40
personality disorders 107–113
poor emotional expression 165
poor motivation 176–177
Positive and Negative Affect Scale (PANAS) 15
positive self-talk 63
post-release criminal recidivism 5
power-hungry officers 216–218
power orientation, defined 132
pressure from others 48
prison gangs 200–202
Progress Checkpoint worksheet 22–23
Progressive Muscle Relaxation (PMR) 52–53
prosocial free time and criminalness 128
psychache 60–61
psychiatric risk factors 6
Psychological Inventory of Criminal Thinking Styles (PICTS) 21–22, 131–134
Psychological Inventory of Criminal Thinking Style-Short Form (PICTS-SF) 15
psychotic symptoms 168–170

Ready, Introduce, Talk, Exit (RITE) routine 197–198
recidivism, criminal 127–131

Recovery Assessment Scale (RAS) 15
recovery rescue exercises 161–162, 166–167, 170, 173–174, 177–178
recreational activities and criminalness 128
Red Light trigger of noncompliance 181–182
relapse into criminality 138–140
Relapse Prevention Packet 9
relationship problems and criminalness 128
resistance, defined 84
restlessness, strategies against 175
restrictive housing 4–5, 42–44
Road Map to Recovery: Creating Your Relapse Prevention Plan: goal-setting 226–230; introduction to 4; keeping busy 234–235; Letter of Progress 236–237; medical management 235; personal history impact 225–226; personal strategies for 231; program overview 24, 31, 224; self-awareness 230–231; supportive allies 233–234; thinking it through 232

sadness 95–99
schizophrenia 110–111, **111**
schizotypal personality disorder 117–118
school problems and criminalness 128
security, feelings of 192
Seeking Supportive Allies: Finding Helpful Others Among the Crowd: antisocial associates 192–195; bullies/bullying 203–207; good *vs.* bad people 188–191; initial prison experiences 196–199; introduction to 4; model inmates 194; prison gangs 200–202; program overview 23, 31; recap of 208–209; Road Map to Recovery with 233–234
segregated inmates 4–7
self-harm behaviors 19
self-injurious behavior (SIB) 63, 175–176; *see also* Suicide and Self-Injurious Behavior: Protecting You From You
sense of purpose 192–193
sensory deprivation 54–56
sentimentality, defined 132–133
setting personal goals 37–40
shame 95–99
side effects from medication 179–181
sight sense 54–56
sleep and segregation 51–53
smell sense 54–56
social withdrawal 165–166
solitary confinement 4–5
Stepping Up, Stepping Out program: adjunctive services and interventions 14; assessment 14–18; assessment schedule 17–18, **18**; completion and graduation policies 13–14; goal-setting basics 11–12; introduction to 3–14, 29–30; module content quizzes 16–17; participant rules 12–13; program goals 4; program outline 18–24, **20**, 30–31; program structure and logistics *8*, 8–9; provider qualifications 7–8; role of hope 10–11; taking personal responsibility 9–10; theoretical rationale and evidence base 4–7; treatment modules 4
stigma over mental illness 120–122
stress 155–159
substance abuse 128
Substance Abuse and Mental Health Services Administration (SAMHSA) 3
Suicide and Self-Injurious Behavior: Protecting You From You: false suicidal intent 65–66; introduction to 4; morbid rumination 63; positive self-talk 63; prevention plan 64; program outline 19–20, **20**, 30; recap of 67; risk of 60–61; self-injurious behavior overview 63; suicide overview 61–62
suicide overview 61–62
superoptimism, defined 133
Surviving Segregation: What to Expect and How to Cope: anger acceptance 49–50; good/best behavior 47–48; introduction to 4; occupying mind and body 45–46; program outline 19, 30; recap of 57–58; restrictive housing 4–5, 42–44; sensory deprivation 54–56; sleep and 51–53

taste sense 54–56
THE Circle of Change 18–19, 34–35, 188
thought interrogation 98–99
thought stopping 77–80
thwarted belongingness 62
touch sense 54–56
toughness 83
Treatment Manual for Justice Involved Persons with Mental Illness: Changing Lives and Changing Outcomes, A (Morgan) 9, 10, 12

Understanding Change and Making It Happen: An Introduction: basics of program 34–36; THE Circle of Change 18–19, 34–35; good (productive) goals 11–12, 37–38; Green Light to Goals 35–36; introduction to 4; program outline 18–19, 30; setting personal goals 37–40
Understanding My Emotions: Identifying and Dealing With Anger, Fear, and Other Frustrating Feelings: aggression 70–71, 81–84; anger 70–80, 88–89; assertiveness 81–84; cognitive restructuring 76–77; conflict resolution model 82; fear 90–94; introduction to 4; passive-aggression 85–88; program outline 21, 30; recap of 100–102; resistance 84; shame and sadness 95–99; thought stopping 77–80; toughness 83; violence 70–71

victims of bullying 204
violence 70–71

Working Alliance Inventory (WAI) 15, 16
work problems and criminalness 128

Yale University Law School 4
Yellow Light sign of noncompliance 181

For Product Safety Concerns and Information please contact our EU representative GPSR@taylorandfrancis.com Taylor & Francis Verlag GmbH, Kaufingerstraße 24, 80331 München, Germany